The Dissolution of the Financial State

Heterodox Studies in the Critique of Political Economy

***Series Editor*:** Andrew Kliman

The outbreak of the global economic crisis in 2007 has led to renewed discussion of heterodox economics and Karl Marx's contributions. Heterodox Studies in the Critique of Political Economy contributes to and seeks to broaden the focus of these discussions. It welcomes proposals from authors working within various heterodox traditions. Contributions to the critique of political economy in the tradition founded by Marx are strongly encouraged, as are other marginalized voices and perspectives. Thus, nonacademics, scholars from Asia and the global South, and proponents of perspectives that are underrepresented in the existing academic heterodox literature are encouraged to submit proposals. Both single-authored works and edited collections are welcome.

Advisory Board

Recent Titles in this Series

Is Marx's Theory of Profit Right?: The Simultaneist-Temporalist Debate, edited by Andrew Kliman and Nick Potts

The Dissolution of the Financial State: A Marxian Examination of the Political Economy of Money since the 1930s, by Simon Mouatt

The Dissolution of the Financial State

A Marxian Examination of the Political Economy of Money Since the 1930s

Simon Mouatt

LEXINGTON BOOKS
Lanham • Boulder • New York • London

Published by Lexington Books
An imprint of The Rowman & Littlefield Publishing Group, Inc.
4501 Forbes Boulevard, Suite 200, Lanham, Maryland 20706
www.rowman.com

Unit A, Whitacre Mews, 26–34 Stannary Street, London SE11 4AB

British Library Cataloguing in Publication Information Available

Library of Congress Cataloging-in-Publication Data
Mouatt, Simon.
The dissolution of the financial state : a Marxian examination of the political economy of money since the 1930s / Simon Mouatt.
pages cm. — (Heterodox studies in the critique of political economy)
Includes bibliographical references and index.
ISBN 978-0-7391-9037-1 (cloth : alk. paper) — ISBN 978-0-7391-9038-8 (electronic) 1. Money—History—20th century. 2. Money—History—21st century. 3. Capitalism—History—20th century. 4. Capitalism—History—21st century. 5. Financial crises—History—20th century. 6. Financial crises—History—21st century. 7. Marxian economics. I. Title.
HG255.M68 2015
335.4′12—dc23

2015013243

™ The paper used in this publication meets the minimum requirements of American National Standard for Information Sciences—Permanence of Paper for Printed Library Materials, ANSI/NISO Z39.48-1992.

Printed in the United States of America

Contents

Acknowledgments

This book would not have been possible without the seminal work of Professor Andrew Kliman to whom I owe a debt of gratitude. I would also like to thank Professor Victoria Chick, Dr. Carl Adams and Dr. Julian Wells for comment, and Professor Nick Potts for his insightful reflection at every stage of the research. Special thanks also to Helen Anderson for her train illustrations used in Chapter 8, Charles Caplen for proofreading, Rachel Searle for background information on the Bank of England and, for tireless support throughout the writing of this book, my wife Catherine.

Figures and Tables

Acronyms and Abbreviations

ACB	Allied Bank Commission
BDL	Bank deutscher Lander
BIS	Bank for International Settlements
BOE	Bank of England
BW	Bretton Woods
DB	Deutsche Bundesbank
ECB	European Central Bank
EMT	Endogenous Money Theory
ERM	Exchange Rate Mechanism
FIRE	Finance, Insurance and Real Estate Sector
FRG	Federal Republic of Germany
IMF	International Monetary Fund
LTFRP	Law of the Tendential Falling Rate of Profit
MB	Monetary Base
MTFS	Medium Term Financial Strategy
MELT	Monetary Expression of Labor Time
PK	Post-Keynesian
QTM	Quantity Theory of Money
STM	State Theory of Money
TSSI	Temporal Single System Interpretation
WB	World Bank
WW1	World War One
WW2	World War Two

Preface

In this book I argue that the post-Keynesian (PK) theory of endogenous money (EMT) can be combined with Marxian analysis in order to give insight into the changing power relations between the state, finance sector and real economy. The *control* of financial resources and money, described in the book as *financial power*, is a primary (but not exclusive) source of *social power* for those that wield it. Since virtually all of modern money exists in the form of credit-money held in bank deposits and denominated in particular currencies, the political economy of the credit system and currency value are worthy of specific focus. In this respect, following the work of Susan Strange, one of the book's key arguments is that financial power is derived from the *control* of money-issue and its purchasing power, both assumed to be determined by the state and market in varying proportions depending on context (Strange 1988). As the subtitle suggests, the theme explored in the book is the erosion of state sovereignty, in terms of this financial power, experienced from the 1930s to the current era of globalization. The assumption is that, during the Keynesian period after WW2, the state acquired a measure of capability to determine money-issue/value that has been subsequently lost. In addition, the growth of financial markets in recent decades, so-called *financialization*, has led many to assume that private finance is an important proximate driver of economic affairs in general. I argue in the book that the impact of the state's lost capability is a democratic deficit and the reduced capacity to regulate the macroeconomy. It is common in the discourse to explain this financial transformation, and lost state sovereignty, with reference to the actual processes of financialization itself. However, this view is somewhat tautological and, therefore, provides insufficient explanation. To discuss various financial factors as causes of financial crisis, for example, risks describing the phenomena without illustrating the root causes. In contrast, the book seeks to argue that systemic drivers of capitalism (rooted in production), probably best understood by Marx, actually *do* provide a more plausible explanation of the causes of the financialization and erosion of state sovereignty. In addition, the post-Keynesian descriptions of monetary processes are considered to best reflect the actual reality of the monetary system. This represents an interesting synthesis of the classical Marx with modern money theory.

The interpretation of Marx that is employed to explain this financial transformation has been named the Temporal Single System Interpretation (TSSI), which illustrates Marx's value theory (assuming certain agent behaviors in the productive economy) across periods and identifies falling profit rates. In particular, the method used by Andrew Kliman, in his study of US corporate profitability since the 1930s, is applied in the European case studies (Kliman 2010). It is claimed that the tendency for the profit rate to fall is an underlying (albeit indirect) driver of the systemic propensity toward crisis and stagnation. The empirical findings presented in the book appear to support this view. The central argument of the book is that the *response* of agents (including the state) to the profit tendency has been a significant driver of the observed financial transformation. Profitability, accumulation, concentration and Marx's theory of the state are then combined with the post-Keynesian EMT, in order to interpret the empirical findings. The book then concludes that this synthesis provides a *more* appropriate explanation of the historical transformation of the global financial system since the Great Depression, than much of the financialization literature, and the sourcing (and operation) of financial power by the modern capitalist state and market.

Chapter 1

Market and State

1.1 INTRODUCTION

The control of money, shared between state and market, is a major source of social power in the capitalist nations of today. In this book, I hope to make a contribution toward an improved understanding of the actual processes involved in these important and changing power relations. In this opening chapter I begin by outlining the nature of the book, and then I summarize the theoretical argument presented. Next, I provide an academic rationale for the writing of the book followed by a discussion of the assumptions made. The next section explores the nature of financial power, and how it manifests in the real economy. The final section considers the key sources of social power and how they interact with each other.

In 1945 the memory of the Great Depression and WW2, in conjunction with the influence of Keynes, had provided the political appetite for the regulation of the economy through informed state intervention. The process had already begun in the 1930s, but by the late 1940s Keynesian ideology was firmly embedded in administrative and political circles in the US, UK and, by implication, in West Germany through allied control. The UK state was also keen to regulate the level and allocation of credit by UK settlement banks. Yet, almost from the outset of the post-WW2 era the banks had lobbied the political process seeking less regulation and their freedom to pursue profit through financial innovation and liberalization (Helleiner 1994). By the 1980s this was largely achieved. Yet, in order to do this, the ideological resistance in the state had to be weakened. As the book title suggests there is an analogy here with sixteenth-century England and the need to remove religious orders (as seats of learning and pastoral care), loyal to the papacy, which had ostensibly stood in the way of the establishment of protestant supremacy. This dissolution of the monasteries, administered by Thomas Cromwell during the reign of Henry VIII, had been a time of great upheaval. Yet, ironically, it was not simply about the removal of religious ideology. The state, in the form of King Henry, gained from the appropriation of incomes and lands from the disbanded worship communities. In the same way, the banks gained from the removal of state Keynesian policy-makers, and their replacement by free-market thinkers who favored financial liberalization. In this sense the new breed of state policy-makers were, from a Marxian perspective, simply serving the interests of market financial institutions—a bourgeois state. In other words, rather than the state gaining from the dissolution of an embedded ideology, private capital was the key beneficiary. This book explores this notion of the erosion of state financial sovereignty from the 1930s to the recent financial crisis, both theoretically and empirically, and seeks to identify plausible explanations of the transformation. In particular, the ability to regulate credit levels and the purchasing power of money is investigated. It is concluded that the analysis of Marx, in conjunction with post-Keynesian monetary theory, offers the best explanation of this current era of financialization that has received so much recent attention.

1.2 THE THEORETICAL ARGUMENT

Which individuals, or entities, control the issue and purchasing power of modern money in capitalist nations? In the popular conception both these matters are the responsibility of the monetary authorities—the state. Yet, in recent decades, we have experienced a reduction in the scope and size of the state generally. Does this extend to a diminished state-role in the national monetary system? I argue in this book that state power has certainly waned but that, importantly, this does not mean finance now drives the real economy. In contrast, I posit that systemic drivers of capitalism that are rooted in production are responsible for the erosion of financial sovereignty, growth of financialization and, indeed, the propensity toward financial crisis. This is not to deny the significance of financial factors, however. Post-Keynesian (PK) theory, for example, has contributed much toward our understanding of endogenous credit money, and the financialization literature has contributed much toward our understanding of this enlarged, innovative and profitable sector of the economy that is proximate cause of many economic outcomes. However, the claim made in this book is that Marx's law of value that is the mechanics of the capitalist mode of production, in particular falling and persistent low profitability, are the *indirect* causes of the migration of surplus capital to the financial sector (and hence financialization), profit-seeking financial innovation and the historical erosion of state financial sovereignty in the arena of credit creation and money's purchasing power. In addition, it is claimed that this also provides plausible explanation of the propensity toward financial crises. The book further claims that the PK endogenous monetary theory (EMT) can be satisfactorily combined with Marxian analysis in order to provide insight into the changing power relations between the state, financial sector and the real economy. This is predicated on the assumption that modern credit-money, in the form of bank deposits, and the practice of fractional reserve banking, is created in response to demand at a given interest rate partly exogenously determined by the central bank as a semi-state institution.

1.3 RATIONALE

While some thinkers, such as Killick, have outlined the existence of restricted fiscal and monetary policy autonomy, as a direct consequence of capital flows, privatization and foreign direct investment, less discussion has taken place regarding the implication of the increasing *private* control of *money-creation and its value* (Killick 1995). This is despite monetary debates, since the classical period, that have been conducted on topics as diverse as convertibility, neutrality or endogenous money. Yet, the ability to determine the creation (and, by implication, the allocation) of money and its purchasing power is an important source of social power. The financialization thesis of recent times has pointed toward the increased influence of the finance sector, in relation to the real economy, "over economic policy and outcomes" (Palley 2007: 2). However, while these interesting perspectives have served to illuminate the real financial phenomena there has been little analysis that unearths the root causes of financialization itself. It is both of these issues that this book seeks to address, by giving more focus to money-issue, value and the underlying causes of financialization.

Also, what about the creation and operation of international money? The US dollar remains the key currency for payments and reserves, yet successful *currency competition* (leading to greater currency use) can lead to significant benefits for a national economy and/or its financial institutions.[1] Has the relative decline of the financial state since WW2 led to an increased *private* ability to manipulate currency and, by implication, alter the international balance of power? Given that money is a key source of social power, the type of questions this book has sought to address would appear to be important ones. A further question suggests that if the state's ability to create money and control its value has diminished, then who or what has gained ability at its expense? It could be that the private banks or the nonfinancial corporate sector (or combination of both) have increased their capabilities or, alternatively, their capability may have simply evaporated. Yet, if both financial and nonfinancial corporations have gained power, how do these two separate entities interact and what are their particular interests, objectives and capabilities? Furthermore, which theory, or pluralist synthesis, can best explain the changing financial reality of contemporary capitalism? It is these types of interesting questions that this book also seeks to address.

In summary, the monetary theory discourse reviewed in early chapters has been varied and prolific. Yet, there is little specific focus on *political* processes involved, that is, the social power relations pertaining to money's issue and value, and the specific ramifications implicit in the questions mentioned above, and what may have caused these recent developments. The book aims to provide a first attempt at remedying this by exploring and synthesizing economic theory from a political perspective and applying this to a post-1930s case study of financial systems in the UK and Germany. Monetary theories that have investigated aspects of money function, without reference to their political implications, are mentioned only as far as they point toward the consideration of power capabilities and interests. The issue of whether price changes drive the money supply, for example, or if the causality is reversed, does not first appear to have direct political ramifications. Yet, since the argument discusses the neutral impact of money, and non-neutrality implies the increased *capability* of financial resource controllers, then it was considered relevant. The overall aim, therefore, was to investigate money-creation and purchasing power, and then to synthesize appropriate monetary theories in order to best explain the empirical realities of state/market practice. The book involved a theoretical exploration of the capitalist state, and an analysis of financial power, that draws on Marx, Hilferding, Schumpeter, Strange, and Hayek *et al.* In addition, the discussion on monetary economics in the early chapters has involved (neo)Classical, Austrian, (post)Keynesian, reform, and Marxian perspectives. The empirical work, regarding the mechanics of money-issue, money's purchasing power and the influence of state/market, necessitates drawing on the mainstream banking literature. These case studies do not pretend to constitute rigorous academic practice but, instead, are designed to simply provide contextual and supporting evidence to the theoretical arguments presented earlier in the book. The political economy approach taken has been unashamedly pluralist drawing on heterodox economics, political science and other subject arenas, and examined the interaction between the economy (including the monetary system) and the political structure(s). The question is asked, who (or what) control(s) money assuming that it is controlled at all?

1.4 SOME GENERAL ASSUMPTIONS

The underlying intuition of the book is that the *private* control of monies has been increasing at the expense of the state, with presumed ramifications. Several thinkers have long noted this development in the present era of liberalized capital flows, financial market deregulation and the private credit creation (Griffith-Jones 1998; Helleiner 1994; Strange 1996). Still, other authors have emphasized the strategic role of state *political* factors, in contrast to the usual economic explanations posited, that have led to these changes (Cerny 1993; Germain 1998; Helleiner 1994).[2] In the globalization discourse of the last twenty years, these same authors have also debated the erosion of state sovereignty, since state capacity to pursue independent fiscal and monetary (and other) policies has been diminished. In addition, hedge funds, investment banks and private equity firms have all substantially increased their activities in global financial markets in a financial environment where there is now an enhanced incentive (and perhaps objective) to manipulate market values of financial assets. These developments, arguably, serve to further undermine the capabilities of the state to issue currency and control its purchasing power. It is this literature, in the field of international political economy, which provided the original motivation for me to undertake the writing of this book. A key question that could be derived from this same discourse, implicit in the book but not explored, asks what are the motives of any private entities (if any) who have increased their monetary power as a consequence of the relative decline in state financial capabilities, and was the process premeditated? In other words, who has gained from the recent financialization processes and was it a plan? It is for the interested reader to speculate on such matters. Be that as it may, the perspective that I assume in the book is the notion that agents are more driven by systems than the other way around. This is, of course, the classical Marx position. In this sense, the erosion of financial sovereignty, financialization and propensity toward crises are primarily driven by the imperatives of the capitalist system rather than any individual behavior *per se*.

A further assumption implicit in the book is that accumulation and centralization of money-resource *ownership* by private financial rentiers occurs, and this then contributes to a redistribution of financial power toward a monied class. In addition, banks have become bigger in terms of assets and scope, which increases the capabilities of decision-makers responsible for financial intermediation. These elites, consisting of both nonbank corporate and banking entities (and their investors), form an embedded *plutocracy* as capitalism evolves. Antecedents of these notions can be found in Lenin, Luxemburg and Hilferding, particularly following the rise of the joint-stock company and, in more recent times, by several academics and monetary reformers (El Diwany

2003; Hilferding 1910; Hudson and Bezemer 2012; Lenin 1996; Luxemburg 1971; Palley 2007; Stockhammer 2004; Zarlenga 2002). Monetary accumulation occurs through the combination of interest (and other commissions, fees and charges), asset inflation, speculation and the control (and allocation) of credit-issue itself. In addition to the monetary accumulation, there is the impact of the increasingly oligopolistic nature of economic activity leading to further concentration of financial power, as the channels of financial intermediation are narrowed. This erosion of state financial capability and monetary accumulation, assuming they exist, together represent a substantial democratic deficit and substantiate rising inequalities. This is arguably to the detriment of the productive economy and society in the longer term.

The mainstream economics profession has not given too much consideration to these matters. Capitalism has clearly generated inequalities and galvanized elites but the usual retort is that created-wealth trickles down toward the marginalized and thus benefits all. The economic system is praised and the significance of plutocratic elites is routinely downplayed. Keynes, by contrast, was concerned about the *beggar thy neighbour* brutality of capitalist mechanics. He argued instead that redistribution, and the mitigation of rentier income, was imperative for a civilized society. However, it was the state's fiscal policies, in the main, that needed to take the overall responsibility to achieve it. Marx, on the other hand, was not convinced that the contradictions of capitalism could be overcome easily. Marx had instead emphasized, with his concept of the circuit of capital, that money as finance capital is the *instigator* (and potential disruptor) of production and is therefore afforded a central role in economic activity (Marx [1867] 1976: 248). Yet, importantly, in Marx's unique analysis it was the production, thus *real* economy factors, that were the significant drivers. The accumulation that takes place, therefore, is primarily driven by productive agents and then manifests in monied elites. Later Marxists, conversely, were keen to emphasize the increasing significance of financiers as drivers of the production process. In Hilferding's notion of *finance* capital investment, for instance, private banks are seen as integrated with (increasingly concentrated) joint-stock firms, but with bankers clearly driving the process of cartelization and general development (Hilferding 1910). Meanwhile, following Marx, the state functions as a complicit extension of the *bourgeois* nonfinancial *and* financial corporate interests. In this conception, and one adopted in this book, the integrated (combined) corporate structure determines key economic outcomes in the system, aided and abetted by a capitalist state.

Challenges to the abovementioned Hilferding view of finance capital have occurred on the grounds that, in the modern era (as Griffith-Jones suggested), finance has become less closely linked to the production sector (Griffith-Jones 1998). It also appeared that while corporate and financial entities have similar interests most of the time, there are periods of divergence, and financial sector agents are able to determine economic outcomes that are contrary to the interest of industrial capital (Mouatt 2011). Yet, ironically, the recent bank crisis of 2008–2009 perhaps illustrated contemporary signs of a weakness in the *private* commercial banking infrastructure. The state had felt obliged to provide liquidity to traditional banks that were technically insolvent, as collateralized debt securities they were holding devalued and the normal interbank lending evaporated. Several factors were (or are) at work. Commercial banks now earn a smaller proportion of their profit from interest and are increasingly exposed to the vagaries of global financial markets, through their own exposure to trading positions. In addition, as argued in an earlier book, the nonfinancial corporations are less dependent on bank capital, as a consequence of retained profits, and are also developing their own monies and banks (Mouatt 2011). The IT revolution has also further facilitated these developments and assisted in the creation of new money circulation channels. New payments software for Internet use, or the increase of so-called nonbanks (non-settlement) for retail banking, is an example.[3] This emerging *corporafinance* (my term), so-called since many nonfinancial firms have entered this market, could incrementally transform the current financial system, as these new processes encroach upon and replace the traditional bank activities. It is within this context of financial transformation that another theme of the book emerges, which discusses whether, as Marx had believed, industrial capital is actually driving the financial transformation since social power is firmly located in production (Mouatt 2011: 103). It is also hoped that the exploration of the relative autonomy of the financial system from the state, within the case studies, should contrast the German stronger state-intervention with the UK political economy culture which, as Keynes had posited, noted by Tabb, could be described as a private finance-dominated "rentier" economy preoccupied with short-term gains (Tabb 1999: 151). In addition, the German propensity toward public banking and cooperative banking also contrasts well with the UK private commercial bank infrastructure.

In order to explore these themes, which are both concerned with the political economy of the credit-based financial system, the book combines the behavior of the productive economy, as predicted by Marx (specifically recurring crises), with more modern theories of money (the EMT) in chapter 4, a Marxian theory of the state (chapter 7) and the Susan Strange notion of financial power (outlined below). The choice of Marx is justified because, unlike other theorists, he did not claim that a steady-state (i.e., sustainable) capitalism was feasible without crisis. Secondly, in contrast to other Marxian interpretations, which deny the *consistency* of Marx's value theory (rejecting the tendency for profitability to fall), the TSSI confirms Marx's value theory and its conclusion of a falling rate of profit as a primary underlying driver of capitalist mechanics as logically consistent. It is argued that these provide a surer economic grounding to the political intuitions outlined. The book then seeks to find out whether or not the financial system has become more autonomous from the state and, further examines the changing activities of the private banking infrastructure and corporate production structure with respect to this. The classical Marx paradigm utilized enables the centralization, accumulation and recurring crises *et al.* of the capitalist mode of production to be theorized as a natural (thus predictable) capitalist process, rather than as anomalies attributed to exogenous factors.

1.5 FINANCIAL POWER

The book is based on the notion that while money is seen as significant in studies of political economy, it is not often placed as the central mode of analysis. This is due, in part, to the mainstream view of money as relatively neutral in the long term. If money is neutral and, by implication, the real economy is akin to a barter economy, then money merely facilitates a more efficient operation of the economic system. In contrast, there are a variety of heterodox economists who view money as non-neutral and having a wider scope of function. From this perspective the control of financial resources (as stated) is a primary source of *social power* in a monetary economy and, subsequently, the politics of money creation and its purchasing power then become relevant and interesting areas of study. This view is fully adopted here.

Power *per se* can perhaps be described as the ability to get someone (or an entity) to do that which they would otherwise choose not to do.[4] Using this definition authors have then explored the exercise of power, in the present capitalist order, and surmised on the sources of this power (Ferguson 2002; Mann 1986; Strange 1988; Strange 1997; Walter 1993; Zarlenga 2002). Arguably the *control* of money and finance, including the provision and expansion of credit, constitutes a primary (but not exclusive) source of this social power and therefore needs to be the central mode of analysis. A corollary of this proposition could be that the control of financial resources largely *determines* power relations, or that control of financial resources *manifests* any shifting power relations (derived from other sources). It is the latter description of *financial power,* which is presented in this book.

Money is defined here as state-produced *base* money, in note and coin form, in combination with legally sanctioned *credit* monies in the form of bank demand deposits that derive from depository institutions.[5] Money performs certain functions in the social economy, such as a means of account, store of value, enabler of exchange and a means of deferred payment.

Yet to operate as money, an entity needs social acceptability derived from the state monetary authorities' ability to maintain scarcity, legitimacy and stable inflation. The standard textbook account is that money has liberated economies from the inefficiencies of barter and, therefore, facilitated growth and industrial development. It can also be argued that, as Strange noted, the technical development of finance directly correlates to the level of economic advancement (Strange 1988: 92). In the modern era money has little intrinsic value (unlike commodity money), since it exists in the form of paper, base metals and digits on computer software. Yet, credit monies are reflective of the physical reality of the economy that they represent, and so money derives its value from tangible production, resources and traded activity. It is also assumed in this book that money is not neutral, in a *Ricardian* sense where money simply enables the economy to operate, since *financial powers* are able to determine outcomes through the *instigation* (and regulation and cessation) of economic activity. This activity might not otherwise occur and may have a long-term impact.[6] Furthermore, the quality of *fungibility* (the ability to change form) increases money's operational flexibility in relation to other assets or sources of power and endows it with additional use-value as money. Indeed it is, arguably, indispensable to the exercise of virtually *all* power. The controllers of assets in other forms (including near-liquid assets) simply do not possess the same abilities despite their value. In order to exercise financial power, they would need to *materialize* it by transferring their assets into a distinct money form. Similarly, social power derived from other power sources is limited, without the access to and control of financial resources. These capabilities, therefore, must be obtained. The conclusions of the book imply, therefore, that these specific qualities of money set it apart as a *primary* source of social power, creating an interesting arena for study.

The control of money resources is actually exercised through the possession (ownership title) of financial resources *per se* (in conjunction with associated property rights) or the control and management of the institutions and systems that determine its use. Financial power thus wielded can then manifest in the real global economy in a variety of modes through, *inter alia*, its spending power impact on global markets, new economic activity, war finance, international capital flows (and their ramifications) and the social relations between creditor and debtor. It is these social power capabilities that enable those that wield financial resources to pursue an extremely wide range of objectives and strategies in almost every aspect of life.

Credit creation, for instance, is a key source of financial power as a direct consequence of the pervasive use (and ubiquity) of credit-money. Credit has enabled economic systems to evolve more efficiently through the recycling of money surpluses to deficit agents (assuming 100% fractional backing). Although in the present era levels of debt have reached unprecedented volumes and substantial political leverage is transferred to the creditors.[7] Any principal and interest repayments required will also restrict the present spending power of borrowers and increase the financial power of lenders. Furthermore, the interest is sometimes compounded. The net effect is that as capitalism develops there is an accumulation of the relative financial power of creditors, since the credit expansion process itself leads to an expansion of their resources albeit mitigated by crises and inflation. In addition, interest payments (and receipts) are also unfairly distributed across society, a phenomena often emphasized by monetary reformers such as Margrit Kennedy. This antagonises any prevailing socioeconomic class divisions and inequalities that exist (Kennedy 1995: 9).

Financial institutions that create credit also grant or restrict actual spending power as well as "manage or mismanage" currencies through the leverage they permit, which then directly affect consumer markets and fluctuating exchange rates. Both of these activities lead to a redistribution of financial resources. Strange explained how this financial power is located in a *financial structure* that consists of two elements. First the systems of credit creation, determined jointly between the state and private banks (in varying proportions), and the processes that determine exchange rates (and value). These exchange rates derive from state economic policies, interstate negotiated regimes and agent activity in the foreign exchange market and general economic fundamentals (Strange 1988, chap. 5). The nexus between state and market (a key theme of the book) consequently becomes a key factor in determining the distribution of financial power. However, since the historical expansion of the modern state itself has coincided with its increasing indebtedness to the private banking structure, in this sense the state could be viewed as the weaker partner in the relationship. This view necessarily implies the existence of a strong *bourgeois* state, one that prioritizes *inter alia* the protection of the private capital in its many (including financial firms) forms. These same financial power elites are also instrumental in impacting capital flows where, in recent years, international transactions have grown exponentially. The *private* capital flows enhance exchange-rate risk and enforce a monetary discipline on those states that are able to manipulate their macroeconomic variables enough in order to further their economic interests. Those states that are not capable find that currency devaluations lead to repressive IMF adjustment policies and an enforced exposure to foreign direct investment that enables multinationals to purchase assets "on the cheap."[8] State sovereignty is subsequently reduced as the capability of private *financial power* is increased (Strange 1990: 266).

Financial power is also manifested through the use of international money. The US dollar, as the main reserve, trading and vehicle currency, fulfils this role, and US financial powers gain substantial *seigniorage*, notwithstanding periodic difficulties in practice.[9] General confidence in the dollar, imperative for international liquidity, can be maintained with both long-term balance of payments equilibrium and prudent monetary management. Yet, the nature of *international money* is such that all currencies (including the reserve) are ultimately valued in foreign exchange markets, which operate (it is assumed) according to the relative strengths of underlying fundamentals. The euro, for instance, could be viewed as an emerging reserve currency, and is clearly indispensable to the present German financial system and Eurozone area. The UK pound also remains influential. This overall *currency competition* (for greater general use), as Cohen has effectively argued, is a geopolitical reality and subsequently leads to a redistribution of interstate (or currency area) financial power and is therefore significant for the future world order (Cohen 2006, chap. 1).

Multilateral monetary regimes such as Bretton Wood (BW), as sets of political arrangements that define the structure of the international financial system and regulate the processes, can restrict the *fungibility* of money and financial power is subsequently curtailed. Exchange rate regimes, for example, seek to maintain currency stability among trading partners, which is useful for sustaining trade but may necessitate capital controls. While these political actions can serve state development agendas, the *capabilities* of interstate *private* financial powers are restricted. Conversely, during the neo-liberal order, floating exchange rates have become increasingly pervasive, and *private* financial power (as Griffith-Jones has noted) is, therefore, increased through global capital movements (Griffith-Jones 1998). In the same manner the legislative and operational influences, on respective national financial systems, will also further affect the functioning of money.

1.6 SOURCES OF SOCIAL POWER

So, how should this financial power described be considered in relation to other sources of social power, since they are often interdependent? In her work, Susan Strange identified five *primary* sources of power but avoided too much discussion on their relative capabilities.[10] In a similar way, Mann, as a historical sociologist, has posited that all societies are "multiple, overlapping and intersecting socio-spatial networks of power" (Olson 1991: 185). In his study of history he notes four sources of social power that interrelate, that of ideological, economic, military and political and suggested that their "boundaries and capacities" are all different and that neither one is predominant in a permanent way.[11] He suggests instead that defining moments of structural change occur through these networks of interaction where, at any given point in time, the "boundaries and capacities" of any of these sources of power may display greater capacities to organize and instigate than others (Olson 1991: 187). This general view of social power is accepted in the book and in this sense the financial power identified earlier can be overruled by social power exerted from another source. Mann further suggests that social relations, and changes to world order, cannot be reduced to an immutable systemic property, or an ideological "normative system," since there is no bounded social system as such due to the *overlapping* and changing networks of power (Olson 1991: 186). Rather, he suggests that key historical change has been instigated by either an "empire of domination" consisting of military and political power combined with geopolitical hegemony, or by "multi-power-actor civilisations" where all four diffuse powers, in varied combinations, were the predominant reorganizing force (Olson 1991: 188). This latter point is true when history is considered at watershed moments but, in terms of industrial capitalism, Mann's networks of power all appear to have consistently supported the interests of private capital. In other words while capitalism can, in theory, be swept away by some unforeseen powerful social movement, in the meantime we can assume that all of the power sources and relations are virtually solely determined by the systemic imperatives of capitalism.

Mann, like Strange, thus avoids presenting one source of power as a primary one (at least in a permanent sense) since the networks "overlap and intersect" and change. But, power almost invariably needs to be exercised through the control of *money*.[12] With Mann's ideological power for example, based on normative systems, the mobilization of virtually all activity requires financing and it is difficult to conceive of structural change occurring without the support (or control) of presiding financial powers. While in Mann's work this is probably implicit, financial resources are not placed as the central mode of analysis. The security structure is similarly dependent. The financial needs of the military-industrial complex are colossal (Mann's military network), both for production purposes and operations. Given the historical connection between money and war-making capability, as Ferguson has reviewed, financial power has been instrumental in world history (Ferguson 2002). Yet in Mann's view of the economic network of power, that consists of the control of resources, wealth generation and commerce, money is seen as merely serving the interests of the production process. In summary, the sources of power that Mann has identified are indeed plausible, but it is contended that they give insufficient attention to monetary factors. Susan Strange, in contrast, identified primary and secondary sources of social power and specifically argued that money represented a key primary source and, as a consequence, she is credited with the inspiration for the writing of this book. The control of financial resources is a source of power, as stated, but (it is noted) that the very same control of financial resources can also be the manifestation of power relations derived from other sources.

1.7 CONCLUSION

In summary, the book asks whether or not there has been an erosion of state sovereignty in terms of *financial power*, defined as the *capability* to determine credit-money levels and the *capability* to influence purchasing power in the modern German and UK financial systems since the 1930s, and whether or not the mechanics of *production* are driving the transformation(s) of the traditional (private) banking sector. The theoretical tools used to accomplish this are a combination of Marx's conception (as interpreted by the TSSI of Marx) of the predicted behavior of the productive economy, combined with the modern endogenous money theory (EMT) adopted by post-Keynesians and monetary reformers (Mouatt 2011). These Marx-based ideas include topics such as the law of value, crises, falling rate of profit, fictitious capital, accumulation, capital concentration and state theory.

The book also combines established monetary theory with a political economy discourse that normally only makes general references to specific economic theories. In addition, the notion of *corporafinance*, in conjunction with Marx's law of value, stands in direct contrast to financialization literature of recent years that seems to emphasize an increasing influence of the financial system on economic outcomes. Finally, the use of the TSSI of Marx, in conjunction with the EMT credit money, is seen as an interesting perspective since the usual practice of the proponents of Marxian economics is to not focus explicitly on the creation of credit-money units in their analysis.[13] The rationale for this synthesis is the *apparent* ambiguity of Marx's monetary theory, discussed later in chapter 6, in regard to credit-money operation, and the explanatory capability of more modern monetary theory. It is accepted, however, that Marx can be interpreted in such a manner that allows for the existence of endogenous money if one chose to do so. In the empirical chapters, a Marxist analysis using credit-money, based on the TSSI of Marx, is then applied to the case studies of Germany and the UK since the 1930s, which, it is argued, provides a measure of supporting evidence to the book's theoretical themes and findings.

It is concluded that the *control* of the issue and value of money resources is an important source of social power and this, therefore, constitutes the central argument. The intuitions and assumptions that have been outlined in this chapter will pervade the remaining discussion. In chapter 2 there is a review of monetary history. In chapters 3 and 4 there is a critical review of mainstream and heterodox monetary theory, in terms of the nature, creation and function of money. The purpose is to analyze the various strands of monetary theory, from the classical antecedents to the present period, in order to ascertain the manner in which the book's themes have been theorized. In chapters 5 and 6 there is a consideration of Marx's political economy and monetary theory respectively. In chapter 7 there is a study of state financial power relations, within the context of the capabilities and mechanics of the modern state. This will necessarily involve an exploration of capitalism *per se* as well as technical detail of relevant monetary processes. Consequently, the changing role of the financial state, and the aforementioned EMT/TSSI synthesis will be theorized. Chapter 8 then uses a light-hearted analogy of a steam train to illustrate and reinforce the theoretical arguments made in the book. Chapters 9 and 10 then review the German and UK financial system(s) operation respectively and chapter 11 explores the operation of Marx's law of value and other aspects of the productive sector as drivers of financial transformation. Chapter 12, the final chapter, then draws together the various findings, arguments posited and provides some general conclusions to the book.

NOTES

1. Hayek probably coined the phrase "currency competition," but Benjamin Cohen has developed the phrase in the modern context (Cohen 1998).

2. Economic arguments for financialization were provided by the mainstream. Arrow and Debreu, for example, had claimed there would be a more efficient allocation of resources due to the development of financial assets as future contingent claims, as a consequence of knowledge efficiencies (Arrow and Debreu 1954). Friedman had also argued that securities prices based on fundamentals would be more accurate as a consequence of greater financial market volumes (Friedman 1953).

3. These nonbanks in the UK are financial institutions that offer some retail banking services but without the traditional bank license and a reserve account at the Bank of England. Their clearing, therefore, takes place in one of the settlement banks.

4. Allen argues that there are different *modalities* of power such as coercion, manipulation, seduction or authority as well as spatial and time complexities in the *exercise* of power (Allen 2003: 2).

5. Sight deposits are accounts that can be drawn on (and spent) immediately. This means that nonliquid time deposits, shares, derivatives, bonds and other financial securities are not included in this description of money.

6. This notion assumes that money is the *catalyst* for productive agents rather than the entity that merely enables economic activity, following instigation by production agents.

7. Adams notes that the developed world has subjugated the developing world to neo-liberal economics; through use of structural adjustment policies by the IMF/World Bank following prolific default (Adams 1993: 162).

8. The Asian crisis of 1997 was an example of such a currency crisis.

9. The so-called Triffin paradox pointed out that in order to ensure liquidity an international reserve currency needs be plentiful and the host currency needs to run a balance of payments deficit yet, conversely, in order to maintain stability and

confidence in the international money a surplus (or at least sustained equilibrium) needs to be obtained (Triffin 1960).

10. Her sources of power included the knowledge, production, state and security structures (Strange 1988).

11. Mann asserted that the networks were not coterminous that is, their boundaries or capacities do not coincide but instead differ. In the past, perhaps, Mann's four networks might have, at best, reached the major regions of the world. In the modern era, however, it could be argued (as Olson points out) that they are all approaching a global scope, and therefore a social totality, and becoming coterminous (Olson 1991: 187).

12. Financial power, in this sense, can be viewed as an *alienable* concept since the control of resources can be transferred from one individual, entity or group to another.

13. Potts does, however, employ pure credit money in his abstract models of the economy, but he does not explore the process in any concrete way (Potts 2005; Potts 2009a).

Chapter 2

A Monetary Economy

2.1 INTRODUCTION

The development of a monetary economy has been as useful to humanity as the invention of the wheel. Without the capacity to exchange efficiently, for example, specialization and the division of labor and hence economies of scale would not have been possible. This chapter explores the fundamental aspects of the monetary economy from a historical perspective. The first section explores the nature, issue and function of monetary systems in general. The next section asks the question how did money first originate? The following section considers the different forms that money can take. The next section then examines the control of credit money—this is important since credit money is by far the most significant money form today. The next section considers the manner in which the value of money is conceived and in the final section there is an exploration of the different money measures and a consideration of money as both a stock and flow.

2.2 NATURE, ISSUE AND FUNCTION OF MONEY SYSTEMS

In any historical examination of the contrasting views of money, two immediate problems emerge. First, monetary theorists, as Niebyl noted in his study of the classical period, have tended to explain the function of money in the productive economy by describing particular conditions that only pertain to a defined historical context. Subsequently, abstract notions or theories of money, that can be universally applied, are rare and subject to inconsistencies (Niebyl 1946: 1). Monetary theories that evolved during the period of the gold standard, for example, are likely to pertain to the specific monetary conditions and therefore have limited explanatory value for contemporary systems. Secondly, to add to our problems, theorists from the same schools of thought have also differed in their view of the nature (and origin) of money, creation of money and its functioning in the economic system—the latter two themes that form the basis of this investigation. As a consequence, any relevant money theories will be presented in context, wherever appropriate, and theorists differentiated.

The standard definition(s) of the nature of money expressed below can be widely found in undergraduate programs and texts and can, therefore, be considered mainstream. So, how do they define money? This commonly occurs with reference to money's *function*, where it is stated that money functions as a means of exchange, store of value, credit facilitator and unit of account (Fuller 1990; Maunder 1995; Begg 2000). Yet, there are exceptions. Hicks, for instance, had argued in 1967 that money could be used as a means of exchange without being a store of value. He had presented a hypothetical marketplace where all transactions are completed (at the end of trading) and no one buys more than they sell. Yet, as a result of the *non-synchronization* of these transactions (in the real world), money is required that is a (at least temporary) store of value, so we are able to dismiss this objection.[1] Meltzer noted that this notion of non-synchronization, as the *raison d'être* for money that is, to enable exchange, forms the standardized view of the historical development of all money systems (Meltzer 1998: 9). So, the tradition of defining money according to its function appears to be common in the history of monetary theory. It then becomes easy to identify money as *any* entity that possesses the necessary properties that enable the stated *social* functionality. Textbooks, for instance, speak of the necessary characteristics (or qualities) that monies *require* such as portability, acceptability, divisibility, scarcity and durability that *enable* money to function as a means of exchange, account, deferral (i.e., credit facilitator) and store of value.

2.3 THE ORIGIN OF MONEY

There are two distinct schools of thought that explain the historical origin of money differently. The *commodity* view, posited by Menger *et al.*, suggests that earliest man had no need of money (Menger 1871; Mises 1912). Hunter-gatherers provided for their own needs and those of their immediate family. As early societies began to form, however, the need for exchange became evident in order to facilitate the division of labor and specialization. Thus barter was established, yet it failed to resolve the dilemma of the "double-coincidence of wants" (having to find someone who has what you want and wants what you have) and the paucity of any necessary market information.

There was also a cost in acquiring relevant information, in terms of any resources forgone (Meltzer 1998: 9). These early monies, in the form of a commodity, are then considered to have gradually replaced barter inefficiencies as a result of the needs of market actors. The debate among monetary theorists, however, hinges on whether money was actually created *endogenously* by market agents themselves (the commodity view) or whether the money origin was sanctioned/initiated by the state (or relevant leaders/institutions) in an *exogenous* sense—the state or chartalist view of money.[2] The monetary historian Michael Hudson has pointed out that this debate has important political implications for present government policy. If, for instance, the chartalist view of money—originally "created by law"—is accepted (which is supported by some evidence), then state credit management is seen as entirely appropriate. Conversely, if historical money origin is seen as endogenous then, it can perhaps appear more natural to "leave it to the market" (Hudson 2003: 1). Historically, there appears little dispute however, that once instigated the political elites (in whatever form they manifested) soon assumed a controlling and regulatory role of any currency forms utilized.

Soon the use of gold and silver (or both together) as a means of payment was established, and from the Byzantine period through the middle ages this was often, as Zarlenga notes, a key source of political power (Zarlenga 2002).[3] The specific authorities managed the minting of coin and assaying of the metals, and in time paper notes were then produced by the (private) banking system, backed by the holdings of specie in the vaults. In addition, those that were able to offer the safe protection of specie, for example, the goldsmiths, Rothschilds or the Knights Templar, received a substantial income for the provision of their services. In terms of the historic use of specie, however, there were natural limits to the creation of the commodity money and any credit based upon it—dependent upon available sources. Nowadays, monies have no intrinsic value *per se*, existing in the form of paper and digits on computer software, and are not convertible to any particular commodity. As a consequence, therefore, there is no significant physical limit to their issue. Modern monies therefore simply represent a claim on the *resources* of the relevant monetary economy, and are subsequently realized in the form of the particular goods, services and assets available. In addition, at any given particular point in time, all monies are owned (in terms of property title), by someone or something regardless of the particular form in which the money appears.

2.4 MONEY FORMS

It is interesting to note that, in all of these presentations of the origin and historical nature of money, there is rarely mention of the political processes involved and the partisan interests that they serve. Money is simply viewed as enabling the economy to work. In chapter 6, in contrast, I consider the specific development of the capitalist financial state in which I argue that the predominant principle of operation is to serve the interests of private capital. In this scenario, the private agents mainly control money-issue, and its operation in the monetary economy, through the medium of the proxy state. However, the start of the case-study period studied in this book is characterized by a small measure of autonomous state financial power.

An interesting monetary debate on the form that money takes, first outlined by Schumpeter, asks whether all money (once formed) is actually credit, called the *credit theory of money* since it constitutes an IOU claim on goods, or whether credit is a distinct entity from money, the so-called orthodox *money theory of credit*, and is directly backed up by *real* (commodity) money that can be used as final settlement (Ingham 2001: 306). If a particular money form has no intrinsic value, and is not backed by any commodity, the question is asked can it be considered real? I take the position that if the credit money unit functions as money, then it can be considered money proper and I therefore empathize with the credit theory of money perspective. Furthermore, money can still be termed credit even if it does not form part of a credit contract, since it is a future *claim* on goods. Yet, the orthodox view of money described above would presumably only regard narrow (high-powered) money as *real*, and providing that it did not constitute part of any credit contract. However, since bank deposit monies constitute legal tender and are acceptable for the purposes of taxation payments, I argue that they are *de facto* money. In the present UK financial system, *high-powered* money (notes, coins and reserve balances at the Bank of England [BOE]) is accepted as final settlement in interbank clearing and could therefore be considered real from the orthodox view. In 2007, the BOE had approximately £4 billion of assets in excess of liabilities suggesting a sizable monetary base of accumulated fiat monies in (at least on the accounting books) existence (BOE 2007). The term *fiat money* (from the Latin "let it be made") is used by economists to denote monies which are publicly available and that are sanctioned and/or produced by the state, as opposed to circulating monies that derive from other (usually private) sources of credit creation. These fiat monies then remain in circulation once issued.[4] When credit is created, in contrast, any monies formed are destroyed when the contacts are resolved. This is in accordance with monetary protocol and legal audit. Yet, it still functions as money prior to settlement. In the UK the phrase *legal tender* is used to describe any notes and coins that are produced by the Royal Mint but bank deposits and transfers are also (legal) acceptable means of monetary settlement.[5] This particular terminology denotes the legitimization role of the state in the UK monetary system, which means that the vendor involved in a transaction is legally bound to accept the stated form of currency for payment when offered. This serves to increase social confidence in a given currency form that, in turn, enhances its efficiency and consequently improves the functioning of the productive economy.[6] Meltzer has further noted that the frequency of use of the given money asset reduces the marginal cost of acquiring information about it and therefore further justifies its social use, as a means of exchange, on efficiency grounds (Meltzer 1998: 13). This is an important point to make since almost all presentations of monetary theory recognize this essentially *social* aspect of money use, which necessarily further depends on communal trust (or coercion) for acceptability. This implies, under normal circumstances, that greater use enhances its *kudos* as money.

To clarify matters, in the modern era most money is held in the form of bank deposits, and when transaction payments are made, a substantial amount of exchanges take place through the electronic transfer of funds from one deposit to another. Most of these deposit monies are known as *credit money,* to denote their origination (from banks as credit providers) and their form. The commercial business of banking had originally involved the safekeeping of money for which a charge was made. As banking developed it soon became apparent that receipts for deposits of specie could be issued that could themselves be exchanged for transactions. In this sense the receipts were a form of *promissory* note that promised to pay the bearer on demand. Subsequently, banknote production became an additional function of banking. Since the banks did not require all of the money deposits, in order to meet the daily transactions demand of customers, they began to lend money owned by others in the form of notes, leading to what is known as *fractional backing*. Credit became an important function of banking. Since this was a profitable activity the banks also began to attract further deposits by offering a rate of interest rather than charging for safekeeping. During the seventeenth century depositors had also begun to issue orders to their banks to transfer money to some third party and cheques came into being. Historically, the key advantage of these clearing systems, as Chick noted, was that this enabled bankers to settle total amounts between themselves, thereby enhancing *liquidity* in the banking system, facilitating the expansion of credit and the use of deposits as means of payment (Chick 1986: 5). The cheque system also enabled the bankers to offer overdrafts on accounts, which helped them circumnavigate restrictions on banknote issue that were sometimes imposed by the state monetary authorities. The development of branch retail banking further enhanced the ability of the private banks to create credit and mitigated the dangers of a bank run. Nowadays the existence of debit cards and direct debits serve to enhance the credit expansion capability of the banking system, through decreasing the transaction demand for cash and increasing the predictability of bank customer deposits. When a bank makes a loan it creates a deposit which then becomes the liability of the bank. The (credit) money supply is thus expanded, until such time that the debt obligations are settled and then it contracts.

It has been traditional in monetary economics teaching, for example, textbooks like Pilbeam that the bank deposits are used as the reserve basis for lending (in the aggregate banking system) and the money supply is thus expanded by a multiple of the deposit reserves, a process known as the bank *credit multiplier* (Pilbeam 2005). These credit monies *per se* denote the existence of a *monetization* of credit in contemporary systems. Yet, since the banking system is constrained by the reserve asset (or cash) ratio determined by the state, and other regulation policies, this constitutes a significant regulatory role for the authorities that are able (exogenously) to determine the level of credit creation in conjunction with the demand for credit. However, as Rochon notes when describing the essence of the so-called EMT in many developed countries, the legal reserve requirement has now been removed and the credit multiplier is therefore no longer an accurate reflection of financial operations in the real world (Rochon 2007: 2).[7] This is certainly the case in the UK financial system.

Credit is provided in response to demand at a given interest rate. In addition, it is now not necessary for there to be an actual physical presence of deposits in order for lending to take place, since credit (and hence credit-money) is formed *ex nihilo* as an accounting entry on asset/liability sheets, rather than as a transfer of a fixed physical entity. Also, any demand for reserves, as Wray notes, is simply *accommodated* by the central bank (Wray 2007). This constitutes the essence of PK theory since the 1970s. In this sense, the national bank functions, as Chick noted as the "lender of first resort" (Chick 1986: 7). The ability of the commercial banks to obtain reserves at the base rate, on a discretionary basis, was introduced in the 1960s.[8] Notwithstanding, according to banking protocol, a bank is not permitted to create a loan that then forms a deposit at the initiating bank, and then use the *same* deposit to make a transfer payment on behalf of the loan recipient. If there is a request for a transfer payment from the created deposit, this has to be financed from: preexisting deposits at the central bank, new reserves (freshly obtained from central bank borrowing at base rate), liquidity resulting from the discount of securities at the central bank (or sales elsewhere) or borrowings from the interbank market. If this were not the case, the individual banks would be able to make loans to themselves and use the created deposits as a base for their own lending. Furthermore, when any default occurs, individual banks suffer losses from pretax profits. It is the case, therefore, that default and changing state policy toward banks directly affects their costs of production (and risk premiums) and, therefore, the levels of credit remain (partly) exogenously determined by the government.

It is argued in the book that the EMT (see Chick, Lavoie, Moore, Rochon, Wray, e.g.,), further discussed later, now provides a better explanation of the contemporary financial reality (Chick 1986; Rochon 1999; Lavoie 2003; Moore 2006). Some of the financial textbooks, surprisingly, still need to be rewritten despite the acceptance of the EMT.[9] Credit monies have increased as the relative proportion of notes and coins has declined. Yet, notes and coins, *cash* in the vernacular, are still widely circulated as money and, in some cases, remain the only acceptable method of payment for goods and services, although in modern times they now only form a small percentage of total global monies. In the UK in 2005, for instance, M0 constituted 3.5% of M4 (IMF 2011).

2.5 THE CONTROL OF CREDIT MONEY

In order to explore the general discourse surrounding the *control* of money it is necessary to turn to the ideas of sociologists, economic historians and political economists, rather than mainstream monetary theory, since these considerations are almost invariably absent from the orthodox economics literature. The industrial revolution and its immediate aftermath had brought many relevant monetary ideas to the fore. As mercantile capitalism was gradually transformed into industrial capitalism, for example, new nonmetallic (credit) money forms emerged. The French credit system under the management of John Law, in the first quarter of the eighteenth century, had been an early forerunner of this. Scottish-born Law (1671–1729) had been licensed to set up a bank in France and issue credit money in the form of paper banknotes, backed by government securities. These were *legal tender* and were accepted for taxation. Law also set up a holding company for which he issued notes and stock. He then (infamously) manipulated shareholder expectations of corporate success until, a speculative asset bubble crashed and his monetary system ended up with worthless banknotes. Marx, insightfully, had labeled him a "mixture of swindler and prophet" (Pringle 2001: 4). Law had, however, been responsible for instigating the notion of paper credit-money that facilitates industriousness, and this new form of *bank credit money,* as Ingham notes, is recognized as a key foundation of capitalist development (Ingham 2001). In the UK, between 1694 and the late eighteenth century, a more stable credit system developed that lasted until the middle of the nineteenth century.[10] Here, only the so-called country (provincial) banks and the BOE could issue banknotes. From 1844, however, the BOE became the sole issuer of notes and subsequently became the model on which central (national) banks around the globe were based (Zarlenga 2002).[11] This had the effect of *centralizing* the control of money-creation in private hands since national banks were privately owned, where it has largely remained ever since. Yet, the overall quantity of banknotes in circulation was still small, in contrast to the exponential growth of the credit money-form that occurred during the twentieth century.

Prior to this preindustrial revolution period the state (or institutions and groups that served them) had to a greater or lesser extent directly controlled the issue of the money-form (with associated *seigniorage*) through the safeguarding of specie, the control of precious metal mining and the manipulation of price ratios between the silver and gold currency areas (Zarlenga 2002).[12] This was in addition to the occasional issuance of perpetual bonds, which do not mature but pay interest in perpetuity, for the purposes of war making. After the instigation of bank credit money, however, financial power (as defined) had been increasingly transferred to an emerging private banking infrastructure.[13] This meant that, despite the state increasing in size and scope, monetary sovereignty was in decline. During the period of the gold standard in Britain, for instance, the state had reduced regulatory powers over the financial system, which had led monetary reformers, such as Keynes, to resist a return to the standard following WW1 (Keynes 1924). This was due to the fact that inflows and outflows of specie directly determined the domestic money supply. When this system was finally abandoned in 1931, support for state intervention arose and an era of enhanced state financial capacity emerged following WW2. During this BW era, as Helleiner has effectively demonstrated, the state regained some regulatory control over money, yet this was subsequently lost as a result of consistent lobbying from the bankers (Helleiner 1994). This proposition of Helleiner is the key theme of the book's narrative and will therefore be examined theoretically and empirically in later chapters. Private money has increased its sphere of influence. In addition, money is now not backed up by precious metals (or other commodity), since the demise of BW in 1971, and is merely maintained by the legal sanction of the (respective) state through their license of the private banking infrastructure.[14] This has substantial implications for the future of political economy.

2.6 THE VALUE OF MONEY

What is the present *value* of money, since there is no longer any intrinsic value? The standard answer to this question is that the value is determined by the quantity of commodities, at a given time, that can be purchased in the given currency area. This concept of money-value implies that the rate of inflation (and exchange rates) necessarily determines any changes in the *real* value of money.[15] This, as I shall discuss, forms an integral part of mainstream monetary theory. A further implication is that if a particular quantity of money represents a given basket of commodities then, as Smith had maintained, there is a given *necessary* circulating quantity for the purposes of commercial activity (Itoh 1999: 11). Yet, the stock of money is a small proportion of the total social *wealth* of an economy, which is, perhaps, an important point to remember.[16] The implication of this, as Meltzer has noted, is that money (in the mainstream conception) is relatively unimportant as a "store of value," in contrast to its exchange function (Meltzer 1998: 10). This, as could be argued, also suits the political aspirations of those that wield financial power who are perhaps keen to *downplay* the role of monetary factors in the economy and emphasize its means of exchange function. According to Marx (and Smith and Ricardo before him), however, the value of money is conceived differently. In his conception, money is viewed as the alienable depository of (abstract) social labor that people possess. It still represents the purchasing power of use-value but then it also measures labor. At any specified time, a fixed sum of money is considered to represent a definite quantity of labor hours (and hence value) in the aggregate, whatever commodities are exchanged for money. If money quantity *per se* were to be increased, *ceteris paribus*, it can be considered to be *fictitious* in the sense that no new value has been created, and the incidence therefore can have a redistributive effect on economic agents. These ideas will be explored in later chapters and are significant for the theories that have been adopted.

2.7 MONEY MEASURES

In the UK there are different measures of money that can be used and, by definition, varying compilations of financial statistics to represent them. M0, for instance, denotes the quantity of notes and coins and BOE reserve accounts, whereas M1 includes sight deposit accounts. In a specified time period a given quantity of money can also circulate at different speeds and, therefore, represent varying levels of aggregate transactions.[17] Yet, it will also be helpful to distinguish between a money stock and flow. At any given point in time there will be a certain amount of money in existence, denominated in separate currencies and all owned (according to title) by someone (or an entity). In this static model, it is possible to identify the relative proportions of monies owned. However, the money supply is constantly changing. During a defined period of time there exists a dynamic creation and destruction of available (credit) monies that suggests a *money flow* and this is somewhat more difficult to quantify. If all outstanding contractual credit relations were to be instantly resolved, in a hypothetical sense, the money supply would immediately shrink. This particular discourse centers on the concept of "inside and outside" money, first theorized by Gurley and Shaw in the 1960s, and is worth a mention at this stage (Harris 1981: 30).

The economy is seen as divided into the private, banking and public sectors. In short, an item that illustrates part of the net worth of an individual may not affect the net worth of the sector in aggregate. All money is seen as a debt category of another entity in the system. Banknotes, for instance, are the liability of the state. If we consider the banking sector's balance sheet, we see assets in the form of cash, loans to the private sector and government securities. The liabilities take the form of bank deposits. It then follows that part of private sector bank deposits are canceled by loans (inside money). It can be assumed that bank deposits, held by the private sector and offset by government bonds in the banking sector, are "outside money" since the bank deposits are an asset of the private sector whereas the government bonds are not a liability of that sector. Yet, if we were to take into consideration the role of taxation (a future liability of the private sector), that is used to meet the debt repayments on government bills, we could argue that there is a further canceling out. In more recent times, similar ideas have found form in the so-called modern monetary theory espoused by Randall Wray (2012).

Wray's exposition of MMT begins with discussion of inter-sectoral balances, where one sector's deficit is matched by another sector's (or a combination of sectors) surplus, since by definition all balances must net to zero in the aggregate (Wray 2012: 4). In this sense, netting to zero refers to double-entry bookkeeping on retail bank balance sheets. A bank deposit, for instance, constitutes part of the net wealth of an individual, combined with other (including nonfinancial) assets, yet it represents a liability for the bank. The MMT approach refers to a *pyramid of liabilities* with the government liabilities at the top and layers of credit below founded on base money, which means that if all debt obligations were to be canceled base money would still remain (Wray 2012: 85). Ignoring base money for simplicity, the private sector balances net to zero but, if this sector has a deficit with the public sector, then the public sector must have a surplus by definition. The public sector will have an asset on their balance sheet (*ceteris paribus*) without a corresponding liability, while the private sector has a net liability on its balance sheet.[18] The key proposition of Wray is the notion that a state that issues its own currency is in a stronger position than decision-makers in a non-sovereign currency jurisdiction so that some states have lost more control than others. Wray presents a sovereign state that retains (at least in theory) the ability to determine financial outcomes, through fiscal policy and debt-management protocols, even if the state is serving the wishes of private capital. In a credit-monetary system, as Wray notes a person (or entity) that is credit-worthy can always decide to spend more if they so choose (Wray 2012: 14). Since a sovereign currency (in terms of base money) issuer is able to dictate the terms of supply, and possesses the right to tax at will (note earlier note on tax), there is no theoretical limit to their ability to borrow. As Wray notes, since government deficits create an equivalent amount of nongovernment savings (p. 126), it is impossible for the state to face an insufficient supply of savings (Wray 2012). But, importantly, *self-imposed constraints* exist that limit the behavior of sovereign currencies and, in the current austerity discourse, these tend to be predicated on what Wray calls the *myth of unsustainability* (Wray 2012). It is these types of constraints that are prevalent in the so-called austerity agenda in the UK and Wray helps us understand this. However, it is worth noting that the relevance of the concepts of inside/outside money has been questioned by some, notably Pesek and Saving, who argued that any difference between inside and outside money is not helpful and that all money can be seen as a net asset even if it might have a dual function as a future repayment of debt. If an entity has the capacity to function as money, and does so, then it *is* money (Harris 1981: 37). This is the ontological approach adopted in this book since credit money actually circulates as means of payment.

2.8 CONCLUSION

So money has functioned as a means of exchange, store of value, credit facilitator and unit of account and has liberated human communities from the inefficiency of barter and its double coincidence of wants. A monetary economy simply works better. In terms of money's origin there has been a debate between chartalist thinkers, who emphasize the engagement of the authorities with money's first appearance in society, and the commodity view that suggests money emerged endogenously as a consequence of the market agents themselves. This debate reduces down to a chicken and egg argument since although the historical evidence tends to favor the chartalist view it is by no means conclusive. Money has also taken different forms. Commodity money, for example, took the form of gold or silver although there are plenty of examples of other entities being used.[19] Fiat monies have also been created at various times in history, such as the circulation of minted coin or paper monies, backed by the legitimacy and force of the state. It is noted by Wray that a key factor in the success of such currency is the ability to pay your taxes with it. This, in turn, creates a demand for the money (Wray 2012). The most ubiquitous form of currency, however, is credit money. In the modern era, private banks operate as intermediaries and create credit contracts, thus forming accounts that serve as depositories of circulating currency. The control of this credit money, of course, is shared between both state and market and the book investigates, as stated earlier, the changing state/market nexus of power relations in this regard. There has also been a discussion of the value of money that is its purchasing power. If prices rise or international exchange rates change, this will impact the nominal value of money. In the final section, I identified that monetary aggregates can be measured in different ways and can also be considered as a monetary flow or a stock. In the next two chapters, the mainstream and heterodox views of money nature, creation and function are considered respectively, in terms of the theme of financial power that has been outlined in chapter 1.

NOTES

1. Hicks had also used these ideas to illustrate the origin of a simple banking process where bankers issue short-term credit (Hicks 1967: 11).
2. Michael Hudson argues (Zarlenga 2002: 14), for instance, that the origin of money was sanctioning by the state, where the Austrian school posit that money derives endogenously from the market (Zarlenga 2002: 676).
3. The management of the currency took place in palaces or temples.
4. The official sanction of a currency is manifested by the *ability* to pay taxes with the monetary medium specified. Wray points out that this increases the social acceptability of money (Wray 2012).
5. Unless the authorities choose to remove these monies from circulation.
6. Legal tender is interpreted differently according to jurisdiction.
7. It is noted that capital adequacy is now subject to international regulation through the Basle accords.
8. This was known as the "open door" policy.
9. The Howells and Bain textbook is an exception (Howells & Bain 2008).
10. The Bank of England was formed in 1694 and led to the increased private control of monies at the expense of the state (Zarlenga 2002, chap. 11).
11. Certain partnerships, however, were still issuing notes until the twentieth century.
12. Also, the state-controlled "tally-stick" system had existed in England for hundreds of years and constituted a form of debt-free money issuance. The Prussians, according to Marx, also practiced a similar form of money-issue (Marx [1858] 1973: 132).
13. Some of the actors involved might have derived from the prevailing financial infrastructure.
14. The gold-exchange standard that followed WW2 enabled central banks to exchange their currencies with the dollar, which was convertible to gold at $35 per ounce. The system faltered as international market forces put pressure on the dollar following US current account deficits.
15. The use of the concept of *purchasing power parity* in international comparisons of spending power reflects this trend in monetary thinking.
16. Meltzer suggests money constitutes as little as 2% of consolidated wealth of an economy (Meltzer 1998: 10).

17. This is known as the velocity of circulation.
18. External balance is also ignored for purposes of simplicity.
19. Paper currency can be used that is convertible into such commodities and this has been very common.

Chapter 3

The Mainstream View of Money

3.1 INTRODUCTION

In this chapter I consider the basis for the mainstream view of money that, by definition, still dominates the policy-making circles in the capitalist nations. I begin by a brief description of mainstream policy from the classical period. In the next section the idea of money neutrality is explored within the context of capitalist apologetics. This includes a review of the classical position and key debates. Next, there is an exploration of the key ideas of Smith, Ricardo and Steuart respectively. In the final section, modern mainstream monetary thinking is explored in the context of general equilibrium, with particular reference to Walras and Marshall.

Mainstream monetary theory can be considered as general orthodoxy, adopted by a consensus of policy-makers, in particular historical and/ or geographical contexts. Leading up to WW2, for instance, the classical pre-Keynesian quantity theory tradition was viewed as mainstream in the UK, before the Keynesian *revolution*.[1] However, in the immediate post-war period, a neoclassical/Keynesian synthesis developed that utilized IS/LM models and exogenous money-creation (Harris 1981: 141). This synthesis of theory derived its roots (and models) from a broad sweep of monetary economists and was instrumental in informing the policy framework of Germany and Britain. Yet, the classical ideas persisted despite existing in a watered-down form. Toward the end of this period there was a revival of the quantity theory, promoted by Milton Friedman, with the monetarist challenge. This was superseded by the neoclassical formulations of money that have survived relatively intact to the present day. In Europe (but not the US) it has also been common to use the phrase neo-liberal to describe the monetary ideas that have applied neoclassical economic ideas to the deregulation of finance and international capital flows. There are now, however, many strands of heterodox thinking which refuse to accept these mainstream views (and Keynesian synthesis) and have provided some stimulating theoretical and empirical research. It is these heterodox ideas that have given us insight into some of the implications of an erosion of financial sovereignty that has occurred as a consequence of financialization. But, what is the essence of the mainstream monetary view and what were the antecedents of these ideas?

3.2 THE THEORY

A suitable starting point is David Ricardo. The classical *Ricardian* notion of *neutral* money, in terms of its impact on the real economy, has arguably exerted the strongest strategic influence on policy circles for 200 years, even though it is clear, as Harris noted, not all of the classical economists adhered to this (Harris 1981: 91). In addition, since advanced economies are monetary ones, and a complete theory of money's function is arguably inseparable from capitalist theory, the focus has been on real economy factors. Ricardo, in conjunction with Smith, Say and Mill *et al.*, had provided a clear conception of capitalism that consisted of the private ownership of the productive resources, capital accumulation, free markets and competition between firms for the pursuit of profit. Neutral money is simply added in order to make the commodity markets work, and the authorities are expected to monitor its quantity to avoid inflation. These Ricardian monetary ideas can be identified in the later work of thinkers such as Walras, Patinkin, Marshall, Wicksell, Fisher, Pigou and monetarists such as Friedman (Harris 1981, chap. 6). Even today the influence is ubiquitous, reflected in the prolific use of new Keynesian DSGE models in central banking that still assume that money is neutral in the longer term but recognize frictions or hindrances to the establishment of the equilibrium.

The classical economists had presented a capitalist economic system that possessed a harmonious equilibrium, which could only be achieved if the authorities avoid misguided intervention and any market rigidities were removed. It was claimed that the unfettered operation of markets would lead to the efficient allocation of scarce resources and economic development. Furthermore, it was later assumed that the "trickle-down" theory would ensure that the spoils reach the marginalized. The eighteenth-century story of the Fable of the Bees, by Bernard Mandeville, was often used as a capitalist apologetic suggesting that as bees (analogous to profit-seeking firms) pursued their own interest, they subsequently maximized the efficiency of the whole beehive (Mandeville 1997). It was therefore concluded that universal capitalism *per se* was the *natural* historic social order that could not be improved upon. Economic history was, therefore, complete.

In this context money and credit are seen as secondary—imperative for the functioning of capitalism but *neutral*, serving merely as a means of exchange and not able to instigate or radically alter (at least in the long term) the operation of economic activity or any real economic variables.[2] Money is thus defined by its function and is also perceived as created by the authorities, either directly by state issue or indirectly through the sanction of privately produced currency. Yet, it could be argued, this concept of neutrality serves the ideological interests of a plutocracy who prefer that money is viewed as secondary to the *real* productive structure, where wealth is produced, since it diverts attention away from the accumulation and concentration of money resources, that are a claim to the same wealth. These political considerations become even more important if monetary factors are instead seen as variables that determine outcomes, as a result of their *instigative* and *fungible* qualities. In this case those that determine the money-issue and fashion its function are then endowed with substantial social power that, arguably, needs to be explored and understood. In the first chapter the interaction between creditor and debtor, war finance, the instigation of economic activity and the impact of international capital flows were all cited as manifestations of the operation of financial power. Yet, a consideration of such matters has been routinely ignored by mainstream economists, from the early classical thinkers to the more contemporary ones, who preferred to focus simply on the productive economy served by *neutral* money.

The foundation of these mainstream ideas is the *quantity theory of money* (QTM), derived from the ideas of Cantillon and Hume *et al.*, which posits that when the money supply is increased *ceteris paribus*, the price level rises but relative price ratios are unaltered (Blaug 1995: 29). The Fisher or Cambridge *equation of exchange* identities used for the QTM both assume that money is issued exogenously that is, determined by forces outside the model. There is a stable velocity of circulation that is not influenced by endogenous factors, the volume of transactions is determined independently of the model, causality runs from money to price rather than the reverse and the problems of adjustment to equilibrium are small. In other words, markets *clear* (Blaug 1995).[3] The early QTM, in Hume's conception, had involved "fictitious-value" money, in the sense that money merely represented labor and commodities in the sphere of exchange. In the aggregate, therefore, Hume posited that the value of money would be equal to the inverse of the price level. His assumption here, contrary to Locke, is that money is *only* utilized for the traded economy as a means of exchange and does not, by implication, represent a claim to accumulated wealth or be subject to hoarding. Hume had also discussed the "international level" of specie money whereby money seeks the "same level," like water, between countries (Itoh 1999: 8). If the source of specie for one state increases then monetary metal flows out of the country, since domestic commodity prices have risen, and a balance of payments deficit ensues until the "level" is found again. Hume had a transmission mechanism to illustrate how this worked in the short term. Extra money puts more people in work and boosts production but, in time, the temporary boost is reversed as output returns to its previous level yet with higher prices. So, for Hume, and later for Ricardo, money is simply a *veil* on real economic activity representing neutrality in the longer term. In terms of the *creation* of money (he did not distinguish between different money-forms) it is implicit in Hume's work that the state should monitor the quantity of money in order to avoid inflation but that the fresh money-issue derives from the mining of precious metals (Itoh 1999). In this sense the monetary thought of Hume, like the majority of mainstream thinkers since, had assumed that the control of the money-issue *per se* was of secondary (political) importance and that the regulatory role of the state should merely be focused on the standardization of the money-form, and its overall money supply, in order to facilitate a smooth running of the productive economy and the mitigation of inflation. This perhaps accounts for the lack of political concern about the erosion of financial sovereignty and growth of financialization.

In context, this classical political economy emerging in the late eighteenth century was in contrast to the mercantilists, who had considered that the primary *economic* aim of the state was to intervene in such a manner as to facilitate an international trading surplus. This would ensure an influx of commodity money in the form of precious metals, which was considered commensurate with wealth. Ironically, the current account surplus of one nation is matched by a corresponding deficit elsewhere and so the mercantilist policies could not be successful for all. The classical school, conversely, held that minimal state intervention in the form of free trade allowed international markets to operate more effectively, leading to favorable efficiencies and increased prosperity for all trading partners. They had also established the principle that national wealth, comprised mainly of commodities, did not reside in trade surpluses but in the *labor* content of produce—the labor theory of value—since labor was the *real* cost of production. This was in stark contrast to the mercantilists, who had held that value (in the form of price) was determined by demand and supply in the sphere of exchange. Understanding these competing value theories is necessary in order to conceptualize different notions of the function of money. Ironically, the neoclassical school, while upholding the belief in free markets, has *rejected* labor value theory in favor of (marginal) utility theory where *value* is established in the market, which is closer to the ideas of the mercantilists.[4]

Utility theory of value is predicated on the subjective notion of perceived satisfaction derived from produce, usually called use-value. These subjective *values* then determine demand, which, with supply factors, form price. In order to appreciate the role of money *per se* in the productive economy it is arguably imperative to discuss value theory more fully since *money* is the most effective and practical depository of *value* in a monetary economy. Notions of utility, as a basis for value measurement, will consequently be considered later in the chapter in the discussion of more modern mainstream theorists.

In the real economy the classical school had maintained that free markets would be beneficial and stable, and this was also extended to the operation of money and credit, although two separate traditions emerged. The *currency school*, supported by Ricardo (also Torrens and Overstone), was based on the idea that stability should exist between real output and total (commodity or fully convertible) money, providing there was no state (or other) interference with market operation. Yet, they maintained that an overissue of credit (in relation to its metal base) would result in inflation, even if full convertibility existed. An excess of paper would lead to depreciating value, in relation to specie, leading to a fall in exchange rates and an outflow of gold.[5] This led to their support for the English Bank Act 1844 that sought to restrict credit. This QTM approach had its contemporary *monetarist* adherents, most notably in the Reagan or Thatcher administrations, and has influenced the mainstream view. Ironically, the monetarists had also advocated nonintervention by the state in goods markets while arguing for state *control* of the *quantity* of money-issue. It is also ironic that original quantity theories had usually been applied to commodity money (e.g., Hume) which, as Blaug noted, tends to be *endogenously* created (from specie sources), and it is, therefore, perhaps irrelevant to consider policies of quantity control in these circumstances since this implies the state capacity to control the money-issue (Blaug 1995: 31).[6] It is perhaps fortuitous that this type of logical dilemma is irrelevant today, since commodity money is not used, but it is still necessary to consider the impracticality of monetary aggregate control in a world where money is largely endogenously determined by the market.

The *banking school* (or anti-quantity theorists) for example, Fullarton and Thomas Tooke, in contrast, had maintained that stability also exists between real output *and* credit money, provided that the credit was extended for productive investment and not speculation, and they were not (therefore) particularly concerned with overissue.[7] In order to sustain this position the banking school had to emphasize specie hoarding and the paying functions of commodity money, that implied that money was *non-neutral* and also functioned as an effective store of value.[8] They asserted that productive capitalists in possession of commodity monies would be more inclined to hoard surpluses rather than spend, and that the *necessity* of payment for commodities and investment goods *instigates* (perhaps permanent) economic activity that would otherwise not occur rather than necessarily fueling inflation.[9] Monies could be extended or withdrawn from hoards, thus responding to the needs of circulation. Rather than the *quantity* of money determining the price level they claimed that the causality worked the other way. Raised prices led to more money in circulation, drawn from hoards. In addition, the school had also distinguished between fiat money and credit money, positing that fiat money could be issued to excess and remains in circulation, whereas credit monies would be subject to the *law of the reflux* whereby credit contracts are canceled through repayment. The banking school thus identified the properties of different money-forms and functions, and these notions have tended to influence the more heterodox views of money as a consequence. These ideas are more fully explored in chapter 4. The currency school and the QTM serve, in contrast, as antecedents of the mainstream monetary view that has pervaded much of the policy space since the industrial capitalist age.

3.3 ADAM SMITH (1723–1790)

Smith, while supporting banking school arguments, has also informed more general capitalist theory. Smith (Smith 1776) had first outlined the origin (and hence nature) of money and explained its role in advancing the division of labor through transcending the inefficiency of barter. Metallic money became the ideal form and this led to state-minted coins based on weight and finesse. The state was able to provide legitimacy, harmonization and efficiency to the weighing and assaying functions. In this sense, for Smith (and Hume), the state has an indispensable role in the *creation* of (commodity) money yet the origin and nature of money are market driven from mining. Smith then explained how, as coins circulated, a system of nominal prices was established once coin denominations had been established. Smith also formulated the classical theory of exchange values (the transaction ratios) determined by the labor content as the regulating factor. Even if nominal prices were to deviate from their *natural* price in the short term, competition would eventually render the natural price. Yet, as Ormazabal notes, Smith did have some ambiguity between his treatment of *labor* value in production and the *labor* value in exchange, in his nonrecognition of the Marx notion of *surplus value* in order to explain profit (Ormazabal 2004). When the profit of a firm is added to the calculation it means that the exchange-price exceeds that of the labor value. Marx resolved the dilemma by identifying that profit is extracted from the labor used in producing the output. Surplus value, for Marx, is the difference between the *labor* value added to commodities by living labor and the *value* of the wage. There has been enduring debate in which the mainstream claims that Smith ditched the labor theory of value when considering profit in capitalism. Yet Ormazabal claims that Marx had illustrated how Smith had merely become confused on this matter. Marx had argued instead that the existence of profit does not *add* value to a commodity, since profit merely exists in the form of (realized) surplus value (Ormazabal 2004). In contrast, the mainstream view of economic history still maintains that Smith had realized the *error* of the labor theory of value. This, perhaps, serves a convenient political purpose since it enables him to be established as the father of the neoclassical (mainstream) school. Smith's description of the "invisible hand," for instance, has contributed clear definition to the logic of free markets and resource allocation in capitalism. Yet, as monetary reformer Zarlenga claims, Smith's support for the banking school, with their policy of less state regulation of credit-issue, can arguably be seen as an attempt to divert attention from the existence of profiteering private banking. The banking sector, consequently, wielded accumulating financial power as the capitalist system evolved (Zarlenga 2002). The counterargument to this view of Smith is that credit instigation and expansion simply responds to demand and the needs of the real economy and is not, therefore, necessarily problematic *per se*. Furthermore, it is more likely to be the systemic drivers Smith, for example, had defended his theoretical position with reference to his "real bills" theory.

Banknotes that were superfluous to the (necessary quantity) *channel of circulation*, according to Smith, were converted to gold and exported for the purchase of imports, rather than raising prices (Itoh 1999: 18). Also, for Smith, the advance of credit did not increase the *capital* of an economy directly, through instigating fresh production (a re-statement of the neutrality of money), yet it speeded the process of capital turnover through creating efficiencies. Money stocks needed for the different stages of production were not needed, for instance, with their associated administration (and opportunity) costs. Subsequently, Smith had felt that banks should advance to capitalists the precise amount that they would have kept as precautionary funds. If they were to advance any more they would discover that notes return faster than usual and the bank would need to keep high levels of reserves in order to meet demand for specie, reducing their profitability. To counteract this the bank should, when they discounted bills of exchange (trader IOU's), only advance to the merchants the amount they need according to commercial requirements, moderated by the *real* nature of the bills. These *real bills* represented real production and trading activity and so, therefore, any credit monies created were backed by this economic activity. Smith hoped that as a result equilibrium would exist between commodities and credit monies. Yet, Henry Thornton contested Smith's bills doctrine. Thornton had loosely adhered to the QTM but recognized that different money-forms had different circulation velocities and, therefore, it was difficult to talk of a *necessary* quantity of money. Thornton also attacked the tenuous distinction Smith had made between "fictitious" bills and "real" bills and also suggested that capitalist sales limited "real" bills. As far as banks were concerned it was *creditworthiness* that mattered most. Furthermore, one lot of goods may give rise to several "real" bills as they pass between traders. Thornton argued instead that it would only be the reflux that limited banknote issue, and that credit expansion levels were linked to the relationship between the varying rate of interest and rate of profit. Thornton had clearly thought that money had an *instigative* function, in terms of production, and saw no natural limit to credit expansion, and, therefore, the level of output (Itoh 1999: 21). Smith's overall position, therefore, implied that there should be an enhanced regulatory role for the state, in terms of moderating banking practice, in order to prevent excessive credit that (he assumed) affected gold reserves. Yet, as a supporter of the banking school, he had clearly felt that the *modus operandi* of the private banking infrastructure (and credit-money creation) was reasonably beneficial and, by implication, was of little political significance.

3.4 DAVID RICARDO (1772–1823)

The English stockbroker and MP, David Ricardo, articulated the finished classical position on labor value theory (as labor embodied in produce) and also adhered to the quantity theory. He argued that if only metallic money circulates there would be a *correct* quantity of money that reflects transaction volume and the *necessary* circulation speed (Itoh 1999: 12). If actual money quantity deviated from the necessary amount then Ricardo believed it would be inflationary or deflationary like Hume. Yet, unlike Hume, Ricardo believed that commodities (and commodity money) had intrinsic value determined by labor content. Ricardo, therefore, had to marry Hume's idea of the "fictitious value" of money with his own intrinsic view. Ricardo figured that if money was all specie then each economy would have enough for its sphere of exchange and a global equilibrium would exist. There would be no motive to transfer money overseas. In this sense, the (international) steady state is actually a current account balance, with trade being akin to barter. A shock to equilibrium, such as a fresh supply of specie, would cause the domestic value of money to fall (raising prices) and then bullion could be exported at a profit. The exchange rate would then fall, reducing the domestic money supply, until equilibrium is re-established. According to Ricardo, paper money did not disturb this natural equilibrium providing the paper was fully convertible into gold. Inconvertible paper, however, drives out (hoarded) commodity money if it increases in quantity, since the aggregate rate of exchange with commodities will be permanently below that of the specie. Ricardo, interestingly, actually thought that paper money was superior to specie, providing that it was convertible. For Ricardo, therefore, money was simply for exchange since he did not theorize on hoarding functionality. Yet, it is implicit in Ricardo's work that he envisaged a *strong* role for the state in terms of money legitimization, the prevention of (excessive) fractional backing and the maintenance of convertibility. Itoh and Lapavitsas suggest that this recommendation of a strong state (financial) regulatory capability caused Ricardo unpopularity with the private bankers at the time (Itoh 1999: 23).

So, in summary, classical political economy had identified that the social expression of money was *commodity* money in the form of specie. This money-form, in terms of nominal prices, was a representation of the exchange-value existing in commodities. This exchange-value, in turn, would be proportionate to labor content rather than the *subjective* use-value. Their general theory of money was, therefore, rooted in this labor theory of value, which posited that market values were regulated by the labor content. They still accepted, however, that market forces would cause nominal prices to deviate from their natural prices in the short term, but that capitalist competition would render the correct prices (adjusted to labor content) in time.[10] Yet, in all their discourse regarding the ideal economic role for the state there is still no meaningful consideration of the *social power* derived from the control of money-issue and function and the varying interests that may be served by this. This subject has been generally left to political theorists, political economists and sociologists.

The currency and banking schools of thought had each represented different traditions within the classical school, and this manifested in their varying approaches to monetary questions. The currency school, for instance, regarded money as relatively neutral and wanted to restrict credit monies in order to avoid inflation. This was the antecedent of the current mainstream view. The banking school, conversely, posited that monetary factors could instigate economic activity and they emphasized the store of value function. However, both groups accepted the logic of capitalist ideology that stressed the benefits of free markets, private property and the competition between firms for profit. Instead, these different approaches to monetary theory were reflected in their different positions on the law of the reflux, the quantity theory, the *real bills* doctrine, and the emerging credit system.

These classical ideas still have influence on mainstream policy, despite the historical critical discourse and any implementation difficulties that have been experienced. The idea that money is *neutral* in the long term, for instance, is still utilized in most professional economic models.[11] Yet, conversely, heterodox economists, such as members of the Marxian or post-Keynesian school, have ideas that have clear links to the banking school tradition and certainly appear to offer a richer analysis of the reality of contemporary money and credit systems. Some of these ideas have also derived from the work of an earlier monetary thinker, Sir James Steuart, and his thought therefore deserves to be reviewed.

3.5 SIR JAMES STEUART (1712–1780)

Steuart, a late mercantilist, had reasoned that the *accounting* function of money, that uses a scale of equal parts, determined its fundamental *nature*. In this abstract sense, money was construed as anything socially (and politically) acceptable that would serve this purpose and, in addition, is a prerequisite for exchange. Consistent with other mercantilists (and neo-liberals), however, he had rejected the labor theory as a determining factor of exchange-value and thought instead that prices (and utility) were simply determined by market forces in the sphere of exchange. Money could, therefore, be considered as a "measure of things vendible" (Itoh 1999: 6). He posited however, in line with Smith, that commodity money, which he termed "artificial or material" money, was an imperfect measure of this abstract form since it was itself subject to changing valuation. The value-measure of vendible entities can be expressed in several money-forms and so, therefore, money *per se* can be seen as abstract. Marx also stressed this difference between *abstract* money, where value is transferred into price, and *real* money that gives price a concrete equivalent containing the essential qualities of (commodity) monies since commodities were the sole form that (in his day) could transcend the boundaries of state jurisdiction. Yet, this did not preclude the successful use of abstract monies in a society (Marx [1859] 1970: 119).

Steuart had also discussed paper money, which he regarded as the "melting down of solid property," which adds to the commodity monies available (Itoh 1999: 9). Using the phrase "symbolical money" to refer to credit money usage (in the form of bank notes, bank deposits, bills, bonds and merchant's books), Steuart suggested that the "exchanges between classes" and general industriousness could be facilitated. There is, however, no discussion of bank deposits (similar to Marx) as a *money form* (deposits are now used as money for payments) which he seemed to view as a form of hoarding and, therefore, as nonfunctioning through their non-circulation. Steuart held instead that only metallic money settled transactions in a *definite* way whereas the various credit monies were a *promise* to pay. Steuart also posited (as the banking school) that these two separate forms of money followed different regulating principles. Whereas an excess of metallic money was hoarded, an excess of credit money was returned to the creditor through the repayment of loans. He called this process the "regorging" of money as returned credit money was converted back to metallic money and was then exported or lent to the state. Steuart had also suggested that if there was a surplus in the balance of payments, there is an appreciation in the exchange rate and an inflow of coin. As a consequence, part of the circulating currency then becomes redundant and is "regorged" leading to lower interest rates and fewer loans held by banks as assets.

So, in terms of the political economy of money creation Steuart had envisaged a key role for the "statesman" who he assumed would ensure that the correct amount of monies required for circulation was available. This might involve monitoring the production of paper money, in the form of endogenous credit money, in order to replace any commodity monies that had been hoarded or were needed to finance new activity. Steuart had therefore viewed the creation, sanction and monitoring of money forms as deriving from both state and market, with the emphasis on a strong role for the state. Yet, despite theorizing on an abstract "money of account" as the ideal form of money, he remained (like the classicists) a *metallist* in practical terms. These ideas of Steuart, however, in addition to influencing heterodox ideas, have also influenced more modern mainstream ideas that have rejected the labor value theory yet upheld the belief that free markets drive price valuation. The essential concept derived from classical thought is that an economy will settle at equilibrium where utility-maximizing consumers/producers, via Marshallian subjective demand/supply schedules, establish a complex arrangement of relative price ratios—akin to a barter economy, where money simply operates as a veil facilitating *real* economic activity.

3.6 LEON WALRAS (1834–1910) AND GENERAL EQUILIBRIUM

The general equilibrium model that was first developed, and later adopted by the mainstream, was based upon the Walrasian theoretical model. In Walras's approach, people come to the market with goods/services (and money) to exchange. They proceed to negotiate and make deals and, as a result, form relative prices. However, it is assumed that the transactions are not settled until the end of the period. The deals are then conditional contracts that can only be honored if *equilibrium* prices have been established. The equilibrium is defined as a state where the traders purchase all that they require and sell all that they require (Walras 1926). It appears *prima facie* that there is no need for *money* here at all, since the economic activity is akin to barter, although the conditional contracts *per* se could be seen as a form of money. It is interesting to note that Patinkin, working in 1965, used this Walrasian model in order to illustrate money's function as a store of value, as a result of this non-synchronicity (Patinkin 1965). Uncertainty has now been introduced. Each trader is unsure whether he or she needs to purchase products before making some sales, even at market clearing prices, and they have a subsequent need for money. The idea is that after the market day, and before the next one, the transactions need to be completed which are the most likely to be nonsynchronized, hence the necessity for money. In the neoclassical thought that emerged after the marginalist revolution, money became the *sine qua non* of the capitalist economic system yet remained, and remains, a *veil* for the exchange economy.

3.7 QUANTITY THEORY, MARSHALL, AND EQUILIBRIUM ANALYSIS

The crude quantity theory (QTM) that had been adopted by Hume, Ricardo and Mill *et al.*, describes the impact of an exogenous change in the nominal money supply *ceteris paribus* that leads to a price level change. The implication is that the money supply affects the goods market, in terms of the price level, but *not* relative prices and/or output. They assumed relative prices (price ratios) to be already preestablished, in accordance with the Walrasian equilibrium. Yet, it is worth noting, as Harris comments, even the classical economists did not adhere to the crude QTM since they recognized the disruptions during the transition to equilibrium, following a disturbance in nominal money supply. If a change in nominal money supply affected interest rates, for example, changes to consumption and investment spending would follow (Harris 1981). QTM supporters argued that these changes in real balances eventually led to a general equilibrium again, where consumption and investment levels (and relative prices) remained as before.[12] In the pre-Keynesian QTM tradition some did not assume velocity to be constant (due to interest rates, price changes or expectations) and they thought prices could also affect the money supply, rather than it consistently being the other way around. As a consequence, Harris recommended viewing the QTM as a historical money paradigm, rather than an idea rigidly adhered to, that could then be used as a reference point for investigation (Harris 1981: 91).

Notwithstanding, Walras suggested that there are different time periods where equilibriums are formed. He posited that prices are established, where there is no excess demand or supply, overseen by an (theoretical) auctioneer. Desired deals can be seen as conditional contracts since any excesses (or deficiencies) need to be sorted out before any transactions can take place. If there is an excess demand for product A, for example, the auctioneer calls out a fresh set of relative prices leading to a new set of contracts. The process continues until a general equilibrium is established with new relative prices, where the aggregate demand for each good is matched by a corresponding aggregate supply. Yet, while the idea of equilibrium certainly has its supporters, it is difficult to conceive of this occurring in the real world. But, surprisingly, the concept has been prevalent in the mainstream for a long time despite the need for a substantial number of catallactic coincidences.[13] The *Walras Law* further states that the *sum of the excess demands and supplies over all markets (including money) must identically equal zero* (Harris 1981). In other words, if there is an excess demand at a specific relative set of prices for one good then there will have to be a corresponding excess of supply for another. This suggests that individuals are subject to budget constraints. An additional concept that is often employed when considering general equilibrium models is the *Homogeneity Postulate* that suggests that the *demands/ excess demands will not change in response to a change in the price level alone* (Harris 1981). This posits money as neutral. In this sense it is believed that we can determine relative price ratios through the process of "truck and barter" yet cannot, however, determine money-prices unless we are given specific information about the monetary system/supply.[14]

But, given the assumptions of the model, if the quantity theory tells us about the price level and Walras's law informs us of relative prices, is it possible to combine these two aspects in the same model? Patinkin has convincingly argued that this is not possible, as a result of a logical inconsistency. This is because if the homogeneity postulate (neutrality) is combined with Walras's law it is found that the barter economy cannot be extended to a monetary one. Harris uses the following example; if the goods and money market are in equilibrium and the price level is doubled, with no change to the exogenous money supply, the homogeneity postulate informs us that the goods market will remain in equilibrium. This occurs because the excess demand (and equivalent excess supply) depends on changes to *relative prices* only. The money market, conversely, according to the quantity theory, cannot be in equilibrium since a change in the prices must mean more monies in circulation or faster velocity (Harris 1981). The (model) inconsistency is still relevant if the homogeneity postulate is replaced by Say's law, since the implication is the same that is, the demand for goods as a whole will equal the supply of goods (supply creates its own demand) (Harris 1981). In order to solve the theory dilemma, Patinkin developed the notion of the *real balance effect,* which draws on the notion of *real* purchasing power. If the price level is increased, it follows that the spending capabilities (real balances) are restricted and the equilibrium is therefore affected (Harris 1981). The neoclassical ideas of equilibrium, with certain developments (like Patinkin's) and assumptions, were thus able to persist.

The neoclassical ideas of money had first been given definition after the publication of Marshall's seminal *Principles of Economics* in 1890

(Marshall 1890).[15] Marshall had formulated, for instance, the Cambridge version of the QTM involving *k*—the inverse of the velocity of circulation—otherwise conceptualized as the demand for money (to hold) as a proportion of nominal income, rather than other financial assets.[16] He then speculated whether various factors, such as hoarding and expectations, might affect the variable (Harris 1981). Many of Marshall's contemporaries took up this research, the so-called Cambridge quantity theorists (including Keynes), and then further mused on the determinants of the demand for money and the causes of economic cycles.[17] Yet, these debates surrounding the QTM are not directly concerned with the political implication of either money-issue or the state management of monetary policy. The QTM notion of neutrality, on the other hand, is significant. Its acceptance suggests that money is a secondary entity in respect of the real economy. This, it is argued in this book, *serves the interests of plutocratic financial powers by downplaying the social power of money*. In addition, the monetary discourse that sought to reconcile the QTM with a simultaneous equilibrium, as well as more general marginal analysis of the late nineteenth century, meant that money was still viewed as secondary and, therefore, served to divert attention away from the political economy analyses of the implications of money-issue, money-value and money-function in the productive economy. Conversely, some of the heterodox monetary traditions that are considered in the next chapter direct the interested reader toward a much deeper consideration of such matters.

The mainstream monetary notions discussed have also found expression in the research work of Giffen, Pigou, and Wicksell (pre-Keynesian monetary economists), in conjunction with Keynesian-inspired thinkers, and were instrumental in informing the monetary policies and theoretical understanding that underpinned the post-WW2 German and UK financial systems during the so-called *golden age* and after. The Keynesian synthesis, for example, contained a mixture of mainstream and heterodox views and is considered in the next chapter. The neoclassical monetary ideas that followed and contributed to the *golden age* era, conversely, based on the monetarist Chicago school of Friedman *et al.*, and then superseded by more contemporary neoclassical (liberal) notions, represented a revival of these mainstream ideas discussed.

3.8 CONCLUSION

Any serious approach toward the study of monetary affairs needs to have an explicit or implicit study of the neutrality (or non-neutrality) of money *per se*. I have argued here that, within the mainstream QTM tradition, money is seen as secondary. It is assumed that market forces have established *price ratios*, which exist simply because they reflect consumer and producer behaviors, determined by subjective notions of relative value. In this sense the economy is simply a barter system to which money is added. In addition, the development or growth of the economy, that is, the transition from one state of equilibrium to another, is seen as independent of monetary factors. The mainstream monetary view does recognize, however, that money serves to enable the economy to work, and that it does so in a more efficient manner than could be achieved otherwise. I reject this mainstream notion of neutrality on three key grounds. First, when spare capacity in the real economy is taken into consideration, it is suggested that the control of monetary resources *can* affect overall output through the *instigation* of investment, and, furthermore, the impact of this on the production structure changes the equilibrium. Production, therefore, takes place that would otherwise not occur and, in contrast to the mainstream, it can be permanent. Secondly, the neutrality of money view assumes an acceptance of the QTM that is explicitly rejected in the book. The QTM is problematic because money is hoarded or re-introduced from hoards, and thus can be withdrawn from circulation. There is also a varying *velocity of circulation* and (I argue) changing price levels that *drive* money supply growth rather than the other way around. It is interesting to note that, according to Caldor, even the monetarist Friedman recognized the possibility of reverse causality (Johnson 1991). Thirdly, the *fungibility* of money provides it with flexibility. Money can change form more easily than other entities and, this means that its range of functionality is perhaps extended beyond that of the functions of money usually stated. Besides, the very existence of financial power alone, as Susan Strange defined it (outlined in 1.3), suggests a more than passive neutral role for money in the productive economy and society.

So, the mainstream view of money remains problematic since it is difficult to conceptualize money as simply a *veil* on real economic activity. In the Walrasian world, of a complex set of exchange ratios determined by catallactic coincidence, it seems impossible that a monetary economy can function in the same manner as a barter economy. Ingham has further suggested that another problem for the mainstream is the inability to identify a plausible explanation of money origin, by emphasizing commodity theories (Ingham 2001). These ideas, usually associated with Carl Menger *et al.*, are predicated on the notion that one commodity evolved, as a functioning money-form, that was acceptable to all market agents (Menger 1871).[18] Yet, as Ingham points out with reference to Hahn, the theory needs to be able to demonstrate the individual rationale for holding money, in order to be consistent with its overall claim of rational agents, and this presupposes the existence of a social norm. This social acceptability, in turn, can *a priori* only be based on social institutions that have been politically sanctioned (Hahn 1987). Ingham further points out that, even if it were logical, the commodity view of money origin is not supported by historical evidence (Ingham 2001).[19] He posits instead that these theories neglect the use of money as a means of account (a function identified by Steuart), where the account unit is *established* prior to trading. Walras had simply assumed a *numeraire* and the existence of "an auctioneer" before the market process begins, an incidence that is unlikely to have just simply appeared (Ingham 2001). If a *means of account* notion of money is assumed, it can therefore be expressed in a variety of different money-forms, which, in turn, all represent abstract value (of underlying real resources). This idea is given substance within state theory of money (STM) traditions, which are considered and developed in chapter 7.[20] It is this chartalist notion of money, defined by its functionality, which has been adopted for the book. In short, the mainstream monetary conception, while interesting, has not really addressed the political implications of the state/market nexus in respect of financial power in any meaningful sense. It is, therefore, for the purposes of the book's key arguments, abandoned altogether.

NOTES

1. Keynesianism has been contested by post-Keynesians who have sought to "restore and extend" Keynes's original monetary ideas (Tily 2007: 2).

2. Blaug notes that there is also the notion of "super neutrality," adhered to by some of the monetarist school that claims the neutrality of money even under specific conditions of an increasing rate of growth of money supply. This was something that Hume (and the later Friedman) had not agreed with (Blaug 1995: 30).

3. Irving Fisher's identity was MV = PT (where M = money supply, V = velocity of circulation, P = price level and T = number of transactions) whereas the Cambridge version Ms = Kpy, where K is the inverse of the velocity of circulation, makes the same point using a different approach (Harris 1981: 104).

4. In this regard modern Marxian analysis is the closest to the classical school.

5. To the currency school, these exchange rate movements were clear evidence of the "overissue." This led to the so-called currency "criterion principle" of Robert Torrens who stated that the only acceptable quantity of banknotes was the amount that facilitated current account (trade) balance. The so-called "Palmer" rule was adopted where the Bank of England had to maintain gold reserves of a third of all banknotes (Itoh 1999: 26).

6. Endogenous money derives from the market as opposed to state-determined exogenous money.

7. Tooke had also famously identified that low interest rates do not necessarily lead to more speculative activity, and higher prices, since they reduce the cost of production as well as stimulate demand (Itoh 1999: 29).

8. They had also accepted bank deposits as money, which was not accepted by others at time but is now universally accepted by monetary economists (Itoh 1999: 28).

9. This, of course, depends upon the particular economic circumstances that prevail.

10. The explanation of profit (in price), however, was more problematic for the Classical thinkers and, though solved by Marx's notion of surplus value, this was not clear in the monetary thinking of Smith and Ricardo.

11. The current macroeconomic model, used for assessing monetary policy at the Bank of England, is an interesting example of this (Arestis 2002).

12. It is worth noting that this requires extra money to be distributed equally across economic agents. It is more likely that any interest rate change has a redistributive effect on real balances and, therefore, price ratios.

13. It should be pointed out, however, that Walras himself had identified difficulties with his model and was really (perhaps) only seeking to find a set of simultaneous equations that could reflect a given hypothetical situation, rather than a real one.

14. This is clearly an inadequate reflection of market realities.

15. Marshall had given the economics discipline, *inter alia*, demand and supply analysis—a common feature of foundational economics teaching around the world.

16. Also, Marshall (like Marx) had not included bank deposits as money, despite the fact that they fulfill all of the (defined) functionality of money, and was also only concerned with the longer-term analysis (Harris 1981).

17. Keynes and Wicksell, for instance, had both examined the impact of interest rates on the demand for money to hold. Wicksell had also theorized a "pure credit economy," the "natural/market" rates of interest and direct/indirect mechanisms for translating exogenous money supply growth into higher prices (Harris 1981).

18. The "regression theorem," of Ludvig von Mises, is another example from the Austrian school, which suggests an endogenous market-driven origin of money (Mises 1912).

19. Ingham points out that it is not only the mainstream that makes this mistake, and cites Marx (Ingham 2001).

20. Ideas derived from Knapp (Knapp 1924).

Chapter 4

Heterodox Monetary Traditions

4.1 INTRODUCTION

In this chapter the ideas of Keynes, Circuitists, Austrian School, (so-called) Keynesians and post-Keynesians are examined, in conjunction with the present monetary reform movement and Islamist economics. These ideas generally posit that stronger state regulation (and, for some, the *issue)* of money, combined with some major changed practice, would form the basis of a more stable productive economy that is both more efficient and also contributes toward notions of social and economic justice. This would necessitate an alteration of the *social* power balance between the private bank infrastructure and state. I have assumed, however, that vested interests mitigate the likelihood of such a transformation. While it is true that all heterodox monetary theories challenge the mainstream conception of money, Marx will be considered separately in chapters 5 and 6. The reason for this is that Marx's ideas have informed the ideologies that anticipate the *socialization* of private capital, so that it ceases to be capital by definition, deriving from the objective (Marx argued) laws of capitalism as a whole. This means that subsequent political agendas deriving from this analysis target the *root* of the system, while other heterodox approaches merely seek to transform *undesirable* capitalist (financial) aspects, leaving much of the *modus operandi* of the free market intact.[1] The implication of these latter ideas is the debatable notion that a steady-state capitalism is, at least in theory, possible. It may be that, given the *realpolitik* of global capitalism, these are the preferable options for the future transformation of the system. In the absence of a reliable future vision it is probably best to leave such considerations to speculation and the ruminations of the reader.

4.2 KEYNES, KEYNESIANS AND POST-KEYNESIANS

While serving the UK HM Treasury (Her Majesty's Treasury) at the Treaty of Versailles in 1919, Keynes demonstrated awareness of the latent disruptive capability of the financial system and financial power, through his identification of unsustainable German reparations (Keynes 1919). In the 1920s, default broke the chain of payments necessary to maintain confidence in the international financial system and the subsequent credit squeeze (as Kindleberger noted, contributed with other factors toward falling stock prices and the depression years (Kindleberger 1973: 15). Keynes's general desire for economic stability, using government intervention, appears to have been a consistent theme throughout the *policy* aspects of his work. A key contribution to economic thought, for example, was arguably Keynes's challenge to Say's law, where supply creates its own demand, suggesting that the macroeconomy could, instead, settle in underemployment equilibrium. He considered this to be inefficient with further social costs associated with unemployment. Keynes advocated the use of fiscal and monetary policies in order to stabilize the trade cycle and stimulate (or mitigate) *effective* demand levels to establish sustained full-employment, theorized using consumption function, multiplier, liquidity preference and circular flow models. Keynes favored state intervention (especially debt-management) in order to ensure the prevalence of cheap and stable (in the short and long run) interest rates, so that the *rentier* was restricted and the growth of the productive economy was supported. To this end he advocated capital controls for international transactions, for instance, to avoid capital flight toward states with higher interest rates. As one of the key architects of the BW system he managed to obtain this objective while remaining unsuccessful in the establishment of a clearing union (*Bancor)*, his own proposal for a world bank with its global currency unit based on a currency basket, which would have aimed to stabilize the balance of payments between states through the discouragement of current account surpluses *and* deficits (Singer 1988).[2] Following diplomatic pressure, the US dollar-gold-exchange standard via central banks was adopted instead, set at $35 per ounce, and a system of fixed exchange rates established. The international payments system then remained in this form until Nixon closed the "gold window" in 1971 and fully floating rates reappeared in 1973 (Helleiner 1994).

Yet, despite these achievements, there have been claims of ambiguity in Keynes's monetary theories, which stem from debates surrounding his thinking on the endogenous/exogenous nature of money and the classical quantity theory (Skidelsky 1995; Ingham 2001; Tily 2007a; Tily 2007b). The so-called Keynesians were able to exploit these ambiguities in their contribution to the *synthesis* of monetary ideas adopted in the postwar period.[3]

The post-Keynesians (PK's), conversely, derive different notions and policies from Keynes' monetary ideas, which draw on his concept of endogenous money and aim to recapture and advance their academic value. In short, EMT claims that the level of credit money is created *ex nihilo* in response to market demand rather that exogenously by the state. Yet, paradoxically, most PK's, as Tily notes, have been reticent in acknowledging the ideas in Keynes' own work (Tily 2007b: 2). The matter needs to be explored further since it relates to the state/market power nexus in terms of money-issue.

In the first three decades of the twentieth century, there had been growing concern with the increased magnitude of the trade cycle oscillations. Keynes, with Wicksell and Fisher, had felt *monetary* policy could instigate stability, and subsequently used the QTM (that assumes exogenous money) to support his ideas. Yet, as Skidelsky noted, this presents epistemological difficulties. The quantity theory also presupposes that monetary and output variables are independent, the classical dichotomy, so it is therefore logically inconsistent to assume that the use of policies based on the quantity theory are capable of influencing output fluctuations (Skidelsky 1995). Yet, there is a clear correlation between rising output and rising prices (and vice versa) suggesting *prima facie* that monetary policies based on the quantity theory *could* stabilize the price level and, by implication, the trade cycle itself. But in order to do this the government must be able to control the level of the overall money supply. In practice this meant that the monetary reformers opposed the gold standard because, as Skidelsky pointed out, Marshall recognized that the vagaries of gold mining and trade led to fluctuations in the money supply and price level that the authorities were historically unable to control (Skidelsky 1995). Also, at the time, there was increased recognition of bank credit, emanating from commercial banks, which circulated and functioned *as* money. Keynes, Tily notes, still maintained that the monetary authorities had the *means* to control the rate and level of this money creation, through the discount rate (for reserves) and other monetary controls, suggesting that money was still partly exogenous (Tily 2007a: 19). The interwar government could, for instance, engage in open market operations, issue bonds, set reserve ratios and enforce credit restrictions. Central banks were also beginning to develop these mechanisms, even under the gold standard. It is interesting to note that these early monetary reformers, like later monetarists, while advocating free-market principles in the productive economy had ironically argued for the vigilant state management of the *quantity* of money in order to stabilize inflation. This position is, as expected, more understandable for Keynes given his overall state-interventionist paradigm. The instruments of state monetary capability, using liquidity preference (and debt-management policy implications) and PK ideas, will be further discussed in chapter 7.

In his account of Keynes's monetary ideas, Skidelsky is mindful to illustrate that Keynes had sought (at first) to modify the classical quantity theory, in order to make it work better, as his thinking developed. Skidelsky traces this in several stages. In his *Tract on Monetary Reform* (1923), for example, Keynes had laid out his view of the gold standard hampering state price-level control, and also mentioned that the short-run velocity of money is variable. In its purest sense, the QTM needs a stable velocity in order to illustrate the inflation impact of the money supply. In his *Treatise on Money* (1930) and the *General Theory* (1936) Keynes produced a sophisticated view of different velocities instead, deriving from varying types of bank money, yet still adhered to the Fisher/Marshall equations in both texts.[4] He also, as an illustration of the stated ambiguity, in debate with Professor Caanan from the LSE (1915–1924), questions the mainstream QTM view that causation runs from money to price.[5] He posited instead that the increased government wartime expenditure and wage-push price rises had led to the evident increased money supply rather than the reverse causation (Skidelsky 1995). A final aspect of Keynes' modification, or rejection depending on the interpretation, of the QTM was his view that autonomous forces (e.g., expectations), affecting the velocity of circulation, directly impacted output and prices, which are therefore "endogenous" to the *traditional* model. The quantity theory, conversely, maintains that all of the separate parts of Fisher's equation of exchange are not co-determining in any way.

Notwithstanding, it sometimes *appears* that Keynes assumed that the government fixed the supply of money. His liquidity preference analysis, for example, illustrated the demand for holding money balances (money stock at a specific time) that depended on the transaction, precautionary and speculative motives, which involved a given *exogenous* money supply (Keynes 1936, chap. 17).[6] This provided an alternative to the usual classical, and neoclassical loanable-funds, view of the determination of interest rates.[7] Later on, Keynes had also included, as Moore noted, capital investment requirements in his liquidity preference schedule (finance motive), which was a function of the expected marginal efficiency of capital in relation to the rate of interest (Moore 2006: 257).[8] The *autonomous* and changing expectancy of profit was the key driver of entrepreneurial behavior, and the interest rate thus constituted a contributory factor toward investment finance demand. Total money-demand in the Keynes liquidity preference schedule, therefore, would need to be adjusted if the *planned* investment constituted a break from equilibrium reproduction. Keynes explained:

> If decisions to invest are increasing, the extra finance will constitute an additional demand for money (Moore 2006: 256).

The key question, however, is where does this new money come from given the exogenously created supply? Keynes further writes:

> Just as an increase in actual activity must (as I have always explained) raise the rate of interest, unless either the banks or the rest of the public become more willing to release cash, so (as I now add) an increase in planned activity must have a similar, superimposed influence (Moore 2006: 256).

These are revealing passages since this implied money resources (at least in theory) *could* be created *endogenously* at a given interest rate, according to investment demand, and that, if so, the authorities were only able to regulate the *rate of issue* through monetary policy according to business expectations. Or, conversely (Keynes leaves it open), the monies could equally be derived from the available (exogenous) money supply just with raised interest rates *ceteris paribus*. He did not accept, however, as Skidelsky notes, the so-called "Keynesian" view that monetary policy was likely to be ineffective as a consequence of the liquidity trap, where speculators, expecting falling bond prices, hold on to their money at low rates, or completely interest-inelastic investment. This was despite the fact these views draw on Keynes' own liquidity preference theory (Skidelsky 1995).[9] Instead he maintained the view that monetary policy *was* effective providing that the measures were taken to ensure aggregate demand, and business expectation was affected. Increased monies would be demanded for investment at lower rates, providing the expectation was there. All of these ideas of Keynes, taken together, mean that Keynes had discussed elements of both the exogenous *and* endogenous view of money creation which, Tily argues, is the closest to the *real* Keynes and the reality anyway (Tily 2007b: 21). Keynes had explained the nature of the underemployment equilibrium, where planned savings and investment equilibrate through the working of the multiplier rather than through the interest rate as the classical (or neoclassical *loanable* funds) theory maintained. Yet, Keynes's overall approach allowed for government monetary policy to be used to engender increased economic activity, through either endogenous money-creation or the *changed* use of a fixed exogenous supply.

So, as Ingham notes, despite some adherence to the QTM and the assumption of exogenous money in his models, Keynes is appropriately cited as providing seminal work on the endogenous view of the creation of money as well as, incidentally, providing an exogenous view of money's historical origin (Ingham 2001). First, Keynes had disagreed with the mainstream historical account of money, deriving from barter exchange, and stressed instead the significance of early institutionalized "monies of account"—a view of history shared with Zarlenga, Hudson, and Ingham (Ingham 2001; Hudson 2003; Zarlenga 2006). Secondly, Keynes is assumed to have clearly understood the rise of bank credit as money that is then seen as an *autonomous* force of production (Ingham 2001). This is backed up by Tily, who has also pointed out that the feasible endogenous nature of credit creation is clearly stated early on in the *Treatise* (Tily 2007: 21). Keynes writes:

> the transition from a lower to a higher scale of activity involves an increased demand for liquid resources which cannot be met without a rise in the rate of interest, *unless the banks are ready to lend more cash or the rest of the public release more cash at the existing rate of interest . . . this means that, in general, the banks hold the key position in the transition from a lower to a higher scale of activity (CW XIV, p. 222).*

This is a clear statement of potential demand-led endogenous credit creation but Tily still maintains that Keynes was right to assume (in his models) the ability of the state to regulate this, due to the specific conditions in the first three decades of the twentieth century. Keynes, as a result of his treasury connections, may have presented the view that banks only lent from deposit savings, and that high-powered money emanated from the central bank open-market operations, but then later identified that bank credit was created *ex nihilo* (out of nothing) in response to demand. Another view is that he understood that bank credit did not require prior deposits all along. This is a crucial point in identifying the difference between the so-called Keynesians and the post-Keynesian position yet it has not always been clear to all that this was Keynes's definitive position, which may account for the lack of acknowledgment given to Keynes for PK ideas. It is now widely recognized (e.g., BOE) however, that demand-led endogenous (bank-credit) money *can* be created, at a given level of interest, that *is* affected by changes in planned spending (investment and consumption) as new loans come into being (McLeay 2014). In this scenario, the regulating factors then become the expected marginal efficiency of capital and the predominantly state-determined rate of interest.

Tily argues that the so-called Keynesians had *bastardized* (Joan Robinson phrase) Keynes's ideas with reference to their theory of *exogenous* money, and that this led to their further claim that rising rates of interest were associated with increased economic activity. These ideas found expression in the IS/LM curves that assumed a fixed money supply. Since these so-called Keynesians viewed money as exogenous, when Friedman posited that monetary policy laxity caused inflation they struggled to find counterarguments. The monetarists, backed with some empirical work, claimed a *stable* velocity of circulation, and a demand for money that was not sensitive to the rate of interest (the Hicks LM and the liquidity preference curve suggested otherwise) but rather responded only to nominal income. This followed from the QTM approach and backed the emerging monetarist ideas that emphasized the correlation between monetary aggregates and inflation. Yet, if Keynes's notion of endogenous money is used (detailed above), the monetarist position is *not* accurate as the PKs maintain. Kaldor, for instance, in his response to Friedman, "sets the record straight" by claiming that the money supply simply "accommodated itself" to the needs of trade. In other words, the increased demand for money led to an increased supply of *endogenously* created money without impacting the velocity (Tily 2007b: 5). This argument, however, arrived too late to prevent the ideological attack on the Keynesian era and led to the post-Keynesian response (that still continues) that *inter alia* seeks to restore and expand the *monetary* ideas of Keynes. While Keynes had argued for the necessity of regulating aggregate demand through fiscal measures it is also important to also remember his primary concern for *monetary* issues as illustrated by the PK's. These policies if implemented would lead to a strong interventionist financial state.

However, there has been a debate within the post-Keynesian EMT tradition, between the so-called *horizontalists* and *structuralists*, which is probably best associated with the work of Basil Moore, Tom Palley and Bob Pollin (Wray 2004). The Moore position states that money is supplied endogenously in response to demand, *ad infinitum* at a given interest rate, where the interest rate is delivered exogenously from government policy-makers. In this sense there is a horizontal supply.[10] In practice, this state interest-rate policy might involve the executive arm of the state or be derived from an autonomous central bank if monetary policy powers have been delegated. It is perhaps important, however, to further discuss the meaning of exogenous. Wray, for instance, distinguishes between exogenous in a *control* sense that is policy driven, and exogenous in a *theoretical* sense, which is as an independent variable in a model. This is significant since, as Wray notes, a variable deemed to be exogenous in a control sense might still be influenced by *endogenous* variables in a theoretical sense, as these separate variables constitute drivers of the decision-making process (Wray 2004). The *structuralists*, in contrast, maintain that the supply curve rises as credit expansion occurs. This is argued on the basis that, during an expansion, bank mark-ups rise as perceived risks rise. Kalecki, for instance, as Sawyer notes, had also identified endogenous money-creation that experienced higher interest rates when finance demand rose, due to the increasing perceived risk (Sawyer 2001). Yet, as Wray points out, the structuralists are viewing interest rates over time whereas, in Moore's horizontalism, the supply curve represents a static period of time (Wray 2004). Basil Moore, when discussing the issue, provides the analogy of haircuts, suggesting that the demand for credit determines its own supply in the same way as haircuts are supplied. He suggests that *output* rather than *price* responds to demand changes in the short run, even though increasing marginal costs will be reflected in changed prices sooner or later (Moore 1991).

Hairdressing salons, for example, need to increase in floor capacity at some point in the future if their customer base increases. This challenges the monetarist position mentioned above. The PK debate above is also significant since the *structuralist* approach suggests that private banking agents, as well as state policy-makers, are determinants in money-issue. It appears that an investigation of the political economy of credit creation, from different PK perspectives, can be quite complex. Yet, it is this analysis of the state/market nexus in money-creation, and changing dynamic, which enables us to understand how financial power relations operate in the modern capitalist nations.

There are also various central bank motivations posited by PK's that provide an explanation of why they *accommodate* the request for reserves from commercial banks. Wray cites four. First, the existence of time lags in reserve accounting mean that the reserves required today result from present *and* historic deposits/lending activity. In this sense, since the creation and destruction of credit-money *ebbs and flows* over time, it makes it difficult for central bankers to constrain credit by regulating access to reserves. Secondly, the central bank needs to be the *lender of last resort*, at least to solvent banks, in order to maintain financial stability. This is particularly important if there is a credit squeeze in the interbank market. Thirdly, the central bank needs to provide an orderly payment system and, finally, the overnight interest rate would be unstable without the accommodation (Wray 2004). Since interbank rates tend to guide market interest rates, the accommodation of reserves is a significant part of monetary policy. Wray also notes the often over-looked fact that the operation of fiscal policy results in substantial banking reserves, derived from the creation of state liabilities held by commercial banks. These expenditure decisions thus constitute an important element of contemporary money-issue and private credit expansion is further facilitated by these low-risk and semiliquid securities held by the banking system (Wray 2004).

The link between credit creation and financial crisis, in terms of facilitating asset bubbles, is another important feature of financial power at work and needs to be considered. If credit is directed toward speculative activity, for example, this arguably increases the importance of the relative (and changing) financial power relation between state and market. The work of Minsky has received recent attention in this regard, as a result of the financial instability following the US sub-prime crisis of 2007–2008. As a PK economist he was a proponent of the EMT and, similarly, had emphasized the time and uncertainty elements characteristic of financial contracts (Minsky 1978: 2). The fluctuations in investment demand, for example, "determine whether or not (past) debts can be validated" and the processes affecting this are, therefore, of paramount importance (Minsky 1978: 14). Minsky had identified three types of financial posturing as part of his *financial instability thesis*: hedge, speculative and ponzi finance. Hedge positions are such that future cash flows are expected to exceed "cash flow commitments on liabilities" for every period. Speculative positions, conversely, are those where cash flows fall short for some, but there is expectancy that they will meet all obligations of principal and interest in the future as asset prices rise. Ponzi schemes, however, involve much riskier positions. This is where future cash flows are going to fall short of meeting all commitments. This means that only those investors that manage to sell or buy before the shock adjustment are the ones that can meet their past debt obligations, the others are "caught short" (Minsky 1978: 15). Minsky makes the point that, as the ratio of speculative and ponzi finance units increase, the system becomes increasingly vulnerable to interest rate changes. When short-term rates rise, for example, more speculative units become Ponzi, with the associate instability (Minsky 1978). He had also argued that extended periods of asset-price inflation actually create the conditions whereby financial agents are more likely to take increasing risks at the margins, rather than mitigating instability. This is generally because it is "rational" for agents to shorten risk premiums, in order to extend profit. These ideas of Minsky, regarding the possible impact of credit expansion on agent behavior, constitute a part explanation of financialization phenomena, particularly during the neo-liberal financial order.

4.3 THE FRENCH/ITALIAN CIRCUITISTS

The work of the French/Italian *circuitists*, such as Barrere, Schmitt, Parguez and Graziani, with a monetary circuit based upon the EMT, is popular with some PK theorists despite some reservations (Graziani 2003; Gnos 2004).[11] Circuit theory places significance on the demand for credit by firms from banks, for purposes of production, and base these ideas on the "finance motive" of Keynes, although the ideas, as Gnos notes (p. 3), can be traced to the early-eighteenth-century *physiocrats* (Gnos 2004) and also Kalecki in the modern era (Sawyer 2001). Money is created through debt and is then destroyed when credit contracts are fulfilled. Firms are identified as bank-borrowers and the households are considered as deposit-holders. The payment of factor costs by the firm (the investment) creates a simultaneous equivalent saving. In this sense the saving is the income received by the households, in the form of money-incomes, which is then held as a bank deposit until spending occurs. The monetary circuit refers to the notion of the continuous outlay and receipt of these money units, which represent the debts of firms (measured by the extent of the household services and subsequent incomes paid) that are repaid to the third-party banks when the households purchase goods and services. While households receive a money-income, the money is only a symbol of the appropriate amount of *real* goods and services that are produced and subsequently purchased in the circuit. In this circuitist model the loans, created by the process, actually *form* the bank deposits themselves (rather than the deposit monies deriving from preexisting deposits by transfer), since they are merely accounting entries. In the circuitist language, however, the borrower spends the incomes of other people, since the firm's spending (of borrowed funds) results in household incomes in the form of money spent on goods and services. This is true, as Gnos notes, whether the money is created *ex nihilo* (out of nothing) or is derived from preexisting deposits (Gnos 2004: 5). The circuitists have, however, courted some controversy with their circuit conception.

Credit-money can clearly originate in consumer credit, as well as from the supply of credit to firms. Chick has consequently commented, therefore, that the circuitists may have departed from reality in their modeling (Chick 2000: 132). Gnos explains that the rationale behind the circuitist models is to primarily focus on credit provided to firms that forms the factor incomes, rather than determine income distribution *per se*, because this household credit denies another household expenditure (Gnos 2004: 3). Yet, as Gnos notes, when banks provide credit to households the purchasing power is not transferred from the deposits held by firms and, therefore, a different circuit is initiated. Another possible objection to circuitist theory is that firms often use preexisting monies to finance their investment rather than starting with nothing, and that this causes problems with the circuit modeling. Yet Keynes, as Gnos noted, demonstrated how capital finance creates a new net *saving* despite the precise nature of original money creation that is, preexisting deposit or *ex nihilo* money (Gnos 2004: 4).

The consideration of profit, interest, rent, working capital and the purchase of capital goods also present a few problems for the circuitist ideas, given their focus on factor incomes in the form of wages. In terms of the purchase of capital goods, the circuitist practice is to separate these transactions from the payment of wages. The reason for this is that the spending on raw materials, for instance, can actually be considered as the fulfillment of a previous circuit, whereas the payment of wages generates a new circuit (Gnos 2004: 11). The payment of profit, interest and rent can also be problematic to theorize for the circuitists. Profit, for instance, is income for firms, but when the factor incomes are produced this does not exist. The Kalecki solution was that firms pay profit to themselves, but profit cannot be pre-supposed it has to occur after the relevant circulation. The Marx approach to this, outlined in the next chapter, involves the concept of surplus value extracted by the capitalist during the production process (but realized in circulation) while the ideas of Sir James Steuart (Gnos 2004: 15), with his notion of *profit on alienation*, emphasized a market price received that is above the factor cost. In this sense the payment of interest, rent and profits represent a transfer from buyers to firms (as a proportion of household income) and firms (and/or rentiers and financial firms) then exist as wage earners. In this notion the circuitist approach is more consistent with the real world and Keynes in the General Theory (Keynes 1936; Gnos 2004).

In summary, the circuitists have emphasized the role of banks in the productive economy, whereas the PK horizontalists, conversely, tend to view the banks as merely supplying credit in response to demand. The circuitists have also ignored commodity and high-powered money and are, therefore, concerned simply with the endogenous creation of credit monies and the destruction of deposits at the end of credit contracts. Finally, their focus on the necessity of the triangular nature of banking operations, between various market participants, is in contrast to the (commodity money) mainstream notions of money's origin and function. Yet, the circuitists, in conjunction with Keynes and the PK's, while contributing toward the establishment of the EMT (suggesting a lesser role for the state that is, simply setting interest rates and credit policy), have not meaningfully discussed the *political* implications of such processes. These matters are not, perhaps, considered to be in their remit and are, therefore, left to other academic disciplines to investigate. The monetary reform movement, conversely, while not always academically rigorous, does discuss these concerns. Notwithstanding, Keynes *et al.* have introduced to monetary theory the notion that money needs to be managed by statesmen more comprehensively than simply by setting the quantity and sanctioning its issue, as the mainstream have historically suggested. In particular, a state debt-management and interest rate strategy is recommended by the PK's (see Tily), based on Keynes's liquidity preference theory, in order to stabilize *expectations* of investment (Tily 2007a, chap. 7). Some of these ideas will be discussed further in chapter 7, where the specific state instruments for controlling money-issue are outlined.

4.4 THE MONETARY REFORM MOVEMENT

Monetary reformers today lament the exploitation of private banking and seek a stronger state regulation of the sector. The movement has its antecedents, as Brown notes, in the times before the colonial war with Britain (Brown 2007: 35). Brown explains how the colonialists, faced with a money shortage, issued their own currency, leading to a sustained period of productive stability, poverty alleviation and full employment. Marx had reflected on this development and commented, with reference to the colonies success that, "gold and silver are not so necessary for the wealth of a nation, as the vulgar of all ranks imagine" (Marx [1859] 1970: 79). Benjamin Franklin, on a visit to England, had commented on the relative level of poverty and unemployment existing in London and attributed this to a *private* debt-based money system. Franklin further stated that the relative prosperity of the colonies derived from their *state issue* of paper money providing it was actually created "in proper proportions to the demands of trade and industry" (Brown 2007: 39) Franklin posited that the sensible state control, regulation *and issue* of money, with a restrained role for the private banking sector, constituted a preferable financial system. In Pennsylvania, for instance, colonial authorities issued debt-free money for government projects, in place of taxes, and the economy had experienced low inflation (Rabushka 2004: 73).[12] In addition, credit monies were provided for the private sector at 5% interest rather than the higher 8% charged by the private bankers. The colonial financial system was heralded as a success in Pennsylvania, but, in New England, an overissue of notes led to their depreciation, thus affecting investments of British merchants. In dealing with the colonial issue in 1751 George II (and continued under George III in 1752), anxious to retain the colonies in their role as suppliers of raw materials, issued a decree banning the issue of new paper money in New England, forcing them to borrow from the British banks instead. Franklin noted that within a year beggars had returned to the streets and sentiments rose until there was sufficient revolutionary fervor to challenge the British in the war of independence.

The main complaint of monetary reformers is that the *issue* of *debt-based* money is solely conducted by private commercial banks, with the minimum of state regulation (Shakespeare 2002; Zarlenga 2002; Brown 2007). They further argue that, when credit-money is created, there is often insufficient circulating currency to repay all the principal *and* interest, and so economic agents then rely upon further credit in order to service existing debt. If interest is compounded, as El Diwany has emphasized (p. 8), the problem is worse (El Diwany 2003). In addition, if credit-money levels grow in relation to base money, the private control of credit increases representing an erosion of state financial sovereignty. At the time of WW2, narrow money constituted a substantial proportion of the money supply, whereas it now only constitutes 3% in the UK, and less than 1% in the US (Shakespeare 2002: 27). In addition, reformers argue there is an *inflationary* impact of interest on the productive economy. Firms, consumers and governments all need to find additional revenue to meet interest payments and this puts pressure on prices, resources and the environment (Kennedy 1995; Shakespeare 2002; El Diwany 2003; Pettifor 2006; Brown 2007). It is further argued that private banks, and related *rentiers*, receive this substantial tribute in return for a service to the productive economy of exaggerated value.

The gold certificates of the goldsmiths, as an early form of credit money, are often mooted as an antecedent for modern fractional reserve banking by reformers. Yet, while the goldsmiths had to ensure notes were an appropriate multiple of specie deposits, their modern bank counterparts are not subject to *de facto* reserve restraints since, as Pettifor notes, reserves are available on demand from the central bank (Pettifor 2006: 62). As settlement banks make loans they become accounting entries on balance sheets and, circulating bank monies are thus created *ex nihilo*. Money is, therefore, largely endogenous and demand led. The Bank of England, in 1694, was granted license to lend to the government and business, replacing the (state-controlled) tally-stick system.[13] This new *private* issue of debt served as *legal tender* credit-money, establishing the statutory and common-law principle for private money-issue with its attendant benefits. This latent profit led banks, after WW2, as Helleiner has argued, to become more proactive in lobbying for an increased role in the financial system, arguably to the detriment of the state and productive structure (Helleiner 1994).[14] Monetary reformers recognize the benefits of banking, however, and these are not the targets for change, but instead they do seek a stronger *financial* state alongside effectively regulated private banks. In the modern era this is argued to be imperative since consumer, corporate and state debt levels are in danger of unsustainability that is, where servicing interest payments is not possible.

There are varying proposals for financial systems. Zarlenga, for instance, from the American Monetary Institute, suggests that the state should create a *money of account* that gradually replaces credit-money to become 100% of the money supply.[15] The money is to be provided interest *and* debt-free. Positive Money and Huber and Robertson (in the UK) also support these ideas (Huber 2000; Positive Money 2015). Under their proposals, money would not be backed by specie, only by law, and private banks are only permitted to lend on a 100% fractionally backed basis (Zarlenga 2002). In his historical study of money, Zarlenga explains how the use of specie had led to significant inefficiencies, derived from misdirected energies in the production of mined metals, and the establishment of a plutocracy that hoarded bullion for the purpose of political manipulation (Zarlenga 2002). Zarlenga also recommends, therefore, that the issue and regulation of his un-backed money should constitute a *fourth* constitutional function of state, with autonomy from legislative process. Despite differences, monetary reformers all claim their proposals would combat inflation on the basis of a rejection of the mainstream conception of inflation, which presupposes the QTM and demand-pull and cost-push factors causing price rises. Money reformers, in contrast, focus on the contributory role of debt service to production costs. This debt-driver theory suggests that the interest reduces incomes and revenues and, subsequently, creates pressures to raise prices and wages in order to compensate for the losses (Kennedy 1995).

Monetary reform, however, does not have to focus exclusively on the whole financial system. There are, for instance, grassroots solutions to the problems of a debt-based money system that have been both theorized and practiced. These include complementary or alternative currencies, which coexist with official monies, or local exchange trading schemes (LETS) and time-banks, that contribute toward social and economic development around the world (Lietaer 2001; Adams 2010; Mouatt 2010; Adams 2011). In addition, barter networks, like the Swiss *Wir* scheme for example, or social credit networks have contributed to counter-cyclical stability through their resilience in crisis. These market- and community-driven money initiatives (including business networks) are, perhaps, partly a response to the expense and inconvenience of formal banking and, by implication, an inactive *financial* state. Since the onset of the financial crisis there has been a proliferation of these. Other monetary reformers are concerned with global finance. Hedge funds, for instance, are able to leverage credit-money volumes (with minimal collateral) for purposes of short-term speculative activity in derivative, stock, bond and currency markets that can, potentially, cause prices to rise or fall in a direction *contrary* to the underlying fundamentals.[16] This leads to misleading price signals for smaller investors. These capital flows have been linked to various currency crises in Russia, Malaysia, Argentina and Mexico *et al.* The crises, in turn, have led to numerous (varying) calls to restore the multilateral regulation of the global financial system, experienced during the BW era, with capital controls or new measures such as a capital transactions tax (Palley 2003a; Tobin 1978; Griffith-Jones 1998; Patomaki 2003). Yet, for others, monetary reform is insufficient as an end in itself. They seek monetary reform as a vehicle for the transformation of capitalism itself. These policies, if implemented, would lead to a much stronger financial state than the one that now operates in the financialization era.

4.5 THE ISLAMIST RESPONSE

Under Islamic law the practice of receiving interest (riba) is forbidden. The literal translation of riba is *increase,* although it is usually understood as usury, which can be extracted when credit is extended or derived from trade. These are termed *Riba al Qarud* and *Riba al-Buyu* respectively (El Diwany 2003: 136). This, as we would expect, presents difficulties for economic policy-makers (and bankers) who are seeking to implement religious law as well as making it problematic for Muslims living in non-Islamic financial systems.[17] This is because when monies are provided in the form of credit, incentives are needed for parting with liquidity and the levying of administration costs, assuming that credit is derived from preexisting deposits, even without the extraction of profit for financial *rentiers*.[18] Islamic banks, and western financial institutions that provide for Muslims, devise specialist services that meet these religious requirements.[19] Islamic economic law also requires the elimination of the present fractional reserve system, replaced by a 100% backed (interest-free) money system (El Diwany 2003: 175). In this system money would simply circulate, via the intermediaries, and the financial authorities would need to ensure that sufficient liquidity and money supply growth was provided to meet the demands of industry, commerce and economic growth. A further feature of Islamic finance is the provision of capital. Whenever money is needed as capital for productive purposes, example, the Islamic expectation is that profit sharing and *risk sharing* between investor and productive capitalist takes place. In this regard the capital provider, or financial intermediary acting like an investment bank on behalf of the investor, receives a proportion of net profit or shares the relevant loss. Islamic economists also recommend a commodity standard, as backing for the currency, as well as the elimination of FRB (El Diwany 2003: 186). There are other principles of Islamic law that cover aspects of financial sector activity. Yet, in order for these policies to be adopted, an Islamic jurisdiction would be needed to ensure the enforcement of the relevant monetary practice, development of new contract law and regulatory supervision. This, however, necessitates *state* centralization of social power, in favor of *imams* and *mullahs,* and is therefore unlikely to be an acceptable option outside of the Muslim communities. In the sense of financial sovereignty, of course, the implication is the establishment of a strong interventionist state (on religious principles).

4.6 THE AUSTRIAN SCHOOL

As we have seen, there are several ways in which the present monetary system can be viewed and, by implication, changed. These range from the elimination of the debt-based money system to the introduction of enhanced government monetary policy intervention. Proponents of reform can also be fans of the free market such as monetarists or Austrians. Austrian free banking, for example, recommends that monies be derived endogenously from the market agents themselves. It is argued that since free markets can be relied on to achieve an efficient allocation of resources then, if the market develops its own currencies, the consumers will gravitate toward the system that they most trust. This trust, as Clarke notes, is an essential ingredient for a stable social currency (Clarke 1992). Furthermore, in terms of credit creation, increased trust generates information efficiencies and lowers default risk, thus delivering cheaper money. The Austrian school (AS), like the PK's, attributes the business cycle to endogenous financial factors, except that they suggest (in contrast) that *state*-managed cheap money, in conjunction with private banks that practice fractional reserve banking, is the *key* factor driving the process (de Soto 2009: 347). In the first instance of a cheap money regime, the AS suggest that credit expansion will be more excessive than would otherwise occur, fuelling asset bubbles, inflation and (most notably) a distortion in prices/returns between sectors. This last point stems from the AS view that money is non-neutral, as new money is not distributed across agents proportionately.[20] As a consequence, the AS school advocates market-determined interest rates that, they contend, will allocate credit more appropriately. In addition, they consider that cheap credit leads to *malinvestment,* in the sense that firms are incentivized to engage in capital expenditure that is more risky. When inevitable recession sets in, many of these resources are liquidated. The AS argues, therefore, that *natural* (their term) rates of interest will mitigate the fluctuations of the cycle, through more sensible investment. Secondly, according to the AS, the practice of fractional reserve banking (FRB) is unsustainable since *ex niliho* credit expansion, rather than being subjected to the reflux, is "rolled over," leading to more credit and subsequent distortions and *malinvestment* as stated above (De Soto 2009: 723).[21] Instead, they recommend free banking as a policy.

In addition, the AS also stresses the importance of the *lack* of currency diversity, as a key-contributing factor to business and credit cycle fluctuations. A single credit-money currency monopoly creates a monetary dependence that often becomes the focus of the problem in a financial crisis (Mouatt 2010). This idea draws on Hayek, who had posited the dangers of central planning in general, suggesting that inefficiency and information deficiency hindered effective decision-making. In this sense, the Austrian school is in favor of the erosion of state financial sovereignty. In the following passage, when referring to the greater use of bank deposits as money, and the social dependence on (single currency) credit from banks that need to ensure their adequacy of reserves, Hayek pointed out that this would lead to liquidity fluctuations and a disturbed business cycle thus revealing its fragility. Hayek writes:

> This unfortunate development came about because for a long time it was not generally understood that deposits subject to cheque played very much the same role [as banknotes] *my addition*, and could be created by the commercial banks in exactly the same manner, as bank notes. The consequent dilution of what was still believed to be a government monopoly of the issue of all money resulted in the control of the total circulation of money being divided between a central bank and a large number of commercial banks whose creation of credit it could influence only indirectly. Not till much later did it come to be understood that the 'instability of credit' [R. G. Hawtrey] under that system was a necessary outcome of this feature; that liquid means was mostly supplied by institutions which themselves had to keep liquid in terms of another form of money, so that they had to *reduce* their outstanding obligations precisely when everyone

> else desired to be *more* liquid. By the time this kind of structure had become so firmly established that, in spite of the 'perverse elasticity of the supply of credit' [L. Currie] it produced, it came to be regarded as unalterable. Walter Bagehot had clearly seen this dilemma a hundred years ago but despaired of the possibility of remedying this defect of the firmly established banking structure. And Wicksell and later von Mises made it clear that this arrangement must lead to violent recurring fluctuations of business activity—the so-called 'trade-cycle'. . . Not the least advantage of the proposed abolition of the government monopoly of the issue of money is that it would provide an opportunity to extricate ourselves from the *impasse* into which this development had led (Hayek 1990: 91).

Yet, notwithstanding interesting ideas, the Austrian school is perhaps subject to the same criticism that can be given to the post-Keynesians, in that it is assumed that the business and credit cycle can be overcome and a steady-state capitalism can be achieved. The only difference in this context is that the AS prefers unfettered free markets and, the PK's advocate the economic and debt-management by the state. Given the political realities these may be the only choices.

4.7 CONCLUSION

The various heterodox approaches to monetary thinking outlined here have challenged the mainstream (classical and neoclassical) monetary ideas in several ways, and some of these ideas are considered important in this book. In particular the EMT, also recognized by circuitists and reformers, now appears to be suitable as an explanation of the processes that actually *exist* in the modern era. In addition Knapp's STM, as Naito noted, emphasizes the *unit of account* and *store of value* functions of money, in addition to the usual exchange function, and is also an important part of PK thought (Naito 2008). These ideas are significant because they focus on the financial role and *capability* of the state (Knapp 1924). In addition, as Tily and Freeman have commented, the PK approach attempts to integrate monetary and production factors following Marx and Keynes, in clear contrast to the IS/LM models of the Keynesian era, and the neutrality of the mainstream conception (Freeman 1996; Tily 2007). This approach is considered in the book to be preferable to the mainstream view of money as secondary, neutral and separate, and is further developed as a consequence. It also suggests that financial matters are more important and therefore, by implication, so are state financial sovereignty and changing state/market power relations.

It is also recognized that the functioning of *interest* in the monetary economy, emphasized by monetary reformers and Islam, is an important feature of the modern financial reality. Credit expansion is usually indispensable for the debt-based money system to function, but it leads to an increase of *rentier* incomes and thus galvanizes plutocratic power. In times of credit contraction, the resulting shortage of liquidity also directly affects the operation of the productive economy. These ideas, and the PK notion of the EMP, are explored throughout the book in conjunction with the tendential behavior of the economy, as predicted by Marx outlined in chapter 5. It is argued that a synthesis of Marx and EMT together offers valid explanation of the empirical realities of financialization discussed throughout the chapters. Most of the ideas for reform outlined in this chapter, whether they derive from the monetary reform movement, PK's, Austrians, Circuitists or Islamists all point toward an ineffective state in regard to the financial sector. Even the Austrian school, that usually regards the state as an unhelpful interfering entity and does not advocate state intervention, recognizes the need for the state to instigate currency competition rather than perpetuate a cartelized finance sector (that exploits rather than facilitates the real economy) and conducts monetary policy that keeps market interest rates lower than they should be. In summary, the literature on heterodox monetary theory provides us with a richer understanding of the dynamics of the various monetary factors and the implications of an erosion of state financial sovereignty.

NOTES

1. The practice of Marx's economic method is a separate issue from Marxist ideology.

2. Keynes also advocated international commodity agreements, an early form of established fair trade prices.

3. The use of IS/LM diagrams, developed by Hicks, is the main example of this synthesis that assumed from Keynes a fixed exogenous supply of money, yet some of Keynes's work outlines endogenous sources.

4. Keynes identified income, business and savings deposits that all had different velocities of circulation.

5. Marx had also adhered to this view.

6. There are some similarities to the so-called *portfolio balance model.* Keynes also maintained that his liquidity preference theory referred to money-demand, given a static amount of money, rather than a demand for *loans* as the so-called Keynesians later assumed (Keynes 1937; Minsky 1978).

7. The classical economists had maintained that the rate of interest brought preexisting savings into line with investment. The *loanable* funds theory, conversely, recognized that the extension of credit was part of the money supply (alongside savings proper and dishoarding) for investment (and other purposes) but, as Tily points out, they maintained (in contrast to Keynes) that *saving* was still prior to investment

and greater supply led to higher interest rates. The logic was then extended in the IS-LM formulations (Tily 2007a: 100).

8. The finance motive was developed as a response to criticism from Ohlin in 1937 (Moore 2006).

9. Moore argues that Keynes later adapts (and then abandons) the liquidity preference theory, where the government can regulate the interest rate indirectly through an exogenous change in money supply, and ends up maintaining an exogenous interest rate determined by government that engenders a certain quantity of demand-led money. These ideas may have been based on confusion between Keynes's theorizing on money as a store of value and money creation and change (Moore 2006: 258).

10. Wray notes that Chick, Moore and Niggle suggest that endogenous money is a relatively new phenomenon, derived either from the level of development of the banking sector or a central bank that "accommodates" the reserve demand. He also notes this central bank action is difficult in a fixed exchange rate regime (Wray 2004).

11. Arestis and Howells point out that (substantial) consumer credit is being ignored as the circuitists focus on investment finance (Gnos 2004).

12. Between 1723 and the 1750s, the provincial government collected no taxes at all (Brown 2007: 39).

13. The "Glorious Revolution" of William of Orange preceded the establishment of the then-private Bank of England, which then, in turn, later became the central banking model emulated around the world.

14. It is often argued that economic forces were instrumental in the liberalization of finance; Helleiner argues that political factors were paramount instead (Helleiner 1994).

15. The money is to be issued as a debt-free, and therefore interest-free, replacement for the maturing national debt during the initial stages of the proposals.

16. In 2006, 8,282 of the 9,800 operating hedge funds were registered in the Cayman Islands (Brown 2007).

17. It is worth noting that the UK has the most developed Islamic banking provision outside of Muslim countries (Straw 2008).

18. It is for this reason that, in the West, the term usury is often associated with the extraction of *excessive* interest beyond that of reasonable cost.

19. Mortgages are provided, for example, by bank purchases of the relevant property and then selling it to customers (at a higher price) who then repay the credit monies advanced in instalments—without interest.

20. AS business cycle theory is also known as "circulation credit theory" (de Soto 2009: 347).

21. It is worth noting that FRB, despite imperfections, does provide credit in response to demand and has served capitalism reasonably well for the last few hundred years.

Chapter 5

Marx's Political Economy

5.1 INTRODUCTION

It is probably safe to argue that Marx has provided us with one of the best explanations of the mechanics of capitalist operation. Marx also had very distinct views on the nature of money, creation of money and its function within capitalism. Marx's monetary theory, however, will be explored separately in chapter 6. I begin, instead, by exploring Marx's general political economy, on which the whole of his monetary theory is predicated. This involves the nature of capitalism in historical context, the role of crisis, material relations of production, law of value, alienation, surplus value, rent, competition and falling profit rates. Next, the various interpretative controversies that have surrounded Marx's law of value are discussed. It is concluded that the TSSI of Marx offers an appropriate method to interpret his theory of value. This theoretical work is significant because the book's overall approach is to synthesize Marx's view of the productive economy, based on his theory of value, with the EMT. The end purpose is to provide account for the financial sector transformation, observed in the case studies, by illustrating the law of value in operation. Readers that are familiar with Marx's political economy, and the interpretative controversies, can skip the early parts of this chapter but the latter two sections on the profit rate and depreciation are recommended since they are important for the propositions claimed throughout the book.

5.2 THE ECONOMY IN HISTORICAL CONTEXT

In contrast to the mainstream, Marx viewed capitalism with its privately owned business, free markets and competition for profit as historically specific and, therefore, subject to change. Marx has also been termed a *historical materialist* since he viewed this transformation from one economic system to another as deriving from the "material relations of production," rather than other determinants of behavior. Hegel, for example, had suggested that a synthesis of opposing *ideas* motivates society to enact the necessary changes. Marx's material relations depended on an agent's *actual* position in the production process. Marx called this materialism the "rational kernel within the mystical shell" (Marx [1867] 1976: 103).[1] During the capitalist era this directly involved(s) the tensions and contradictions (conflicts of interest) between the *bourgeois* owners and controllers of productive resources and the *proletarian* class who were solely dependent upon selling their "labor power" (Marx [1848] 1996). Marx contended that these conflicting pressures might eventually lead to a new economic and social system, founded on the common ownership of the "means of production." Since any distress felt by workers would be removed, and labor exploitation from wages paid below the value of their output would also be removed, the state would then soon become obsolete as an engine for social transformation. Notwithstanding these humanitarian deficiencies, Marx viewed the capitalist mode of production as potentially interminable given certain countervailing conditions, which he carefully outlined in his work. System collapse, for Marx, was certainly not inevitable, as some have suggested.[2]

5.3 CAPITALIST CRISIS

Marx recognized the wealth accumulation dynamic in capitalism, yet in contrast to many of his contemporaries, he did not posit this prevailing economic order at the pinnacle of human achievement. For Marx, a key tension inherent in the market-based system was the nature of endogenous crises/cycles, which he attributed to the falling rate of profit rather than the role of unstable money, policy mistakes or indeed any other exogenous factors (Marx [1894] 1981, chap. 13). This was rooted in his idea that it was only *labor* that added value to output. Profit rates declined in boom periods, as the organic composition of capital increased that is, the ratio of capital to labor, and recessions were caused by capitalists seeking to restore profitability.[3] However, Marx had clearly argued that there were various *tendencies* and *counter-tendencies*, including monetary factors, which all contributed to the fluctuations of any crisis characteristics. In his political economy, as Potts noted, money has a role within capitalist *crises* in addition to its more expected functioning within capital formation and the circulation of commodities, and this is significant for the consideration of financial power (Potts 2005). However, having a role in crisis is not the same thing as determining capitalist mechanics.

This, for Marx, was rooted in production and the circuit of capital. Marx had considered, like Smith that money improved the efficiency of production and the circulation process and, while not creating value, *rentiers* providing interest-bearing capital would certainly share in any *surplus* value (the basis of profit) that is produced.[4] Marx had also predicted that industrial capital, that is, investment monies for corporations where production decisions are made and *value* is created, would gradually subjugate financial capital in the form of precapitalist moneylenders. As capitalism developed, newer credit forms appeared that replaced the old. Nowadays, there are signs that a similar process may be happening again evidenced by the systemic weakness of the traditional commercial bank infrastructure and increased (nonbank) corporate monetary activity (Marx [1859] 1970: 468).[5]

Marx espoused that it was an objective law of the capitalist mode of production for capital to increase unless all profit was consumed.[6] Furthermore, in the form of money, the capital is the "prime mover, giving the first impulse to the whole process of production" (Burkett 2004: 461). Marx claimed that money capital (M), therefore, takes the form of productive capital (C) and then is *realized* in an increased money-form again (expressed M–C–M') known as the "circuit of capital." Capital by nature, therefore, changes form. The capital advanced to the production process is known as *capital value*. This, in turn, is made up of *constant capital*, which is the sum of value used to acquire the means of production, and the *variable capital*, which represents the sum of value used to acquire of hire the required labor (Marx [1867] 1976: 200). Marx later (chap 1) decided to rewrite the circuit of capital as M–C (labor and constant capital) –P (productive capital) –C'–M' (Marx [1885] 1978).

5.4 THE LABOR THEORY OF VALUE

Marx's entire political economy is predicated on his law of value, based on abstract labor. The classical economists, as stated in 2.5, from William Petty to Ricardo had adopted the labor theory of value (Marx used the term *law of value*), albeit in somewhat crude forms in comparison to Marx, which suggested that labor was the *source* of all exchange-value (Mandel 1969: 18). Consumables that require no human effort to produce them contain a subjective use-value but have zero exchange-value and hence are free to all. In essence, in order to ascertain value comparisons between different commodities, that all contain social exchange-value, it is imperative to utilize an entity that is common to all as an *objective* basis for measurement. The use of a nominal monetary *numeraire*, with its changing intrinsic value in abstract labor-time terms, is inadequate in this regard. This is because market prices established in exchange would be determined by subjective notions of utility by market agents. Marx claims, at the beginning of *Capital* that it soon becomes apparent that *labor* is the only entity that can be *objectively* measured in this manner, since all commodities that necessitate a valuation are themselves the product of human labor (Marx [1867] 1976). It is possible to develop an alternative value theory system based upon the subjective notion of utility, although this, as Mises has demonstrated, is fraught with measurement difficulties (Mises 1912: 97). Historically, it is perhaps logical, as Mandel has argued, that the more generalized commodity production becomes, the more the exchange-value of a commodity is governed by an accounting system based upon labor hours (Mandel 1969: 15).[7] Market prices may fluctuate around labor values as axes, according to the subjective vagaries of supply and demand in the short term. In the long term, however, it is assumed, as Mandel argued, that the underlying tendential *law of value* would exert its influence, if we assume similar ratios of fixed capital to labor (Mandel 1969: 25). In this sense, market prices merely act as signals to which the producing agents react by reallocating resources. So, for Marx, labor-time *creates* value, residually congealed (dead labor) in produced commodities. Specific use-values are produced in the commodities that, in turn, contain an exchange-value when traded. Marx, in order to determine the labor value of commodities, used the notion of (abstract) *socially necessary* hours. Clearly, some workers are more efficient than others and, therefore, a unit of "socially necessary labor" is set at the average productivity during the stated period of production. The present value of a commodity then becomes the fragment of total "socially necessary" labor at the average efficiency during the production period, that is used for the production of the commodity and is expressed either in the form of labor-time or money. The individual value of a commodity changes, by implication, if the productivity of labor changed in some future production period (Kliman 2007: 22).[8] Marx was keen to emphasize his view that a worker does not add value in proportion to their productivity, since an hour of necessary labor always yields the *same* value. In other words the value of a commodity only reduces as a consequence of its embodiment of less socially necessary labor units *currently* needed to produce it. In addition, in order to account for the existence of skilled labor, Marx had assumed for purposes of analysis that the value created during a skilled labor hour exceeds that of an unskilled one commensurate with the labor hours involved in acquiring the skill (Mandel 1987: 13).[9] This enables objective measurement of labor-value, despite such calculation probably being difficult to achieve in practice.

Kliman first explains how Marx, had measured the value of commodities in terms of either labor-time or money units interchangeably (Kliman 2007, chap. 2). Secondly, Marx distinguishes between the value realized (money received at a given price), by an individual firm or industry, and the value *produced* by the firm (meaning labor value). Kliman argues that this distinction is often the subject of confusion (Kliman 2007: 24). Kliman, following Marx, also posits that prices are *formed* at the end of each production period, determining the value received (by the total labor hours and price ratios), before circulation simply distributes the commodities. Table 5.1 illustrates this difference between value *produced* and the value *received* (or realized), in order to illustrate that *both* can be expressed in either money or labor-time.

In the table we can see how the value produced (w) and value received (p) are both measured in money *and* labor-time, and that they are different from each other. The value the firm receives (price) is 10% below the value it produces (value), meaning that elsewhere in the system a firm(s) is realizing more than they produce. This is because the economy-wide total of value produced will equal that of the value received (realized). But, how do we convert between labor-time and money? Marxian economists have taken to using the notion of the monetary expression of labor time (MELT), in order to explain how value can be expressed in both labor and/or money. Total price is simply divided by labor hours to obtain a monetary value of an hour of socially productive labor. Changes in this MELT then reveal price inflation, from one period to the next, in terms of labor hours. In Table 5.1, for instance, each hour equates to $6. The value of the inputs (cvt+v) are usually determined by their prices in money, formed at the end of production *last* period, with their conversion to labor-time being determined by the MELT established in the same (last) period. In order to express both the value received (realized) and value produced at the end of production *this period*, however, we must now convert using a new MELT (if it is different), established with prices at the end of production *this period*. Kliman argues that the MELT can be calculated by "the economy-wide ratio of the total money-price of output to the total labor-time value of output" at the end of a production period (Kliman 2007: 39). This is the method of MELT calculation that is adopted. However, it should be noted, there are different ways the MELT can be calculated.[10] For the purposes of the book, however, the total money price is divided by the labor hours engaged in the output. I have also chosen to use the phrase *produced* value to describe commodity production-value (measured in either

Table 5.1 Value Produced and Value Received

	Fixed Costs[a]	*Wages*	*New Value*[b]	*Total Output*	*Price Realized*	*Surplus Value*	*Profit*
Dollars	$300	$24	$240	$540	$486	$216	$162
Labor	50 hours	4 hours	40 hours	90 hours	81 hours	36 hours	27 hours

[a]100% of the fixed cost value is transferred in to the product.
[b]The variable capital (wages) is combined with surplus value to form new value created.

labor-time or money) and *received* value (also measured in labor or money) in order to describe the value received (sometimes called appropriated or realized value) that is, the price when sold.

5.5 ALIENATION, EXPLOITATION AND SURPLUS VALUE

In previous modes of production the producer would generally be in possession of his own produce but, in the capitalist era, the worker is not and has to experience the subsequent distress of *alienation* from the product, his labor, other individuals and humanity in general (Marx [1844] 2014, pp. 136–52).[11] In this sense Marx had distinguished between commodity (produce for sale in a market) and non-commodity production. In capitalism the individual proletariat worker also, therefore, has nothing to sell but his own labor power, for which he receives a wage, and is consequently completely dependent upon the capitalist. In addition, there is a difference between the value of the wage (to reproduce and sustain the worker) and the value of the produce that is the source of *surplus value* (or profit) explained below and, this is the root of capitalist labor exploitation for Marx (Marx [1867] 1976: 293).

The classical economists, while adhering to the LTV, had struggled to explain the existence of profit, and Marx's key contribution to the economics discipline had been in identifying expropriated surplus value as a basis to profit (Ormazabal 2004).[12] The breakthrough came by theorizing that the value of the goods and services required to *reproduce* labor (the subsistence of food, shelter, etc.), manifested in the form of wages is less than the labor-power value of the produce of labor. The capitalist then expropriates the surplus as it is *realized* in money-form. Productive labor (as Potts notes) involves commodity production, which produces surplus value, a new value above the wage, compared to unproductive labor (e.g., banking) that while important does not (Potts 2007: 362). In his analysis Marx used the symbol *s* for surplus value, and *v* for variable capital (labor value of wage). Here, *s/v* then represents the *rate of surplus value* or, as it is sometimes known, *rate of exploitation* (Marx [1867] 1976: 670). In the economy as a whole, aggregated surplus value is split between the productive entrepreneurs, landowners/rentiers, government (in the form of taxation), retailers and the bankers/money capitalists who extract interest (and fees, commissions and charges). These groups could perhaps be seen to be in competition or collusion to secure or enhance their relative proportion of surplus value, which necessarily consists *a priori* of a "zero-sum game." This is because no *additional* value is created in exchange, Marx claimed, where a buyer/seller only gains at the expense of another in the medium of circulation. The decline in state capability to control the issue and value of modern monies matters, since these very capabilities are a source of potential *seigniorage* that is, benefits deriving from money-issue. This represents a claim on the *appropriated* surplus value and real resources of an economy.

5.6 COMPETITION, CAPITAL MIGRATION AND EFFICIENCY

The competition between firms is an essential characteristic of capitalism and, Marx asserted, this leads tendentially, taking account of any counter-tendencies, toward the harmonization of profitability between branches. Competition is presented by the mainstream apologetics as beneficial since it arguably leads to the efficient allocation of resources, when combined with the "invisible hand" of the free market (Smith 2003). Marx did not disagree with this aspect of capitalist behavior since, in the mid-nineteenth century, a reasonable amount of free-market competition existed. Now, however, larger firms with substantial market concentration and barriers to entry, *inter alia*, mitigate the potentially beneficial impact of competition. Be that as it may, according to Marx, if some capitals or branches of production were economizing on socially abstract labor and realizing a greater proportion of surplus value (prices above value), then capital would migrate toward them in search of higher returns. Market prices, driven by demand and supply conditions, would then *tendentially* adjust until price/value (and other) discrepancies were removed (Mandel 1969). This is illustrated in the discussion of the so-called transformation problem discussed next.

5.7 TRANSFORMATION PROBLEM AND INTERPRETATIVE CONTROVERSY

The Marx law of value has courted controversy in what has been called the "transformation problem." The debate centers on the procedure in which Marx dealt with the changing of production input values into so-called *prices of production*. Prices of production are the term that Marx used to describe the necessary prices that would be required in order for separate firms to realize the average amount of surplus value (average profit) from the market (from a given capital outlay) that would, in turn, represent an equalization of profit rates between capitals (Mandel 1987). In such a case some of the (prices of production) prices of firms will be above their produced values and some will be below them. This is because, as Kliman *et al.* notes, with varying ratios of constant capital (means of production) to labor (the organic composition) it is not possible for value profit rates to be the same for all firms (Brewer 1984; Kliman 2007: 141–44). Marx then proceeded to demonstrate, assuming firms with varying organic compositions in conditions of normal capitalist competition, with his hypothetical tables, that profit equalization *could* occur (at least in theory), providing that these *prices of production* are established. Some of these prices, as stated above, will be above value; some equal and some will be below value (Marx [1894] 1981, chap. 9).[13]

However, critics have claimed that Marx's description of the relation between input values and prices of production is problematic. Mainstream economists, for instance, have been critical of Marx's overall method, since they expect input values to match output values in a simultaneous equilibrium. Marx, in contrast, theorized in terms of sequential production periods (Kliman 2007). In 1907, Bortkiewicz had first promoted the idea that Marx cannot use his output values to determine new input values and thus "reproduce" production, which Bortkiewicz assumed he should be able to do simultaneously (Bortkiewicz 1949). Mandel, however, rejects this as an irrelevant and explains that Marx uses two time-frameworks rather than a simultaneous equilibrium (Mandel 1969). Kliman further explains that since Marx is sequential he is simply wishing to demonstrate an expansion of capital and accumulation for capitalists, from one period to the next, from the extraction of surplus value. For Marx, input values/prices are not expected to equal output ones although they might equate by chance, since the input values are calculated on the *currently needed to produce* (at the time of use not historic purchase, if it was earlier) labor-time/monetary costs, and the outputs are based on their *replacement* costs during circulation after production (Kliman 2007: 21).[14] The change, during production, in the values of inputs and outputs, is expected because the average social productivity will vary from one point in time to the next.

Kliman points out that there are two different profit rates for the individual firm (or sector), the *produced* rate of profit and the *realized* rate of profit. They are both measured in terms of the total capital advanced, but the first relates to values produced and the second relates to value received when sold, and the surplus value realized. As stated, capital migrates toward the highest return, and this will mean that, even assuming a constant rate of exploitation and the same level of productivity, there will be different value rates of profit for different capitals if there are different organic compositions of capital. Nevertheless, (as stated) there can be equal money profit rates realized (called average profit) for all firms, when market prices are the same as the "prices of production" mentioned above. The price convergence to the prices of production itself occurs because, when capital leaves an underperforming branch of production, it will force the market price (of the same branch) up due to the supply effects. The reverse will occur in technologically advanced sectors. Marx believed that these types of processes were simply laws of competitive capitalism as capital migrates toward the highest returns across periods.

In Marx's schema, that is, his input/output tables with prices of production established, he also posits three fundamental aggregate equalities, which do not depend on whether the necessary competitive equalization has taken place where *prices of production* are established. The first is that the sum total of prices, monies realized in circulation after a given period of production, is equal to the sum total of labor values (Kliman 2007). In the second postulate Marx states that the sum total of surplus value is equal to total profit realized. The third postulate is that the economy-wide value and price (produced and realized) profit rates are equal. It is interesting to note that, if Marx's *own* (sequential) theoretical method of analysis is utilized (as found in his tables), then *all* of the above postulates can be seen to be consistent.[15] This is a significant foundation of Marx's political economy. Yet, there appears to have been several historical efforts to discover inconsistencies in his method, perhaps in order to undermine his political economy and discount any potential influence on policy (Freeman 1996; Freeman 2008). In addition, there was likely to have been a substantial effort to demonstrate empirical inconsistencies during the case-study period, due to the political expediencies of the Cold War. To untangle some of this discourse, I now consider the key approaches to the interpretation of Marx's methodology that draws heavily on the work of Andrew Kliman in *Reclaiming Marx's Capital* (Kliman 2007).

Dual-system interpretation theorists, such as Morishima, have their origin in the Bortkiewicz so-called "correction" of Marx's method (Bortkiewicz 1949).[16] In these approaches the value in labor terms and the price in money of inputs/outputs are determined *independently* of each other and form two distinct systems. It is understandable for these thinkers to separate value and price systems, when they are being measured using separate terms of refer ence that is, labor hours and a monetary numeraire. Yet, according to dual-system theorists, when the value and price of inputs/outputs are measured in the same units (e.g., money), it is claimed that they are *still* determined independently. When Marx is considering the production cost of a commodity to the capitalist he uses the term *cost* price. This refers to the monies *actually* paid for the constant and variable capital. Dual-system theorists maintain, as a consequence, that there are *two* cost prices rather than one (Kliman 2007). Clearly, the *labor*-value of the inputs cannot be expected to equate with outputs if there has been a change in productivity. Since the dual-system thinkers want to use simultaneous models that equate the values of inputs and outputs (in monetary terms), they actually *need* to utilize two independent systems.

These dual-system thinkers have always maintained that there are two separate value and price variable capitals (Kliman 2007). In the 1980s a dual-system *New Interpretation* began, however, with the work of Dumenil and Foley, that held that the *actual money wage* of the workers was the variable capital of both the price *and* the value systems (but different for constant capital). The rationale for this was based on the reality of the wage bargaining process, as a determinant of wages, rather than the "labor" values of the goods and services consumed by workers (Dumenil 1980; Foley 1982). Yet, as Kliman notes, the acceptance of either of these dual-system approaches requires the rejection of an array of textual evidence from Marx. If either of these approaches were accepted, furthermore, it would also result in the existence of two separate sets of cost prices, profit rates, capital advances and aggregates. The three postulates of Marx would, in these circumstances, be found to be inconsistent.

In single-system interpretations the prices and values are determined *interdependently*, in two important ways. First, the prices of production (and average profit) that can theoretically be established during a period of production depend on the general *value profit rate*, so there is not an independent price system. Secondly, the prices actually *paid* for inputs determine the value magnitudes that are considered by Marx, and so there is no distinct value system either (Kliman 2007). The constant capital advanced and the value transferred depend upon the *realized* value of inputs purchased, not the produced values measured in labor terms (Carchedi 1996). This is a very important point for this book since, as Freeman notes, this reclaims the significance of monetary factors in production in direct contrast to both the mainstream and the Keynesian synthesis view (Freeman 1996). In addition, the single-system interpretations agree with the notion of the New Interpretation (mentioned above), that variable capital is determined by the money wages actually paid, not the produced values of the goods they consume. So, prices and values co-determine each other across successive periods of production. Marx, it should be noted, had generally assumed that realized values were the same as produced values for much of his analysis in *Capital* for simplicity purposes.

Kliman explains, however, that all of these interpretations outlined so far, with the exception of the TSSI, are simultaneous models. Simultaneous valuation, as mentioned above, assumes that the per-unit value (or price) of the inputs *must* equal the per-unit value (or price) of the outputs, measured by their prices of production. This has been justified on two grounds. First, it is argued that since Marx spoke about commodity values of unsold items being determined by the current replacement cost, not the historic cost, then inputs for analysis depend on these current costs also. The TSSI advocates, who claim that Marx never implied that the input values must match the output ones because of the separate time periods, dispute this. Furthermore, TSSI proponents argue that it is the prices that currently need to be paid for the inputs, when they enter production, which is a determinant of products' values. These might differ from their historic cost values, since this was when the "means of production" inputs were made, and also be different from the prevailing cost of replacement at the end of the production period. This is important, since if the replacement cost is used as an input value, *a priori,* this leads to the assumption that labor does not add any value to the output and tends to lead to what is termed *physicalist* thinking.[17] Physicalism posits that increased quantities of homogenous entities constitute an expansion of value. Physicalist thinkers, such as Steedman or Sraffa, argued that productivity increases and real wage rates, determined by goods that can actually be purchased, are what adds or detracts value to (or from) the physical output (Sraffa 1960; Steedman 1977). In the section on the LTFRP there is an illustration of this. Secondly, they argue that Marx implied a simultaneous view since he felt that his "prices of production" would be the ones found in the marketplace (Kliman 2007). This notion of Marx's thinking is perhaps unrealistic, however, given the attention to detail Marx gives to the circuit of capital and production periods (Marx [1867] 1976; Marx [1885] 1978). The TSSI advocates, like Freeman, Carchedi, Kliman and Potts, deny this proposition on mathematical grounds (Kliman 2007). The TSSI advocates reject physicalism since an hour of labor-time, following Marx, always yields the same value even if there has been an increase of productivity and an hour of abstract labor *produces* more. All that happens is that the same commodities are cheapened in labor terms (Kliman 2007).

Finally, there is the so-called value-form interpretation of Marx that claims exchange makes labor *count* as Mohun describes it (Mohun 1984). These thinkers, such as Arthur or Reuten, do not claim to be consistent with Marx but, conversely, do not feel that they need to be (Reuten 1993, Arthur 2001). They argue that labor only becomes *abstract*, in the sense that Marx intended, when commodities produced are exchanged for money. These ideas are based on the notion that a product with no use-value is, therefore, a waste of labor. Yet, as Kliman notes, if value is created when the product is sold (rather than when it is produced) there is not any meaningful sense in which labor creates value and it is, therefore, unlikely to be what Marx meant (Kliman 2007). The value-form idea, nevertheless, instigates an interesting debate, since there is logic in the method, but it is argued here that it is *not* Marx's approach.

The TSSI work of Freeman, Carchedi, Kliman and Potts has contributed much to our understanding of Marx's *own* solution to the oft-debated transformation problem, which is notably internally consistent with Marx's overall postulates (Freeman 1996; Kliman 2007). In Table 5.2, for instance, a simpler version of Marx's solution is illustrated, without Marx's use of five branches of production and fixed capital that is, means of production that last beyond one production period, in order to reinforce his essential point.

In the table c, v, and s stand for constant capital, variable capital and surplus value, respectively; $w = c + v + s$ is the value of the output, π is average profit, and $p = c + v + \pi$ is the output's price of production. $s/(c + v)$ and $\pi/(c + v)$ are

Table 5.2 The Transformation Solution

Firm	*c*	*v*	*s*	*w*	*π*	*p*	*s/(c+v)*	*π/(c+v)*
A	$45	$10	$10	$65	$9.7	$64.7	18.2%	17.6%
B	$25	$5	$5	$35	$5.3	$35.3	16.7%	17.6%
Total	$70	$15	$15	$100	$15	$100	17.6%	17.6%

the value and price rates of profit. The table has utilized dollars but it does not matter whether the value and price sums are expressed in units of money or labor-time. In the table $c + v$ are data inputs that depend on the "prices" paid, in keeping with the TSSI (and Marx), and derived magnitudes are the prices, profits and prices of profit. If the output at the end of the period were sold at value, there would not be an equalization of profit rates. Yet, when the prices of production are established (p), then this becomes possible. Marx's solution, albeit subject to criticism, also leads on to the successful and consistent (at least in theory) establishment of his three aggregate equalities stated earlier.

The TSSI approach usually begins with a criticism of the mainstream view of the economic system as a large marketplace that experiences a simultaneous equilibrium, as products are produced and traded. Equilibrium consists of a set of relative prices that assumes an equalization of profit rates across the economy. Money (see chapter 3) is considered to be *neutral*: that is it exists merely to transform these relative prices in to nominal prices. Mainstream economists then focus on modeling disturbances from an established equilibrium to another, which they attribute to exogenous factors such as trade unions or government policies, rather than the mechanics of the market itself. Since these ideas assume a simultaneous equilibrium, as stated above, when they considered Marx's tables they had to make sure that input values equaled output ones, in order for simultaneous reproduction to take place. In the TSSI, however, it is the prices *actually paid* for inputs (or outputs used as inputs for the next period of production), formed at the end of production, that determine the values used in TSSI modeling (Kliman 2007). In these cases inputs are usually not expected to be the same values as outputs. In reality, as Carchedi noted, market prices are established first and then the tendential prices of production may gradually emerge, providing there are no countertendencies, over successive periods thus determining outcomes (Carchedi 1996). The TSSI, it is argued here, thus better reflects the reality.

5.8 THE MARXIST THEORY OF RENT

Marx's theory of rent pertains to the entities that receive part of the aggregate surplus value in the form of rent (Marx [1894] 1981, chap. 40–45). Marx introduces the concept of absolute land rent, required on all land (and other property) leased by producers, since the owner will expect at least a minimum return (Marx [1894] 1981, chap. 45). The tendential redistribution process of surplus value in the economy, which leads to profit equalization, is hindered by absolute rents (Mandel 1987). In other words, the necessary *prices* that would equalize profit across capitals and industries are not established because, the prices are raised higher as a direct consequence of absolute ground rents. If certain conditions prevail, of course, then these rents can be sustained for a long time. In the modern era, monopolys, any leased means of production and technology patents are all further examples of such entities that lead to absolute rents being extracted. In addition, a monopolized credit system could perhaps be seen as a recipient of a portion of the surplus value created in the economy, in the form of absolute rents. Marx's argument posits that landowners will not release land unless they receive something for it, and this is the basis for absolute rent. Marx suggests that in order to yield average profit and cover absolute rent, with the worst soil, the price must rise above the level that would prevail without absolute rent (Marx [1894] 1981, chap. 45). Marx then asks if this is a *monopoly price*, which he defines as a price above value (which is possible with monopoly). He then concludes that, since the organic composition of capital is below average in agriculture, the price of agricultural commodities can rise without exceeding their value (Brewer 1984). Differential rent, as Marx describes it, can then also be paid to entities that rent this better quality land, which allows the producers productivity to rise. As the producer with higher productivity realizes more value, this extra value can be paid to the owner who controls this source (land) of improved productivity, perhaps shared with the capitalist. So, as a result of scarcity, or institutional blockages, absolute and differential rent can be sustained for some time. This can include tribute toward the financial sector. Furthermore, in the modern era, these rents hinder profitability and contribute toward the propensity toward crises and/or the transformation of the financial sector.

5.9 THE LAW OF THE TENDENTIAL FALL IN THE RATE OF PROFIT

This section of the chapter explores the tendency for the rate of profit to fall across successive periods of production. The section deliberately contains more detail than other sections, because of the significance of the LTFRP for the key propositions and conclusions of later chapters. In chapter 11, for instance, I argue that the LTFRP is a valid explanation of financial sector transformation, and the subsequent erosion of state sovereignty. If rates of profit in the nonfinancial sector are lower, and the expectancy of future profits, this will increase the attractiveness of investments in the finance sector despite its risks.

In general, as stated, profitability in the nonfinancial sector can be expected to tendentially equalize between sectors, as capital migrates toward higher returns, although within sectors it does not tend to equalize. This is because new labor-saving technologies is profitable for leading firms, in a particular sector, as it creates a transfer of profit from other firms in that branch of industry.[18] Non-leading firms (laggards) will adopt labor-saving techniques in time but by this later stage will not be able to realize any surplus profit. If they do not try to catch up, alternatively, they are unlikely to make a profit at all. Since the leading firms, as Potts notes, realize surplus profits they are better placed to invest in research and development and are thus likely to remain as the leading firms (2007). So, according to Marx, as the capitalist mode of production evolves, competitive firms introduce labor-saving technologies in order to increase productivity. Yet, when such an increase in the *organic composition of capital* actually occurs, Marx states:

> Then this gradual growth in the constant capital, in relation to the variable, must necessarily result in a *gradual fall in the general rate of profit*, given that the rate of surplus value, or the level of the exploitation of labor by capital, remains the same.
>
> (Marx [1894] 1981: 318)

This is because an hour of abstract social labor always yields the *same* labor value. So, therefore, technical innovation will produce less *new* value per pound (£) of advanced capital, since constant capital for example, machinery has been expanded relative to labor.[19] This seemingly counterintuitive aspect of Marx's political economy illustrates that in a boom time of increasing productivity, the profit rate has a tendency to fall. Increases in productivity thus lower the labor-value of individual commodities and, given healthy competition, should also lead to a reduction in prices. Kliman notes that even monopolies are likely to lower their prices when their costs of production fall, since they are then able to increase their sales and hence increase their mass of profit. This occurs even if their profit per unit sold has not been increased in line with the falling production costs (Kliman 2012: 16). He further explains with use of an example that assumes a constant rate of exploitation (surplus value) and a physical output that is expanded at the same rate as the physical capital that if prices remain the same so does the profit rate. Yet, if prices fall, the profit rate will fall (Kliman 2012: 16).

The TSSI of Marx has reclaimed Marx's LTFRP from the position of simultaneous Marxists who have assumed that profitability is based on the physical output quantities (Freeman 1996; Kliman 2007; Potts 2009a).

Kliman explains how the use of simultaneous models (as stated above) to explain Marx leads inevitably to *physicalism,* and it is then rational to reject the LTFRP on theoretical grounds as Okishio did in 1961 (Kliman 2007). However, since the TSSI has re-legitimized the consistency of Marx's original method, it then becomes possible to utilize the LTFRP for purposes of explanation. This prediction of the *tendential* behavior of the productive economy, based on Marx's law of value, is therefore used here for the purposes of analyzing financial power. Table 5.3 illustrates how in an accumulating economy that assumes everything is reinvested, the profit rate in physical terms rises while the profit rate in terms of value falls, as Marx predicts in his method.[20] It is interesting to note that the capital, output or surplus value can be measured *in either labor time or money,* and since it is only the physical output profit rate that increases, the Okishio theorem as stated above is therefore disproved. In the table, C = constant capital, V = variable capital, S = surplus value and E = rate of exploitation (i.e., S/V). The physical values are denoted by the superscript p.

It is also important to note that, for Marx, the falling profit rate law in capitalist mechanics was simply a *tendency* that, by implication, was subject to counter-tendencies. If the rate of exploitation is increased, for instance, then the profit rate will be raised (assuming nothing else changes). Marx describes that this can occur as a result of a prolonging of the working day, a so-called increase of *absolute* surplus value, or if the worker is remunerated less (as wage-goods are cheapened by productivity increases) an increase of *relative* surplus value takes place (Marx [1867] 1976: 432). However, any technical innovation *normally* increases productivity through the replacement of labor and results in a greater proportion of constant capital. This means that the profit rate will fall since profit is derived from labor power. The significance

Table 5.3 Physical and Value Profit Rate with Constant MELT

Period	*C*	C^p	*V*	V^p	*S*	S^p	*E*
0	200	20	50	5	50	5	100%
1	200	20	50	5	50	5	100%
2	250	25	50	5	50	8	100%
3	303.95	33	46.05	5	53.95	12	117%
4	363.55	45	40.40	5	59.60	16	148%
Period	*Output*	*Output*^{p}	*P Rate*	P^p *Rate*	*Unit V*	*Price*	*MELT*[a]
0	300	30	20.00%	20.00%	10	10	1.000
1	300	30	20.00%	20.00%	10	10	1.000
2	350	38	16.67%	26.67%	9.21	9.21	1.000
3	403.95	50	15.41%	31.58%	8.08	8.08	1.000
4	463.55	66	14.75%	32.00%	7.02	7.02	1.000

[a]The MELT (labor hours/$) is measured at the end of production.

of this point is illustrated in Table 5.3, in Period 3, where the value of variable capital falls from 50 to 46.05 and the mass of surplus value has increased to 53.95, which means that the rate of exploitation has also risen to 117%. Yet, since the productivity increase was achieved at the expense of the rising organic composition of capital, of greater proportion (i.e., something else did change) than the cheapening of wage-goods, the value profit rate falls from 20% to 16.67%. Meanwhile, the physical profit rate rises from 20% to 26.67% due to the increased productivity. To summarize more succinctly, as stated above and illustrated in Table 5.3, the *mass* of surplus value increases as the wage-goods are cheapened and workers are paid less but this is offset as capital employed becomes more productive *with* accumulation because while the physical profit rate is rising the price/value profit rate is falling simultaneously.[21] Marx explains that these circumstances will create the impression that the capitalist has intended to gain from greater sales from more produce, in full knowledge of the simultaneous fall in individual commodity values, and the receipt of less profit per commodity. Yet, in reality the capitalist gains from the increase in the mass of surplus value in this period resulting from last period's productivity increase. Marx writes:

> The phenomenon arising from the nature of the capitalist mode of production, that the price of an individual commodity or a given portion of commodities falls with the growing productivity of labor, while the number of commodities rises; that the amount of profit on the individual commodity and the rate of profit on the sum of commodities falls, but the mass of profit on the total sum of commodities rises
>
> (Marx [1894] 1981: 337)

It should be pointed out, however, that the rising rate of surplus value that is, lower wages as a proportion of new value is problematic, even though it can offset any fall in the profit rate, because there are natural limits to this. To illustrate the point Kliman uses the example of a firm employing five workers from whom the capitalist extracts five hours surplus value each that is, 25 hours in all. In time, if productivity improvements lead to a reduction of the workforce to one worker, the maximum surplus value that could be extracted is still only twenty-four hours (Kliman 2007). In addition to this, the actual act of reducing the wages of workers is a difficult process for capitalists to achieve in reality.

Marx argued that the profit rate is restored through a crisis, reducing the prices of the means of production, and through capitalists finding it easier to increase exploitation of workers. In crisis, with capital assets lying idle, there is a *physical* deterioration of capital value when capital "falls prey to the destructive power of natural processes" (Marx [1867] 1976: 289). In addition, there is the process of what Marx called the *moral depreciation* of fixed assets that occurs when the price of the means of production falls as a consequence of obsolescence. This is explored more fully in the next section. During crises, both these asset write-downs have the effect of cheapening the means of production and, therefore, increasing the profit rate after the initial losses. This is illustrated at its extreme in a crisis when a capitalist goes bankrupt, liquidating assets, and a new capitalist buys the firm at a fire-sale price.

In summary, any combination of these mitigating factors outlined above will reduce the prices paid for means of production and restore the profit rate. These processes, as Kliman notes, lead to the destruction of capital that, in turn, is a central element of what Schumpeter dubbed the *creative destruction* of capitalism, that induces technological revolutions and cycles (Kliman 2012: 210).[22] Notwithstanding these counter-tendencies, some commentators have suggested that Marx pointed toward the ultimate collapse of capitalism, driven by these processes. Kliman notes, for instance, that Ernest Mandel had made this proposition (Kliman 2007). Yet, Kliman claims the actual textual evidence to suggest Marx had considered the inevitability of system collapse is very weak. A gradual transformation toward an alternative economic system, in contrast, driven by political/social/cultural factors is an entirely different suggestion altogether. The dynamics of capitalism driven by Marx's law of value do lead, however, as Marx predicted, to the increasing expropriation of capital by other capitalists as part of the general law of capitalist accumulation. Marx writes:

> It will be further remembered that, with the development of the capitalist mode of production, there is the increase in the minimum amount of individual capital necessary to carry on a business under its normal conditions. The smaller capitals, therefore, crowd into spheres of production which large-scale production has taken control of only sporadically or incompletely. Here competition rages in direct proportion to the number, and in inverse proportion to the magnitude, of the rival capitals. It always ends in the ruin of many small capitalists, whose capitals partly pass into the hands of their conquerors, and partly vanish completely.
> (Marx [1867] 1976: 777)

In this competitive capitalist environment, firms need to be vigilant in order to protect their survival, and profitability strengthens their position by providing resources for research and development. Leading producers, as stated above, are therefore able to realize more surplus value than they produce, in contrast to average or laggard producers, as a consequence of their superior productivity. Laggard firms are not so fortunate, however, and they often find themselves squeezed out of the market altogether. Market prices are established in sectors, and the leading firms are more profitable because they produce a larger output per portion of advanced capital. In addition, capital will also migrate between sectors in search of higher profit. This has the effect of increasing (or decreasing) supply in varying sectors and contributes toward the tendential formation of *prices of production*, that equalize profit rates across sectors, in the transformation process. Yet, as I argue in this book, the process of profit equalization is less likely to occur *within* a particular sector, due to the existence of lead firms, notwithstanding its theoretical feasibility. Many firms may also respond by attempting to gain more market power. Monopolies are continually able to realize more value than they produce, thus reducing the amount of surplus value for distribution among the competitive parts of the general economy. Monopolies and cartels are therefore, as Marx noted, not subject to the same transformation process between sectors (Marx [1894] 1981: 1001).

In addition to the counter-tendencies to falling profit rates mentioned above, mitigation could also occur through increasing *commodification* as capitalism develops. Some freely available products of nature, such as water that contains a use-value but is without an exchange-value, have been privatized and commodified by firms, creating an exchange-value that did not *previously* exist. This, in turn, leads to a corresponding expansion of output value and, providing the market contains above-average profit, an increased profit rate (Petrella 2001).[23] In addition, the development of new commodities, and their markets, can occur *ex niliho*, particularly in the service sectors in an underemployed economy, as new *needs* are discovered or formed by consumers/firms or state spending requirements.

The fall in profit rates, as the economy accumulates in booms, is even more remarkable when it is considered in conjunction with any of the (abovementioned) mitigating factors that may be counteracting the tendency for the fall. I argue in this book, therefore, in line with Marx, that *this law of the tendency for the rate of profit to fall has led to increased systemic need (and practice) to compensate through mitigating factors and this, in turn, has led (albeit indirectly) to the changes experienced in the financial system.* Marx had remarked, for instance, on the increasing role that banks played in the accumulation process generally. He writes, with remarkable prophetic vision of the corporate-raider activities of (leveraged) private equity firms in more modern times, about the credit system of his day as follows:

> In its first stages, this system furtively creeps in as the humble assistant of accumulation, drawing into the hands of individual or associated capitalists by invisible threads the money resources, which lie scattered in larger or smaller amounts over the surface of society; but it soon becomes a new and terrible weapon in the battle of competition and is finally transformed into an enormous social mechanism for the centralisation of capitals.
>
> (Marx [1867] 1976: 777)

In this passage, Marx indicates that credit monies and related banking activities are important elements of the capital accumulation and centralization of capitalism, since they determine real *outcomes* in the competitive process. Marx had argued that they would facilitate the centralization of the means of production in the hands of a decreasing class of capitalists, and concentrate capital in larger joint-stock units. This process has indeed continued unabated in the history of capitalist economies. Marx thus maintained that the *key* driving forces and mechanics of the capitalist mode emanate from *production* itself and, in particular, general accumulation and the tendency for the profit rate to fall as objective laws of its operation. Marx had also claimed, as Kliman illustrates with reference to several key passages from Marx, that this tendency for the profit rate to fall was his single most important contribution to political economy (Kliman 2010: 3). The LTFRP is considered as the *central* explanatory tool for the theoretical purposes of this book, since I claim that falling profitability (directly or indirectly) affects and transforms the financial sector, which in turn erodes state financial sovereignty as defined, and then leads in the absence of counter-tendencies to crisis. It is important, therefore, to outline these processes in more detail since they are significant for the later empirical analysis. We first consider the Potts depiction, derived from Grossman, and then the Kliman approach (Potts 2010, Kliman, 2012). These key theoretical arguments, regarding the behavior of the circuit of capital and falling profit, form the basis for the claims made in later empirical chapters.

Potts argues that the migration of surplus capital toward the financial markets, and thus any subsequent financial sector development that erodes state sovereignty, is driven by falling profit as capital seeks higher returns (Potts 2010). He defines surplus capital as simply the monies that remain when capitalists cut back on productive investment, following a fall in the profit rate (Potts 2011c: 75). Marx writes:

> The rate of profit, is the spur to capitalist production (in the same way as the valorisation of capital is its sole purpose), a fall in this rate slows down the formation of new, independent capitals and thus appears as a threat to the development of the capitalist production process; it promotes overproduction, speculation and crises, and leads to the existence of *excess capital* [my emphasis] alongside a surplus population
>
> (Marx [1894] 1981: 349)

Potts then illustrates how Grossmann had employed Marx's concept of surplus capital to predict the imminence of looming crisis accurately, in the form of the Great Depression, as a consequence of superfluous capital, poor investment prospects and the rising unemployment (Potts 2011c: 77). Grossmann writes:

> Superfluous capital looks for spheres of profitable investment. With no chance in production, capital is either exported or switched to speculation. . . . Despite the optimism of many bourgeois writers who think that the Americans have succeeded in solving the problem of crises and creating economic stability, there are enough signs to suggest that America is fast approaching a state of over accumulation. . . . The depressed state of industry is reflected by an expansion of speculative loans and speculative driving up of share prices. . . . Today's America is doing its best to avert the coming crash—already foreshadowed in the panic selling on the stock exchange of December 1928—by forcing up the volume of exports. . . . When the Germans and the British match these efforts, the crisis will only be intensified
>
> (Grossmann 1929: 191)

The work of Potts further illustrates the point. In a theoretical model that Potts developed in 2009, Potts illustrates how the return on shares for a hypothetical company, which keeps wages constant in use-value terms and experiences rising productivity and thus a rising rate of exploitation, will rise as surplus value mass rises in a boom despite falling profit rates (Potts 2011c: 76). A point arises in the simulation where the return on the shares exceeds that of investing in production. Capitalists then switch to investing in fictitious capital, further reducing productive investment and stimulating more share-price inflation. These bullish conditions continue until a stock market crash ensues. As Potts notes:

> Rather than explaining bubbles in terms of pure speculation, the concept of surplus capital explains why such bubbles should cyclically reoccur. It is not a matter of irrationality; it is simply a consequence of supply and demand. If productive capitalists wish to productively invest less, the financial system is left with more capital to invest elsewhere.
>
> (Potts 2011c: 78)

It is interesting to note, as Grossmann had pointed out that the Hilferding notion of integration between banks and firms, with banks driving outcomes, is an unrealistic one:

> For if Hilferding were right in arguing that the banks dominate industry, this would only shatter Marx's theory of the crucial importance of production itself to the structure of capitalism. The crucial role would then be played not by the production process but by finance capital, or structures in the sphere of circulation. . . . At more advanced stages of accumulation industry becomes increasingly more independent of credit flow because it shifts to self-financing through depreciation and reserves. . . . In countries like Britain, France and especially the USA, it is simply not possible to speak of industry

> being dependent on the banks. . . . According to Vogelstein, this is one of the reasons why banks have been turning to the stock exchange by way of investments.
>
> (Grossman 1929: 199)

Grossmann points out that, as Potts notes, banks can only perform a leading role in business behavior if capital is in short supply (Potts 2011c: 78). In addition, it is the surplus capital instead, Potts argues, derived from low profitability in the productive sector that is the more plausible explanation of crisis than attributing crisis to financial factors (Potts 2011c: 78). This is extended, as expected, to the transformation of the financial sector in general.

Kliman has a similar approach to the issue, except for a slight difference as a direct consequence of his empirical work. Kliman discovered that, in his study of the US since the Great Depression, the rate of accumulation has tracked the profit rate closely, meaning that the proportion of profit used for productive investment has remained constant leading to sluggish growth and speculations of all kinds. While he accepts capitalists cut back on investment following low profitability, and then some surplus profits migrate to the financial markets, his empirical work in the decades leading to the 2008 financial crisis suggested that the investment share of net profit actually rose prior to the crisis in the US despite the LTFRP (Kliman and Williams 2015). Kliman argues instead that profit rates only *indirectly* (albeit importantly) affects the financial sector, via *low* profitability, in that they create the instability for crises (Kliman 2012: 13). Kliman further points out, in addition, that falling profitability cannot be a direct cause of crisis because, for instance, profitability actually rose in the years preceding the financial crisis in 2007.

But, what are the transmission mechanisms that Kliman identifies, linking falling profit rates to systemic crises? Kliman identifies two such intermediate links: a lower average profit rate (and its impact on firms), and the credit system (Kliman 2010: 29). These links will be the *same* as those responsible for the *observed* loss of state financial sovereignty, evidenced by increased commercial banking activity, since the same *financialization* phenomena have led to crises. First, a falling profit rate lowers the average rate of profit. This means that even if the profit rate is rising immediately before a crisis, *marginal* (in terms of unviable) businesses will simply not be able to survive. Minimal profit is an imperative for all firms, at least in the longer term. Secondly, in terms of the credit system, a falling profit rate leads to the increase of securities speculation and asset bubbles to secure some profit, followed by default of debt obligations and sharp devaluations, which then become the immediate cause of crisis. In addition, the low rates of accumulation will also tend to lower interest rates, furthering speculation and asset bubbles.

Marx writes about the preliminary activity, before the indirect impact on the credit system, of a falling profit rate:

> If the rate of profit falls, on the one hand we see exertions by capital, in that the individual capitalist drives down the individual value of his own particular commodities below their average social value, by using better methods, etc., and thus makes a surplus profit at the given market price; on the other hand we have swindling and general promotion of swindling, through desperate attempts in the way of new methods of production, new capital investments and new adventures, to secure some kind of extra profit, which will be independent of the general average and superior to it (the average profit rate).
>
> (Marx [1894] 1981: 367)

This is a key passage, since it reveals how Marx perceived the impact of the tendency for the rate of profit to fall on general capitalist behavior. Firms will seek, for instance, to gain extra profit from any productivity growth achieved, promoting overproduction, at the expense of other firms before profit equalization takes place, or seek out new investments and new markets, mergers or financial speculations. The financial speculations can, in turn, lead to excessive debt in relation to value creation and asset bubbles. In addition, these are likely to be enhanced in a boom, when profitability falls as a consequence of heightened *animal spirits*, and lower interest rates from the surplus capital. Excessive debt and asset bubbles then lead, as night follows day, to default and burst bubbles. In short, crises soon follow.

Marx's view of falling profitability, interpreted by Potts, Grossman and Kliman, is posited as an explanation of general reproduction and the transformation of the financial sector. Since credit-money *is* contemporary money, and provides for almost all modern money transactions, it can be viewed in separate categories that are subject to different forces and mechanics. The falling profit rate, therefore, impacts value-production first and, then indirectly impacts financial sector transactions through transmission signals, and/or surplus capital migration, which are based on underlying asset values of financial securities. Financial sector activity, as we would expect, often creates clear winners and losers. While all financial intermediaries providing interest-bearing capital should be expected to share (barring default) in the surplus value created in the productive economy, activity in the financial markets frequently involves profiteering from the fluctuating market prices of securities where *no* extra surplus value is created. In these specific instances of zero-sum exchanges, the various agents experience simultaneous proportionate gains and losses. In the securitized modern era, this should also be a factor in the increasing the further establishment of plutocracy and the centralization of financial power. It also increases instability.

5.10 AN ILLUSTRATION OF DEPRECIATION AND MORAL DEPRECIATION

In this section the focus is on the question of moral depreciation (Marx's term), which is also significant for later chapters, that occurs as a consequence of obsolescence. Marx saw this as a significant systemic imperative, which engenders an entrepreneurial urgency to utilize the firm's capital assets quickly or risk suffering greater loss. The loss incurred at the outset of production, therefore, represents a wealth *loss* for the capitalist and, an increase in the obsolescence rate raises the reported profit rate in the next period. As Kliman remarks:

> That the measured profit rate ultimately tends to rise because of moral depreciation means that technological progress *first* caused profitability to fall. In other words, the subsequent rise in the rate of profit is not due to technological progress itself, but to the writing down of losses.
>
> (Kliman 2010: 81)

If we first assume a simple reproduction model, where there is no moral depreciation and output is completely sold at its value, then the advanced capital and profit rate will remain the same from each production period to the next, since any *wear and tear* depreciation value *passes* through to the output. If the capitalist were to put the monies aside in a depreciation fund,

Table 5.4 Depreciation from Wear and Tear

	Fixed Capital	*Asset Fund-AF*	*Variable Capital*	*Working Capital*	*Capital Advanced*	*FC in to Produce*[a]
Year 1	$20,000	$0	$6,000	$8,000	$34,000	$4,000
Year 2	$16,000	$4,000	$6,000	$8,000	$34,000	$4,000
Year 3	$12,000	$8,000	$6,000	$8,000	$34,000	$4,000
Year 4	$8,000	$12,000	$6,000	$8,000	$34,000	$4,000
Year 5	$4,000	$16,000	$6,000	$8,000	$34,000	$4,000

	WC in to Produce	*VC/SV to Produce*[b]	*Value of Output*	*Year End FC Value*	*FC/AF+ $ Realized*[c]	*Profit Rate*[d]
Year 1	$8,000	$11,000	$23,000	$16,000	$39,000	14.7%
Year 2	$8,000	$11,000	$23,000	$12,000	$39,000	14.7%
Year 3	$8,000	$11,000	$23,000	$8,000	$39,000	14.7%
Year 4	$8,000	$11,000	$23,000	$4,000	$39,000	14.7%
Year 5	$8,000	$11,000	$23,000	$0	$39,000	14.7%

[a] The fixed capital (FC) depreciates and this value lost is passed in to the produce. The capitalist then puts this value in to the depreciation fund (AF) when the output is sold.
[b] The value of the surplus value (SV) that is, $5,000 is added to the variable capital (VC).
[c] The remaining fixed capital value is added to the output sales and asset fund (AF).
[d] The surplus value as a proportion of the capital advanced that is, $5,000/$34,000.

as suggested in Table 5.4, then they will be able to purchase a new fixed asset after it has fully depreciated.

In Table 5.4, the advanced capital is \$20,000 + \$6,000 + \$8,000 = \$34,000, and a surplus value of \$5,000 is also generated during production. The brand new fixed asset (in Year 1) has a value of \$20,000 and adds \$4,000 each year to the commodities produced. As the monies are returned to the capitalist, the same \$4,000 is put aside in a depreciation fund in order to purchase a new fixed asset every five years. The advanced and total capital values are both the same amount each year, because the depreciation fund is included, and the profit rate remains stable at 17.65%. Finally, the \$5,000 each year is spent on capitalist consumption. Yet, what would happen if moral depreciation takes place? In Table 5.5, new machines fall in value from \$20,000 to \$10,000 at the end of Year 2. The machine currently being used has already transferred \$8,000 of value to the output and is held in the depreciation fund in money form after sales. Now, however, the machine is worth \$6,000 (rather than \$12,000) representing a capitalist loss of \$6,000 thus more than wiping out their \$5,000 profit (surplus value) for that year.

In Year 3 the machine only passes \$2000 of value to the output (and is then realized as money) and the depreciation fund rises to \$10,000 the following year. Assuming no further moral depreciation, the replacement fund already has the necessary monies to replenish the fixed assets. As a consequence, in Year 5, the \$2,000 is not needed. In Year 4 and Year 5, interestingly, the profit rate has risen to 17.9% in Year 4 and then 19.2% in Year 5. Yet, if we consider the total surplus value actually realized by the capitalist over the five years in both illustrations, the profit falls from

Table 5.5 Depreciation from Wear and Tear and Obsolescence

	Fixed Capital	*Asset Fund*	*Variable Capital*	*Working Capital*	*Capital Advanced*	*FC in to Produce*
Year 1	\$20,000	\$0	\$6,000	\$8,000	\$34,000	\$4,000
Year 2	\$16,000	\$4,000	\$6,000	\$8,000	\$34,000	\$4,000
Year 3	\$6,000	\$8,000	\$6,000	\$8,000	\$28,000	\$2,000
Year 4	\$4,000	\$10,000	\$6,000	\$8,000	\$28,000	\$2,000
Year 5	\$2,000	\$10,000	\$6,000	\$8,000	\$26,000	\$2,000

	WC in to Produce	*VC/SV to Produce*	*Value of Output*	*Year End FC Value*	*FC/AF+ \$ Realized*	*Profit Rate*
Year 1	\$8,000	\$11,000	\$23,000	\$16,000	\$39,000	14.7%
Year 2	\$8,000	\$11,000	\$23,000	\$6,000	\$33,000	0%[a]
Year 3	\$8,000	\$11,000	\$21,000	\$4,000	\$33,000	17.9%
Year 4	\$8,000	\$11,000	\$21,000	\$2,000	\$33,000	17.9%
Year 5	\$8,000	\$11,000	\$21,000	\$0	\$31,000[b]	19.2%

[a]The capitalist actually realizes a loss of \$1,000 which could be denoted as (0.029%).
[b]The \$2,000 asset fund contribution is not needed in Year 5 and thus adds to profit.

$25,000 in the first example to $19,000 in the second. Moral depreciation has created losses for the capitalist, despite the increase in profit rate, which is why, in the real world, they seek to utilize the fixed capital as quickly as possible.

5.11 CONCLUSION

We have seen in this chapter that Marx's political economy, summarized in his *law of value*, exerts its *tendential* influence on capitalism across successive periods of production. Marx also provides the reader with a holistic economic system in historical context and, one subject to contradictions and tendencies. The general impact of its operation has led to change, alienation, exploitation, larger firms and the centralization of capital. These processes are all rooted in a clear value theory that is objective and, therefore, are measureable in principle, although this would probably be difficult to calculate in practice. It has also been argued that the mechanics of capitalist production, and market competition, exhibit a propensity toward recurring crises from falling profitability. It is an important claim of the book that it is the *specific* responses to the LTFRP from economic agents that has led to the transformation of the financial sector and the erosion of state financial capability. The asset depreciation from obsolescence (that Marx called moral depreciation), especially in the modern IT era, has also been shown to restore profitability after the initial capitalist loss endured. I now turn, in the following chapter, to Marx's conception of money that had been fully predicated on his *law of value* that has been outlined in this chapter.

NOTES

1. Much of Marx's philosophy had been in response to the German idealism of Hegel and Kant (Rius 1999).
2. Mandel had argued, for instance, that Marx predicted capitalist collapse after recurring crises but this is rejected by the Marxian scholar Andrew Kliman, who claims the textual evidence is weak (Kliman 2007: 31).
3. Profit is called *surplus value,* derived from labor, and will decline *a priori* given an increasing proportion of constant to variable capital (capital goods to labor), known as the rising organic composition of capital.
4. This can take the form of interest, fees, charges or commissions.
5. I contend that Marx saw finance capital as secondary (and/or derived from) to industrial forms (Mouatt 2011).
6. As Marx put it "accumulate, accumulate! That is Moses and the prophets" (Marx [1867] 1976: 742).

7. In a simple barter economy, for instance, economic agents would probably expect to receive goods and services that contained the same labor hours as their own produce being exchanged, as a fair trade.

8. However, if labor productivity were to increase in one *single* firm, the value of its output will increase (almost) proportionately. This is because the individual firm's increase in productivity is unlikely to substantially impact the industry average on which "socially necessary" hours are calculated (Kliman 2007: 22).

9. Debates that investigate the empirical validity of the calculation of these labor-hour totals form what is known as the "reduction problem" (Mandel 1987: 13).

10. Potts, for instance, explores Kliman's definition of the MELT and compares it with Freeman's different treatment (Potts 2011a).

11. Marx identified four types of alienation. First, the worker is alienated from the produce because he is not producing for himself. Secondly, this means that in the process of labor he must also "deny himself," since he is working for the market not his own needs. Thirdly, in exchange-relations the economic agents confront each other through the imperative of the market and not free social relations. Finally, the worker is alienated from his "species" that is, humanity, since the species is not able to engage with nature (to meet species need) in the way nature intended as a consequence of private property and property relations (Marx [1844] 2014, pp. 136–52).

12. Kliman notes that Marx used the phrase "law of value" rather than the LTV (Kliman 2007).

13. It is also worth noting that market prices, determined by demand and supply, will usually deviate from these *prices of production* but still fluctuate around them as axes. Marx was perhaps wanting to *illustrate* that profit equalization was possible, rather than demonstrate any empirical reality.

14. Marx used the actual *prices paid* for constant and variable capital inputs, rather than their specific labor values since this is the real cost to the capitalist (Freeman 1996).

15. The Temporal Single System Interpretation (TSSI) of Marx advanced by Kliman, Freeman and Potts is such an interpretation and dismisses the work of Marx's critics as a misinterpretation (Potts 2005b).

16. Bortkiewitz was an advocate of the (simultaneous) Walrasian general equilibrium (Kliman 2007: 47).

17. Kliman uses an example of corn (Kliman 2007: 79). If ten bushels (used as seed and to pay workers) becomes twelve at harvest then there is no increase in aggregate value (since, by definition, productivity does not increase it) because each bushel of corn will have reduced in value during production. However, in physicalist terms, a profit of 20% is produced because input and output value equate by definition.

18. In Marx's political economy, as Kliman notes, the unit-value does not depend on the activities of the individual firm but the average. If a firm produces twice as much output as before, with the same labor, they produce (and hopefully realize in money) *almost* double the labor-value (Kliman 2007: 22).

19. The constant capital is termed *dead* labor and its value is simply transferred into the product.

20. In Period 0 the surplus value is not reinvested and can be considered as capitalist consumption.

21. Marx notes, "if the variable capital diminishes, and at the same time the rate of surplus-value increases in the same ratio, the mass of surplus-value remains unaltered" (Marx [1867] 1976: 418). In this circumstance, despite the total labor input falling, relative surplus value allows surplus value to stay constant as variable capital falls.

22. The shorter technological life span of fixed assets has also led, according to Mandel, to shorter business cycles which he links to the life of fixed assets resulting from depreciation due to obsolescence (Mandel 1969: 59).

23. Without exchange-value, as Marx notes, an entity has no value as a commodity (Marx [1867] 1976: 166).

Chapter 6

Marx and Money

6.1 INTRODUCTION

In this chapter, I explore Marx's conception of money. The opening section first considers his notion of the social power that money provides and the commodity view of money's origin. In the next section, I outline Marx's description of metallic commodity money, the limits of the standardization of specie by the state and the nature of discounting. The next section deals with money creation, and is followed by a section on Marx's view of money's function in logical order. The final two sections deal with fictitious capital and crisis and the ambiguity in Marx's writing on credit relations.

Marx recognized that in a monetary economy, where money is the only legitimate claim on wealth and is the only truly fungible entity, there is substantial *social power* wielded by entities that control financial resources. This was particularly true of the state during the mercantilist era, when the nation-state focused on the accumulation of specie stocks in order to enhance its political aspirations. These ideas, as De Brunoff has noted, had been developed by Marx in the *Critique of Political Economy* but were not pursued further or discussed elsewhere in his writings (De Brunhoff 1976). It could be that Marx had wanted to focus on the material relations of production and the law of value, as drivers of human economic behavior, and leave the full discussion of the implications of financial power to the more subjective realm the political science of his day?

Marx had a view of money's origin that began with an abstract discussion of the endogenous *origin* of money, which is *socially* established as a monetary equivalent with intrinsic commodity value, through to the development of complex credit forms within the evolution of the capitalist mode of production (Marx [1867] 1976; Marx [1894] 1981).[1] Surplus value is *realized* in the market in the *form* of money. Marx thus identifies a central role that money performs in an economy. Money simply represents abstract social labor. Money capital is transformed into the means of production, and labor power, and then is transformed into commodities and finally back into money-form again, the circuit of capital (Marx [1885] 1978). Capital accumulation is also manifested in monetary nominal terms and money also constitutes the instigator of economic activity and is therefore indispensable to production. This means that the wielders of financial resources have substantial influence on social outcomes through the granting and decline of credit. In essence, Marx's monetary ideas are an extension of the LTV. From this start point, Marx outlines his conception of the nature and function of money.

6.2 THE NATURE AND FUNCTION OF MONEY

For Marx, the function of money follows from its nature as a commodity. In other words the commodity is able to perform the functions of money because it *is* a commodity. In Marx's time this referred to gold mined using human labor, which provided a use-value as money as well as a precious metal use-value, and hence contained an exchange-value. There is the inference that in order to possess the *social* acceptability that money requires, an entity needs to possess this commodity status. Yet, as Itoh notes, it is irrelevant whether or not the commodity money has value other than its use-value as money and that, therefore, accounting prices could actually be set in valueless units of currency in an abstract sense (Itoh 1999).[2] However, while Marx appreciated the existence of an abstract money, that transfers labor value into price, and *real* money that transfers price in to a "concrete equivalent" that contains the "qualities of money," it has been generally assumed (perhaps erroneously) that Marx did not consider or at least outline in his text anything other than a commodity money containing such qualities (Itoh 1999; Zarlenga 2002; Mouatt 2008). In the modern era, alternatively, we have a complete fiat money and credit money system that is not convertible to any commodity, and is fully legitimized and sustained by the modern state. Furthermore, following Knapp, since these electronic bank monies are acceptable for the payment of taxes, they can be considered money proper (Knapp 1924). In more recent times, Wray has pointed out, as stated in 2.3, that it is the tax payment capability that ensures the demand for money in a modern capitalist economy (Wray 2012: 53). Marx in his analysis had utilized gold for illustrating the settling of final payments, although this certainly does not preclude the *a priori* possibility of another legally sanctioned currency fulfilling the same purpose (Marx [1859] 1970). In fact, Marx does discuss the use of inconvertible paper "issued by the state and given forced currency," and also recognized the use of credit-money, but this depended on the abilities of the state (Marx [1867] 1976: 224). In a later footnote, for instance, Marx criticizes Fullarton for suggesting that inconvertible paper notes could render commodity-money superfluous (Marx [1867] 1976: 225). Marx, in contrast, had recognized the *unique* capability of commodity money to transcend the boundaries of the nation-state, if the state ceased to exist for any reason (Marx [1859] 1970). In contrast, a means of account currency that is created and sanctioned by the state is most likely to be unable to survive the demise of the state. Marx, in summary, was unlikely to have been a *metallist* that is, advocating the use of specie as currency backing as an imperative, but rather he theorized monetary matters using specie instead because this simply represented the practical reality of his day (Mouatt 2008).

Marx was also aware of the limitations of commodity money standard. In his *Critique of Political Economy*, for instance, Marx gives an illustration of a debate that had raged in the eighteenth century centered on the "doctrine of the standard of money" (Marx [1859] 1970). The "standard of price" as it is more commonly known is the rate of exchange between the nominal value of paper or electronic currency and the commodity used for backing, which is arbitrarily set by the authorities. At the time of the accession of William of Orange the mint price of silver was 5s 2d per ounce but its market price had risen to 6s 3d. This was because clipping, abrasion and possible dilution of the metal content had reduced the silver content of coin. A study revealed that £57, 200 of coin weighed 141, 000 ounces when it should have been 220,000 (Marx [1859] 1970: 77). With commodity money there is always the practi cal difficulty of relating the metal price to its nominal value (mint price) to consider, where the market value may deviate from the officially set value, as well as deciding the correct quantity of minted coins in relation to circulating commodities. Those that recognized the former problem, such as Sir James Steuart, felt that those with money or tax obligations, due to creditors or the state, should be able to repay less coin as a result of any devaluation. This could be achieved by changing the mint price to reflect the changes. However, at the time, dominant political figures like John Locke ensured this did not happen and this amounted to a *de facto* surplus for government and creditors (Marx [1859] 1970). Marx was no doubt fully aware of the inequitable implications of this in his day.

So, for Marx then, gold was considered as money and its value was determined by the labor content that was embodied in it. Yet, as Brewer notes, in contrast to the quantity theorists, he felt that it was the value of money determining the quantity in circulation rather than the quantity of money determining its value (Brewer 1984). If the labor value of gold falls, more gold will be required to represent the same value, and so more circulating currency is needed to maintain commensurability. Marx's adjustment process suggests that, as gold production is cheaper and is initially more profitable, more gold is then produced and exchanged. The extra demand pushes up prices through the system until a new equilibrium is reached with a new amount of circulating currency. In these cases the *value of gold* and the nominal *volume of exchanges* determine the amount of circulating money. Marx had shown that the quantity theorists of money had causality going the wrong way round (Brewer 1984).

In addition, Marx noted that paper money could be created by the banking system, which he referred to as a "money sign" (Mandel 1987). In this instance, the paper money represents the money commodity nominally and can be exchanged for it. Mandel further implied that, for Marx, if the production of paper notes used for the circulation of commodities is in excess of the quantity of commodity money, *ceteris paribus*, there would be a need for a new standard of price. For paper money, *prima facie*, this appears to be an expression of the QTM, yet Marx's views were different. This is because, in contrast to the QTM theorists, he viewed price changes to be a determinant of the volume of money in circulation. Marx adhered to the views of the *banking school* who felt that any excess of paper money above the necessary quantity of commodity backing not used for economic activity, would return to the banking system and repay debt obligations according to what has been called in monetary theory the "law of the reflux" (Itoh 1999).[3] Marx and the banking school thus tended to emphasize the hoarding and paying functions of money, which mitigates any inflationary impact of money increases. If more money was needed to meet the circulation requirement, money could be drawn from hoards or circulation velocity could be increased. If less money were required, the reflux would apply. In this sense the money supply can be seen as partly endogenous and non-neutral.

Marx had also considered the activity of discounting bills of exchange by the banking sector, which is what he meant by the *credit* system and this is reviewed later. Marx thought that this activity economized on the use of money as a means of payment (Brewer 1984). It is interesting to note, however, that he did not discuss the growth of the cheque clearing system, which utilizes bank deposits as money and also economizes on paper money in circulation. In the modern era switch payments and direct debits use bank deposits in the same way. Modern economists all view bank deposits as real money but Marx, and most of his contemporaries, thought otherwise. Marx, it appears, was only interested in that which fulfilled the necessary money function in the context of his time (Brewer 1984). In this sense, bank deposits *per se* simply did not fulfill the criteria.

6.3 THE CREATION OF MONEY

Marx seemed to underplay the role of the state in money creation, and his theory is similar to the Austrian school that had suggested that historical development of commodity money had been market driven (Menger 1871; Mises 1912). As previously stated, Marx also believed that the producing and exchanging agents, who first produced the commodity that eventually evolved to be used as money, were the originators responsible for money creation. Subsequently Marx recognized, like Smith, the role of the state in steering the management of money-system function (Smith 2003). Marx tended, however, to view token monies, that were sanctioned by the state for purposes of a "means of account" and with no intrinsic value, as temporary in the sense that they pertain to the historic and jurisdiction boundaries of the state and could therefore easily be replaced (Marx [1859] 1970: 119). Marx also was aware of emerging bank monies, such as the discounting of bills and overdraft facilities, which served a necessary finance function in the development of the productive economy. Yet, Marx did not appear to view these monies as particularly autonomous from the processes of industrial capital. Marx, as previously stated, had assumed that older forms of money lending in precapitalist days, in the form of financial capital, would be gradually tailored to meet the evolving needs of industrial capital as the economic system developed (Marx [1863] 1971). This was because monies lent as "interest-bearing debt" were dependent on the expansion of value realized in the market for their continued existence, and monies advanced to noncapitalists were secondary to it (Marx [1863] 1971). Yet, it is worth noting that some of the more modern monetary thinkers would attribute a stronger social power capability toward those in a position to control modern monies, whether this is the state issue of *fiat* currency or the provision or denial of credit by the private banks (Strange 1998; Zarlenga 2002).

6.4 THE MARXIAN THEORY OF THE FUNCTIONS OF MONEY

In Marxist analysis there is a logical ordering of the *functions* of money in the capitalist economic order and these are, respectively, the measure of value, the means of exchange and money as money that is, for purposes of hoarding, payment and world money (De Brunhoff 1976; Itoh 1999). Marx further stated that the function of "measure of value" was dependent on the oscillations in the value of commodity money, as mentioned above. Yet, Marx also talked about the "standard of price" that referred to the actions of the state in setting rates of exchange between the commodity money and the official currency. In Marx's time an ounce of gold was set at £3 17s 10 and 1/2d

(Brewer 1984). What is significant is that for Marx, the accounting system of prices is clearly abstract but has a social foundation, in terms of their commodity values, and is therefore independent of the state-driven standard of price. The second function is the means of exchange. Here Marx is mindful of the velocity of money circulation that is characterized by constant movement. He recognized, in line with Ricardo that the *necessary* quantity and velocity varied according to commodity values. Yet, Ricardo had simply stated that money was exogenously created whereas Marx thought that meeting monetary requirements depended on the complexities of any commodity money output that is, endogenous factors, circulation processes and the existing hoards of money (Itoh 1999). The market participants themselves also drive drawing money from hoards to meet any productive requirements. Marx had also partly accepted the Ricardian notion of money as a "veil," since he felt that it was the production and circulation of commodities, rather than the functioning of the money system, that determine prices tendentially and (for Marx not Ricardo) subsequent money quantity (Itoh 1999). However, as Itoh notes, Marx also felt that money functioned outside of circulation as a store of value and, in this sense, is not simply a "veil" (Itoh 1999). Yet, as we established in chapter 1, money needs to be at least a temporary store of value in order to function as a means of exchange. For Marx, therefore, exchange was not akin to barter since relative *produced* values have been established in production, and the commodities' *realized* values are determined by price formation, whereas barter is a reflection of the static "subjective behaviour" of negotiators based on their individual perceptions of utility (Marx [1859] 1970: 90). This not to say that Marx did not recognize the subjective demand conditions, that exert their pressure on prices, but rather it appears he was simply concerned to posit and emphasize the tendential pressures of the law of value on the nominal price system.

For Marx, the hoarding of money was an essential part of his overall political economy since the capitalist, through withholding of monies, was able to instigate new production or choose not to, whereas the proletarian was simply forced to sell his own labor power. So, Marx presents precautionary hoards as enabling capitalists to deal with market price fluctuations of raw materials etc. in order to maintain the continuity of capitalist production. It is interesting to note that, as Itoh points out, Marx was probably basing these ideas on the mercantilist thinking that recognized the *social* power of money hoards in contrast to the normal position of the classical economists who viewed money as neutral (Itoh 1999).

Another function of money, in Marx's economics, is the function of payment. During the course of circulation, *real* money is used to finally "settle" any promises to pay. Commercial debt is subject to clearing that is, the exchange of one debt for another, but any balancing items are settled during a given period. This clearing activity, of the credit system, economizes on the function of money as a means of purchase. Marx surmised that this extension of credit served to increase the velocity of circulation of money (Marx [1859] 1970). Marx had also, in line with the Banking school, adhered to the idea of the "cyclical" nature of credit money in terms of the law of the reflux. It is worth mentioning, as Itoh notes, that Marx saw credit money as contributing to the expansion of capitalist accumulation in general and, therefore, as non-neutral and endogenous (Itoh 1999).

Finally, Marx had viewed commodity money as serving the function of *world* money, for purposes of "payment" and hoarding for all sorts of motives, in contrast to Ricardo who had viewed bullion as a *pure* means of exchange.[4] For this purpose, Marx had felt that gold was most appropriate as it breaks "through the barriers of domestic circulation" (Marx [1859] 1970: 149). Ricardo and Hume had talked of specie flows that restored equilibrium in international trade, akin to a current account trade balance, so that the necessary means of circulation of gold was always available. Higher prices would lead to a deficit and a gold outflow, followed by deflation until the harmony is restored.[5] Marx challenged these ideas on the basis that prices determine money quantity and specie is hoarded. He used the example of crop failures, between 1800 and 1820, where Ricardo had argued that gold was exported not because of the need to purchase corn but because the value of gold had fallen. However, Marx points out that the evidence contradicts Ricardo, and demonstrates that rather than the availability of spare money due to less grain for purchase there was a shortage because prices have risen (Marx [1859] 1970). It could also be argued here that Marx's ideas on international money are discounted simply by looking at the development of global finance, from the pre-WW2 gold standard to the dollar gold-exchange standard and then toward the financial liberalization without gold backing of today. Yet, financial crises in the global economy seem to be a recurring symptom of the global economy and there are many people, like De Bono, who have argued for the stability that might derive from a commodity-backed system (De Bono 1993). It could be argued that the increase in world gold prices 2008–2010 perhaps validate Marx's notion of the significance of commodity money, as investors seek greater levels of security in times of enhanced uncertainty.

6.5 THE CREDIT SYSTEM

Marx's discussion of the emerging credit system within capitalism is found in volume two and three (parts four and five) of *Capital* (Marx [1885] 1978; Marx [1894] 1981). Marx initially presents money hoards as reserve funds of latent money capital for purposes of advancement as capital, derived from the previous expansion of value from production that has taken place (Marx [1885] 1978, chap. 2). Marx argued that this accumulation of value is the normal state of affairs for a capitalist economy, which takes place when part or all of the surplus value is advanced as new capital instead of being spent on consumption (Marx [1894] 1981, chap. 17). This accumulation then makes the further increase of hoards possible, as surplus capital is directed toward them. Marx viewed, following Tooke, these hoards as facilitators of monetary circulation, as they were withdrawn and released from use (Lapavitsas 1994). Marx had also recognized the social power of these hoards of monetary resources, for those that controlled them, and further recognized that they represented a *de facto* claim on the annual produce (Marx [1885] 1978, chap. 17). In addition, Marx posited that it was the capitalist ability to draw from these reserves that constituted a key-defining feature that separated the *bourgeoisie* from the *proletariat* (Marx 1848). This gave the bourgeoisie substantial decision-making power in general society.

So, Marx viewed these idle capitalist funds as the foundation of the emerging credit system, as they became interest-bearing capital and were lent to capitalists for the further expansion of value (Itoh 1999). Indeed, this 100% fractional backed credit was one of the contributory factors to Marx's proposition, as previously stated, that industrial capital would subjugate more traditional forms of lending as the idle funds of capitalists replaced the money-lender resources of old (Marx [1863] 1971). In addition, as a modern development, much new corporate investment is financed from retained funds by the capitalist class and, therefore, credit may not be required at all. However, according to Marx, idle funds enabled credit to be advanced. Itoh explains how the existence of reserves then enabled capitalists to accept promissory notes, IOUs in a money-form related to a specific commodity transaction, since the spare monies could be utilized to ensure the continuation of the production process during the time period before the debt settlement date (Itoh 1999). Bills of exchange, in Marx's day, represented a more generalized form of commercial credit since they had at least two names as signatories, who had responsibility for payment, and thus the bills benefited from greater acceptability (Itoh 1999). The bills of exchange could then be extended further, to other commercial agents, thus economizing on the use of limited stocks of idle funds (Itoh 1999).[6] The bills were discounted, which represented the interest derived from the provision of credit, by the banking system that then provided banknotes that could be converted by the owner into the commodity money. Marx had also, as Itoh notes, discussed the role of the money market in recycling any available funds, and further discussed the role of the generic central bank in the provision of a means of settlement between banks and wholesale commercial agents (Itoh 1999).

Yet, despite the efficiency that credit affords to the capitalist mode of production, Marx's theoretical foundation for the operation of the system was the existence of idle funds. In the EMT modern era, conversely, money is created *ex nihilo* by the private banking infrastructure and does *not* require the preexistence of funds prior to the lending contract. In addition, even the necessary liquidity to meet reserve requirements (legal and operational) does not have to preexist in order for lending to take place (Pettifor 2006; Rochon 2007). However, it could be argued that Marx's theoretical treatment of the credit system does not preclude the possibility of monies created in such a fashion, if money is defined in a certain way. Bills of exchange and their associated banknotes that function as monies, for example, could be conceived as contributing to the quantity of circulating currency if the banknotes are defined as money or, as Marx perhaps implied, simply economizing on the use of real money that exists in the form of a commodity. If banknotes *are* money, then the monies could be conceived as being created *ex nihilo*, it all depends on the definition of money used. Yet, in contrast to the modern era, it was perhaps more sensible, with the ubiquitous commodity money and credit of Marx's day, to make the separation between real and credit monies.

6.6 FICTITIOUS CAPITAL AND CRISIS

It has been stated that, for Marx, money mediates the exchange of commodities and also accumulation allows hoards of money capital to be established. The decisions not to spend and rather to hoard money mean *de facto* that Say's law, that is, supply creates its own demand, potentially fails to hold in a monetary economy. Crises then ensue as commodities fail to sell in sufficient quantities with various capitals experiencing losses (Bottomore 1991).[7] In addition, within these capitalist crises, hoarding can represent an unwillingness of capitalists to advance further monies when faced with the prospect of further shortfalls of demand in markets if the commodities were to be produced and enter circulation (Bottomore 1991). A further inhibitor to the advancement of monies as capital, from funds held in reserve, is the aforementioned falling rate of profit (LTFRP). In all of these instances capital can be tempted, as Potts notes, to migrate toward fictitious (non-value creating) capital in the financial markets, induced by the prospects for some of greater returns (Potts 2010).[8] Yet, since the very existence of fictitious (Marx's phrase) capital amounts to a zero-sum game at the time when the transactions are made, the activity can be precarious for agents and simply constitutes a redistribution of current nominal money and stocks, hence social power. Those that gain, therefore, do so at the expense of others and no surplus value has been created in the process. Later, the trading in assets ceases to become zero-sum as the securities appreciate at varying rates. In addition, the market forces associated with this capital migration and/or financial sector activity, which has been indirectly driven, then facilitate the formation of speculative *bubbles* and the subsequent crises. Stable expectations of asset appreciation, as Kregel notes, then contribute to the evolution of bubbles as a result of rational behavior, as agents seek profit maximization, rather than a psychological deficiency on behalf of the market participants (Kregel 2008). If greater profit margins are achieved in the productive economy, therefore, the circumstances would be different and bad behavior in the financial sector is less likely to occur. The later evidence from Germany appears to support this view.

Marx posited that during an upturn in the trade cycle, there will be an expansion of credit and capital advanced from hoards, while the reduced expectations of capitalists during a downturn would lead to a contraction of credit and capital advanced (Marx [1894] 1981, chap. 30). A severe contraction of credit, potentially sparked by a collapse of fictitious capital bubbles, would inevitably lead to a liquidity crisis. A credit squeeze, therefore, thus leads to the inevitability of default and unsold stocks. So, for Marx, the migration of capital toward fictitious capital is an indirect feature of the trade cycle and LTFRP. It is also posited that these processes affect the transformation of the financial sector. Marx's ideas, in conjunction with the EMT, are adopted in the book as explanatory tools to analyze the financial systems of Germany and the UK in the empirical research. Marx's political economy and its monetary theory, as claimed in the book, are compatible with inconvertible modern credit-money. It is acknowledged, however, that others have discussed credit money in Marxian analysis in the monetary literature but that the EMT has not been specifically combined with the TSSI by anyone. Most recently (2011) Moseley, for instance, has identified a fiat-money version of the MELT (see chapter 5), denoted as MV/L where M represented inconvertible fiat money (Rieu 2012: 2).[9] He derived this notion of the MELT from Marx's treatment of fiat money that exists alongside commodity money (Marx 1976: 225). Moseley then further posits that this can be extended to the treatment of modern credit money, which he sees as partly exogenous and partly endogenously created (Moseley 2011: 100).[10] However, while Moseley's version to its credit was not predicated on the Marx notion of the *economizing* nature of credit monies, using *units* of bank credit money instead, it was not combined with a full discussion of the EMT (Marx [1894] 1981: 653). It is posited in this book that *ex nihilo* credit entities can also be used in the normal reproduction schema of Marx in the TSSI tradition since, at least for the duration of the term that the debt obligation(s) pertains to, credit monies can serve the full functionality of money as defined. Moseley's concept of the MELT, in contrast, is theorized using a *simultaneous* interpretation of Marx that, as a consequence of its internal logic, as Kliman has explained, precludes the possibility of LTFRP (Kliman 2007). Since this book claims that the decline in state financial power, and the concurrent transformation of the financial sector, can be adequately explained by the LTFRP, the Moseley conception of the MELT has been rejected.

It is recognized that the difficulty of reducing credit-money into units of social labor renders *changes* to commodity values expressed in monetary terms more complicated, and this may be the reason for their previous non-use by Marxian economists. It may also have been problematic to model the credit system in general. Alternatively, it has been suggested in this chapter, as Marx intimated, credit money theory may not be used since it is only specie that has the *sustained* ability to transcend the boundaries of the nation-state (Marx [1867] 1976: 240). Notwithstanding, it is this synthesis of EMP credit-money, theorized as *units* of money, with Marx's political economy as understood by the TSSI, that the book claims is theoretically valid since it reflects the monetary reality in capitalist nations. Just as the MELT allows us to express the produced and realized value of commodities in either labor-time or money, the MELT also allows us to estimate the costs of circulation in labor-time or money. The costs of circulation, or the money unit costs of production in other words, will be a deduction of surplus value for the productive economy and income for the financial sector.

6.7 MARX AND MONETARY AMBIGUITY

Marxian thinkers have concluded that there three key areas where Marx's textual analysis of monetary matters would arguably benefit from greater theoretical development, particularly in the context of modern money and the actual historical evolution of financial systems (De Brunhoff 1976; Lapavitsas 1994; De Brunhoff 2006). First, the theoretical use of commodity money needs to be modified since, in the modern era, money has no substantial intrinsic value or backing and exists almost exclusively in the form of digits on computer software. Secondly, as previously stated, Marx did not include bank deposits as money, since he seemed only concerned with the actual monies, perhaps drawn from deposits, utilized in successive periods of production and circulation.[11] Thirdly, Marx also did not provide a clear view of *ex nihilo* endogenous money-creation, despite his theorizing of bills of exchange and overdraft facilities. In his general discussion of banking and the provision of financial capital, for example, he presents the recycling of funds from surplus to deficit agents from a static stock rather than (as posited by PKs, circuitists and reformers) bank monies derived from a balance sheet accounting entry (Marx [1894] 1981). Yet, it is this PK view that is generally now accepted as the main method of money-creation and is the one adopted in this book (Gnos 2004; Wray 2004; Pettifor 2006). It could be suggested, however, that Marx implied the *possibility* of the *ex nihilo* creation of money from the banking system, in his treatment of bills of exchange, promissory notes and overdrafts, but it was not made explicit in the text (Marx [1894] 1981). Indeed, as Itoh notes, Marx had instead discussed the significance and role of idle funds in the development of the capitalist commercial credit system, something that is not necessary in the financial system of today (Itoh 1999: 87). Unfortunately, as De Brunhoff noted, part of the interpretation difficulty that stems from Marx's work on credit is that it remained unfinished by Marx (even in draft form) when Engels came to complete the work for publication after Marx's death (De Brunhoff 1976).

6.8 CONCLUSION

Marx provides us with a holistic political economy that utilizes an objective, and therefore measureable, value theory based upon units of abstract social labor. This has led to the monetary conclusions discussed in this chapter. Marx's objective basis, rather than subjective notions of utility, also gives Marx a scientific approach. In addition, all of Marx's monetary ideas discussed that follow from his *law of value* are used in the book, albeit with certain PK modifications that reflect the nature of modern monies. The subjugation of financial capital during capitalist evolution, by industrial capital, is also claimed to provide further evidence that the production structure rather than finance is the key driver of capitalist mechanics. In addition, the notion of the falling profit rate tendency provides a theoretical explanation for the possible migration of surplus capital toward the financial markets, and the indirect impact on the financial sector transformation. Finally, Marx's prediction of the tendential behavior of the economy, in terms of the accumulation and concentration of capital and LTFRP, is also a useful explanation for the increasing plutocratic financial power that persists in capitalism.[12]

Most economists generally accept the EMT, as Naito notes, and it is claimed that the approach outlined above will be an important step toward a modern Marxian monetary theory (Naito 2008). Indeed, as also argued in the chapter, when Marx considered the credit system in the nineteenth century it can be argued that his ideas on monetary creation were endogenous anyway, despite some textual ambiguity mentioned above. It is perhaps fortuitous for the book that Marx's ideas do not preclude the existence of monies derived endogenously in response to demand, from the private banking infrastructure in the form of credit, despite Marx's view of the *endogenous* historical origin of money that has similarities with the mainstream and Austrian monetary historians.[13] Furthermore, it was noted that Marx clearly thought ownership title to monies certainly confers social power and is therefore significant.

It has also been stated that Marx had developed theories on the different functions of money, and was careful to illustrate different money-form behaviors, exploring each within their specific context. Marx thus outlined his study of money, in a logical order, with the initial establishment of the monetary equivalent as a measure of value. Next, the exchange-value of money as a medium of circulation was established and then, finally, money as a means of payment, hoarding and universal function was considered (De Brunhoff 1976). In addition, there is a later development of a capitalist theory of credit, based on bank discounts of bills of exchange and overdrafts that were relevant in his day. This was discussed in volume three of *Capital* but was completed by Engels (Marx [1894] 1981). In the circuit of capital, money and credit have a significant decision-making role among interdependent entities in the financing of real production, the *instigative* and *fungibility* functions that I emphasize in the book, and Marx therefore also challenges the notion of monetary neutrality (De Brunhoff 1976).[14] Marx instead emphasizes the role of money as a *social* relation, which is relevant when considering the relative financial power capabilities of state and market. In addition, I claim that the tendential behavior of the productive economy, as predicted by Marx, provides us with a valid theoretical explanation for some of the financial phenomena in the financial system today. In the next chapter, chapter 7, I consider the financial capabilities of the state in more detail.

NOTES

1. Hudson has challenged the endogenous view of money's origin (discussed in chapter 1), in contrast to the chartalist view, supported with historical evidence. I mentioned in reduced "chicken and egg" argument—see Hudson and Shuklian as examples. Marx's own ideas on the endogenous origin of money, where money simply derives from the market participants themselves, has been open to debate since this presupposes the existence of (social) exchange (Lapavitsas 1994; Shuklian 2002; Hudson 2003).

2. In later chapters, there is an outline of the monetary unit that is adopted for the empirical work in the book. While this is not a commodity and thus does not *contain* abstract labor, this does not mean that transactions with this credit money are costless. The costs of circulation are borne by productive capitalists and consumers.

3. Lapavitsas argues that Marx had developed his monetary ideas more deeply than the banking school by describing the different functions of commodity, fiat and credit monies (Lapavitsas 1994).

4. Marx had believed that "socially necessary" labor-time would determine the exchange-value of the commodity money—as it operated internationally. In practice,

however, "political factors" were historically prevalent. For instance, as Zarlenga has noted, the gold/silver ratio differential existed between East and West for centuries (Zarlenga 2002).

5. It is worth noting that Hume had maintained money was a "valueless" token, whereas Ricardo had stated its commodity value based on the LTV.

6. If the bills of exchange are made *payable to bearer* then this becomes possible.

7. A further consequence of crises is the concentration of capitals as resources are reallocated toward centralizing firms from those experiencing liquidation and foreclosure.

8. It is important to note, however, that Andrew Kliman maintains that the falling profit rate has an *indirect* impact (albeit deterministic in terms of underlying conditions) on financial sector activity. In this sense, the productive sector sets preconditions that affect the financial sector (Kliman 2012: 13).

9. Moseley recognizes that the term fiat money is sometimes used to refer to credit money as well as forms created by the state. However, he posits, following Lapavitsas, that since government creates fiat money, it remains in circulation and is separate from credit-money (Moseley, 2011: 98).

10. The Moseley paper appeared in *Review of Radical Economics* at the same time as my chapter that outlines a similar theoretical construct (Moseley 2011; Mouatt 2011).

11. This is, perhaps, defensible given his general treatment of money hoards, and their release of monies into the circulation of commodities.

12. In the next chapter we will see how the Marxist (and Gramsci) theory of the state adds understanding to the theoretical themes of the book.

13. This is developed more fully in the next chapter.

14. His ideas on hoarding, as well as his related view that prices determine money supply, challenge the mainstream neutrality of money.

Chapter 7

The Financial State

7.1 INTRODUCTION

The aim of this chapter is to investigate and develop the mode in which the *financial* state, and power in general, has been theorized in order to contextualize the key themes of the book. In the first chapter the nature of *financial power* was outlined, defined as control of financial resources as a source of social power, and focused on the political processes associated with the *issue* and *value* of money. Certain monetary definitions and common key debates were also discussed in chapter 2. In the common conception, the role of the state in financial matters has been in relative decline as the capabilities of other agents have increased. The other entities include private banks, corporations, market agents and external powers, in the form of other nation-states and multilateral institutions/regimes. In chapters 3 and 4, the monetary literature, from the classical period to the present, was reviewed in terms of these ideas. Subsequently, the conclusion was made, perhaps unsurprisingly, that the implications of the state's role in financial matters has been an underdeveloped dialogue. Economists, it seems, have chosen not to reflect too heavily on such political matters, preferring to focus on pure economic processes. This is despite an increasing awareness of the role of money in economic and political life in general, particularly from the heterodox perspectives. In recent times, for example, the financialization discourse and PK thinking has helped to remedy this. In chapters 5 and 6, the political economy and monetary theory of Marx were explored, and Marx's prediction of the behavior of the productive economy, that is, indirectly driving the financial sector, has been considered a valid depiction of events, in conjunction with the EMT associated with the post-Keynesians. This chapter now investigates the realm of political science, banking literature and international political economy in order to gain greater insight into the *political* nature of financial power and its exercise. Yet, conversely, these approaches have tended to ignore or underplay the specific *economic* theories that pertain to the subject matter. This book, as a consequence, seeks to bridge this gap through the exploration of the *political economy* of money, while remaining firmly rooted in a synthesis of economic, albeit nonmainstream, theory based on Marx's view of the productive economy and the EMT.

We begin with a discussion of different notions of power, followed by an exploration of general theories of the state. Next, the popular conception of the financial role of the modern state is investigated with an exploration of the generic instruments, actors and institutions actually involved in the creation and functioning of modern monies. The chapter ends with a review of interstate relations in monetary affairs, and the global economy, and a clarification of the ideas to be pursued in the empirical chapters.

7.2 NOTIONS OF POWER

There are several *sources* of social power following the extensive work of Michael Mann and Susan Strange (Mann 1986; Strange 1988). Legislators, administrators, systems, institutions, corporations, private banks, the military, religious groups, mafias, lobbyists and the market *inter alia* all wield power. But, to begin, what is the nature of power *per se*? Power needs to be differentiated from authority and legitimacy, despite these being social power sources, and is manifested in an agent's *realized* capability to affect specific outcomes, regardless of the intentions of others. This was described in chapter 1 as the "ability to get someone, or an entity, to do that which they would otherwise choose not to do," a rather crude definition loosely based on the definition of the late Susan Strange. Power capability *per se* can also be considered as a fluid concept, in an alienable transferable sense, or alternatively, as Allen noted, it can be considered to be *amorphous* in nature, with an inconsistent form that might simply evaporate (Allen 2003: 29). In this sense, power does not simply transfer from entity to entity. So, unsurprisingly, there have been debates on the semantics and ontology in the discourse on power. In her work, Strange had suggested that "power is simply the ability of a person or group of persons to affect outcomes so that their preferences take preference over the preferences of others" (Strange 1996: 17). This is a broad interpretation of social power that encompasses all the various *modes*, from violent coercion to subtle manipulation, which power can take, as well as allowing for a plethora of contexts for its exercise. A consideration of these different modes of power is often attributed to the seminal work of Weber (Allen 2003: 2). More narrow definitions might be more appropriate, however, depending on the objectives for particular studies. The investigation of interstate "national interest," for instance, in international relations, might benefit from a more narrow definition that reduces the notion of power to state political processes and capabilities. Yet, for the purposes of exploring the erosion of state financial sovereignty, a broader definition of power and its specific forms and contexts seems more appropriate. This is justified because I am seeking to identify changing power relations that are manifested in *actual* capabilities, exercise and outcomes rather than conducting a theoretical exercise. It is difficult, for example, to consider the power capabilities of an entity without observing its exercise. Latent or any possessed capabilities are somewhat meaningless without their exercise.

A fundamental feature of the concept of power is its asymmetrical, and hence social, aspect. Strange *et al.* have argued that to have any real meaning, power needs to be considered in a relational context (Strange 1996; Allen 2003). In this sense it is the *exercise* of power that becomes more important as opposed to the mere *possession* of a power capability. Power is all too often theorized in terms of a quantifiable alienable resource or capability that can, by implication, be measured against the others and this, as Strange and Allen note, leads to substantial problems. First, power can then be viewed as "zero-sum" so that the loss of capability is matched by a corresponding increased capability of another entity, or set of diffused entities. While this may be true in many cases, it cannot be applied to situations where a power capability has been lost with no obvious beneficiary. Secondly, power resources may be misused or be subject to incompetent use. To combat this, Strange suggests adding the terms *will* and *skill* to our understanding of the utilization of capability, derived from varying sources of social power, that focuses on the *exercise* and *impact* of power rather than the mere possession of a power resource (Strange 1996). The history of world affairs is replete with examples of entities imbued with the possession of superior power resources yet, are unable to secure outcomes in relation to other entities with inferior resource capabilities. Thirdly, as Allen argues, this notion of power, in terms of the possession of resources, naturally leads to the unsafe prediction of outcomes based upon quantifiable techniques, a criticism directed at Weber (Allen 2003). Fourthly, in international political economy, the notion of power as a *possessed* capability has historically led to the use of so-called "hegemonic stability theory" which, Strange had posited, is a restrictive approach to global power relations, despite its wide use in the discourse (Strange 1996).

Kindleberger had introduced his hegemonic stability theory, relevant to state financial power, with reference to the economic woes of the Great Depression. Kindleberger identified that a financial leader or hegemon would have provided stability to international money, a role that the US was reluctant to take prior to WW2 (Kindleberger 1973). Consequently, the political economy discourse on power in the 1970s and 1980s was focused on hegemonic power, measured by their *possession* of capabilities. In the post-WW2 era many theorists pointed toward certain capabilities that enabled the US to discharge this role and, therefore, any decline in these quantifiable capabilities was used as an explanation of increasing instability through US decline. It was for this reason that Strange was keen to distinguish between *structural* and *relational* power. Structural power refers to the operation of systems, where an entity has wielded established powers through tradition and the general *modus operandi* of procedures, whereas relational power derives from social power from sources in a specific relational context. While the US, as Strange argued, could be shown to have lost certain relational power *capabilities* in the later post-WW2 era, including financial, its structural power was and is still decisive in many specific outcomes (Strange 1990). The hegemonic entity also does not need to exercise any relational power capability in its possession, in order to achieve desired outcomes, since the threat of use is usually sufficient. State financial power, discussed in the book, is exercised through use of both relational and structural power.

So, as Allen has noted, we need to distinguish between power exercised and the possession of capabilities "disguised as resources" that are mobilized in order to exercise this power. In addition, Allen notes the importance of distinguishing between "power over others" and the "power to act" in association with others, as separate forms of the exercise of power (Allen 2003). While the former involves a leverage of one entity "over" another, the latter exercise of power is "associational," in the sense that collective action enables the *empowerment* of those taking part in the process. Allen also identifies the specific impact of *geography* on the exercise of power, a consideration that he views as neglected by all but a few of the historic power theorists (Allen 2003). Allen cites Foucault and Deleuze as exceptions to this rule.

Many theorists have appeared to view the operation of power as geographically neutral, in the sense that the exercise of power remains static regardless of distance. Mann had identified that social power was exercised through overlapping and intersecting networks, therefore recognizing the fluidity of power, but did not seem to consider the implication of distance on the exercise of power itself (Mann 1986). As Allen puts it "power relations extended over space and time through the networks seem to remain relatively untouched by the experience" (Allen 2003: 60). Foucault, in contrast, was concerned with the "immanence" of power that operates on and through people/entities, and is also derived from almost anything, that then finds *definition* in its impact (Foucault 1982). This emphasizes the exercise of power while, simultaneously, rejecting notions of power based upon quantitative possessed capabilities from clearly defined sources. In this approach, therefore, there is less concern with *who* has the power, but a greater emphasis is placed on the *techniques* and *practices* of its exercise instead, where random unexpected factors can also be at work. Allen points out, however, that this approach should not be taken too far since, in empirical work, it can usually be demonstrated that certain entities wield power in a reasonably consistent fashion which, at least, give the appearance of *possessed* capabilities (Allen 2003). Yet, Foucault had provided important insights into the geographical implications of power exercise. The techniques of power exercise will necessarily vary according to space that suggests it is not sufficient to view the operation of power as consistent through a given spatial network. The operation of so-called Hungarian *Goulash Communism* prior to the collapse of the Soviet Union, for example, was known to be substantially different in form to the operation of power in Russia, even though they were derived from the same political edicts from Moscow. Geography is, therefore, of substantial importance to the exercise of social power.

In terms of the book's focus on financial social power, these considerations of power *per se* are important to clarify. It is necessary to ascertain, in line with Foucault for instance, which people or entities *actually* discharge the capability to control the issue of modern money, and manage its overall circulation processes, rather than just *possess* the theoretical *capability*. This necessary empirical work may reveal or contradict popular conceptions or professional opinions of the operation of financial power. So, it is this actual *exercise* of social power, sourced from the control of financial resources that is significant and constitutes the approach adopted. It is acknowledged following Foucault that confluences of several factors normally exist in the formation of general social outcomes, which are derived from a multiplicity of direct or indirect power sources of a primary or secondary nature. In addition, these power sources are often interdependent. Yet, in the book, I make no attempt to compare and contrast the varying power sources, since this presents us with several epistemological and ontological challenges. Financial power is solely regarded as a *primary* power source, as discussed in chapter 1 that is exercised in conjunction with other powers and influences depending on context. Yet, the particular motives, established outcomes or objectives of entities that wield social power are not the focus of study, despite the undoubted interest these could engender.

7.3 THE CONTROL OF FINANCIAL RESOURCES AND FINANCIAL POWER

The control of financial resources, in terms of the creation and purchasing power of credit money, is clearly a source of social power. This is dominated (but not exclusively) by the private banking infrastructure and the national bank. However, the *ownership* of property, including money, does not necessarily entail comprehensive property rights for the owner(s), where the resources can be controlled and directed at will. According to UK statutory law, for example, freehold property ownership does not include the mineral rights to land and if required, it is possible for the state to enforce a compulsory purchase. It is for this reason that it is the *control* of financial resources, money and other liquid assets denominated in money form that is the focus here rather than the mere ownership of money *per se*. Financial power is derived, as we would expect, from the actual *control* of the monetary resources. Freezing monetary assets, for instance, gives financial authorities social control over resources owned by others. The existence of property rights is particularly significant when we consider that, in the modern era, the overwhelming proportion of global monies is *issued* in the form of credit-money, circulating through bank accounts, that are formed through the instigation of debt contracts. This illustrates, as Strange had emphasized, that substantial social power is wielded by private decision-makers who are able to grant or decline credit (Strange 1988). In terms of daily monetary management by the state, it is also assumed that there is social power wielded through the operation of fiscal and monetary policies. In addition, the state (or independent national bank) is able to exercise social power through the operation or nonuse of "lender of last resort" facilities, the buying and selling of securities to adjust liquidity, credit controls, reserve regulations and currency transactions.[1] State capabilities can also be limited by exchange regimes, or liberalized capital flows that restrict the full scope of sovereign actions, although they are *subject* to any international agreements. So, it is the *actual* control and exercise of financial resources, rather than presumed capability of agents, that *engenders* social power, and necessarily forms the central focus of this book. Yet, social power *exercise* can also only be substantiated with reference to empirical study. In the later chapters, therefore, there are case studies that investigate the political economy of money-issue and value over time, and also investigate whether productive sector factors are likely to have determined any financial sector transformation.

7.4 THEORIES OF THE STATE

It is perhaps unsurprising, there is no common agreement on the nature of the modern state, a word that derives from the Latin *stare* (to stand) and the word *status* meaning standing or condition (Vincent 1987). Yet, it is so important to everyday reality, and the purposes of this book, that a short trek through the theoretical complexity is indispensable. Every state, regardless of historic context, has a geographical boundary, legal system, judiciary and the usual monopoly of force within its own jurisdiction. This is in spite of the various territorial disputes that exist around the globe. In addition, the state with occasional exception claims and manifests hegemony over all other associations within the jurisdiction, wielding the power to determine rights and obligations in both a *de facto* and *de jure* form. It is important, for example, to be able to make jurisdiction effective. Weber had defined the state in this manner, as the entity where a human community lays claim to the "monopoly of legitimate physical violence" within a particular territory (Weber [1919] 2004: 33). Also, within these jurisdictions, there is a *society* with commonalities for example, the rule of law between citizens, and various sub-communities that contain certain distinctions and bonds. The society has often led to the term the nation-state, meaning the geographic jurisdiction of a defined group of people. The state can also be viewed as derived or created by the society, where the real sovereignty lies, or as a corporate entity that itself creates the sub-groups or associations according to its predominant ideology. The first view is similar to the ideas of many political philosophers, such as Hobbes and Locke, who had viewed the state-society relationship as a *social contract* between the state and the governed. Rousseau, for example, writing in eighteenth-century France, argued that the state should be the context where the "general will" of society should be manifested and implemented in the form of policies (Rousseau [1762] 1968). In the UK historical tradition, Mill's notion of "representative government" has become established, where the legislative body or parliament is usually seen as a proxy for the political expression of society (Mill [1859] 1974). More autocratic states, in contrast to this, might have societies whose natures and various associations are more determined by the ideological preferences and whims of the rulers.

Yet, what is the state? Perhaps the easy answer is that it constitutes a bounded geographical jurisdiction, although this discounts the impact of international law, regional associations and multilateral institutions, etc. that all affect sovereignty. The crucial characteristic of this jurisdiction, as Vincent notes, is the "continuous public power" in the form of various *offices* that are imbued with authority, and discharge a variety of roles in society (Vincent 1987). In this sense the state needs to be differentiated from the notion of *government*, which is concerned with, *inter alia,* the initiation, legislative process and implementation of law (previously established and newly formed) during a *given* period. The main responsibilities discharged by the modern state vary in practice, and some may be contested as well. These include, *inter alia*, the provision of external and internal security, the maintenance of financial stability (including currency value), development and industrial strategy, welfare and redistribution, macroeconomic management, taxation, trade negotiations and general infrastructure. In some states, as Weber suggested, there are semiautonomous organizational entities that develop certain traditional procedures and practices. Alternatively, the individual agents that constitute the state apparatus, with their particular whimsical and rational choices, may have a more significant role in determining the *modus operandi* of the discharge of responsibility (Olin-Wright 2002).

The state can be large according to context and time, in terms of scope and resources, or as advocated by Friedman, smaller in size (Friedman 1985). This existence and functioning of the state, once defined, can be constituted in different ways and a variety of forms are to be found in the modern era. These range from constitutional monarchies to republics, with federal or unitary systems, through to autocratic planned economies, that all involve specific political processes and are therefore rooted in separate theories of the nation-state. These interpretations include *inter alia* the absolutist, constitutional, class, autonomous, and the liberal democratic (and pluralist) theories of the state.

The absolutist approach to the state is associated with the notion that it is *necessary* for the state to embody complete sovereignty, whether this is manifested in a ruling group or single person. The sovereign has the sole capability to discharge the *raison d'etat* according to their judgment of state interests. Papal lawyers in the twelfth century, perhaps with the intention of mitigating the fear of misused centralized power, had put forward the notion of the "office theory of rule" whereby the "office" could not be permanently owned by an individual or group and would always pass between hands (Vincent 1987: 62). Nevertheless, the absolutist theory of the state was (and is) somewhat crude, and consequently, when it existed in a real form, it was often justified by an appeal to spiritual principles such as the "divine right" of kings. In political science the defense of the notion of *necessity* for absolute sovereignty has probably been best associated with Thomas Hobbes, who had argued that in "the state of nature," where a form of anarchy existed, life was always "nasty, brutish and short" (Hobbes [1651] 1968). In these circumstances, a social contract with an absolute sovereign was preferable to the alternative anarchy. Hegel had also argued that freedom for the individual could only be realistically achieved through a strong centralized state that provided uniform rules, as well as encapsulating the *zeitgeist* of human consciousness (Vincent 1987: 121). In this sense order is a prerequisite for quality of life. However, in the modern political discourse there is little support for these absolutist notions of the state in most areas of the world, except in certain circumstances where rival factions are being kept at bay and social instability is thus averted.

Constitutional theories of the state are based on more sophisticated thinking and involve the formulation of a constitution that, by definition, has involved a process of establishment. In this conception, the state can be *designed* according to the particular political philosophy desired. Hegel thought for example, that individuals pursuing their particular goals, according to caprice, really needed to be restrained by the parameters of social norms encapsulated in the state, in order to realize a concrete freedom (Vincent 1987). In many ways this idea is similar to the notion of *liberal democracy* in the western world today. In this conception the liberties of individuals need to be protected, ensuring that each person or group does not infringe on the liberty of others, within a framework of "representative" democracy that also protects the individual from state-abuse derived from the "tyranny of the majority" (Ball 1977). The liberal ideas of the French political philosopher Montesquieu, for instance, were instrumental in forming the "checks and balances" specifically designed and embedded in the original US constitution in order to protect the individual from abuses of government, through making the centralization of power very difficult (Ball 1977).

The Marxist class conception of the state, following Marx, is that the state simply represents an extension of the interests of capital (Miliband 1977). This has been theorized from the perspective of earlier competitive capitalism and the more recent monopoly capitalist (high degree of market concentration) form (Miliband 1969; Poulantzas 1974). These interests of the capitalist class can be considered to be *inter alia* the protection of private property (in terms of the means of production), a business legal infrastructure, state-supported banking, free markets, minimal regulation and competition law. If we examine the historical activities of the state in western civilization over the last 500 years, it is difficult to argue convincingly that these core capitalist essentials have been under serious threat at any point. Furthermore, as Kliman has recently argued, the state is often involved in direct action to protect the system from crisis or collapse in what has been termed "state capitalism" (Kliman 2008). The Marxist view can be separated into two distinct viewpoints, even though they amount to the same political outcome. The first, associated with the ideas of Poulantzas and Therborn for example, identifies a political structure where the institutional entities that constitute the state are clearly formed from class relations (Barrow 1993). The second viewpoint, alternatively, suggests that the political process has a power balance, at any particular point in time, which is consistently biased toward maintaining the key interests of the capitalist class (Olin-Wright 2002). The Marxist notion of the state is normally challenged with reference to the liberal democratic state that is presented as having a *pluralist* nature. The state is seen as independent of the interests of private capital, or any other interested party, and operates in the midst of a disparate plurality of powers for example, business, banks, societal groups, external forces (Ball 1977). It is in the political process that this power *mélange* determines outcomes. Yet, this does not contradict the observed reality, which appears to demonstrate that the *key* interests of capital have remained unchallenged in any serious way in all of the modern era. One consequence of the previously mentioned views of power, as a *possessed* capability, is the emphasis that this gives to the international society (and their competition) of states. Later Marxist thinkers, however, have developed ideas that have pointed toward an alternative view. The approach of the *Gramsci*-influenced Cox, for example, enables a much broader concept of world order, which takes account of the international dimension, and is concerned about power relations at varying levels instead. Cox focuses on classes rather than states whose condition, in a Marxian sense, is determined by their material relations in the now global production structure. Since the production structure creates the *resources* that are indispensable to other sources of power, for example, military power, the relations and hierarchies of production are responsible for forming the political authority that is, the state (Cox 1987). The state, in turn, reinforces the same political hierarchies of production that galvanize a "system of accumulation." In this sense, power and wealth are accumulated by the "exploitation" of some groups over others (Strange 1996). The French "regulation" school with their theory of "regimes of accumulation" share this view (Lipietz 1983). Gramsci (and Cox) was also not merely concerned with the evident material relations of production since the existence of *consciousness*, which finds its form in dominant paradigms and ideologies (called the *blocco storico* in Gramsci's Italian context or hegemonic historic blocs in Cox's), is a prime driver of human behavior as well (Cox 1987; Gramsci 1991).

Yet, following Marx, the hegemonic bloc, in terms of the dominant ideological paradigm, is broadly a reflection of the values pertaining to the production structure anyway. It is worth noting, as Lipietz has noted, that Marx had also clearly recognized an "enchanted world" of appearances and subjectivity as an instigator of specific human outcomes, although it would be reasonable to suggest that he viewed these as secondary to the material relations of production and the law of value. I argue that, in this sense, the subjective realm of ideology and its determining influence on outcomes does not have to be inconsistent with Marx's materialist method provided that the material relations of production are recognized as instigators (Lipietz 1983). Strange further explains how, for Cox, there are three levels of world order: the production structure with its associated material relations of production, the international society of states and the international political economy. The levels are separate yet interact and, the historic bloc, the dominant cultural paradigm, acts to maintain and pervade the existing order. Cox maintains, therefore, that substantial transformation will only occur if a "counter-hegemonic bloc," in the normative world of ideas, works at all three levels in order to engender change (Strange 1996). This concept of a global productive sector, with its *material* relations of production, could arguably provide a partial explanation of the driving forces behind any diminished state financial sovereignty that may have occurred. This Gramsci-inspired view of the state is plausible, in the sense that the ideological paradigm has been (arguably) indispensable for the historical survival of capitalism.

7.5 THE FINANCIAL STATE

The state has clearly discharged different functions in the monetary system depending on historic context and place. Karl Polanyi, for example, pointed out that power has ebbed and flowed between state and market, depending on the historical epoch in question (Polanyi 1944). The aim in this section, however, is to illustrate the financial control that is *actually* discharged by the *modern* capitalist state, as determined by professional, academic and informed popular sources as a prelude to the empirical chapters. Clearly, as Knapp had noted in a 1905 seminal work, the authorities are responsible for the sanctioning of the currency by law, which, in turn, finds its legitimacy in its *acceptability* for the payment of state taxes (Knapp 1924). Yet, the common fallacy that suggests it is the government that *solely* issues the currency is simply not true. So, if this is the case, what does the banking, and educational literature, say on the matter?

It was noted in chapter 3 that monetary theory, in the history of economics, has provided exogenous and endogenous views of money-issue and also provided varying explanations of other monetary processes. Yet, in reality, it is the combination of the state, including the national bank as a semi-state agency in conjunction with the private banking infrastructure that is responsible for the money-issue. One of the common difficulties is that the economics literature (e.g., Pilbeam) still persists in presenting the credit multiplier as a demonstration of private bank credit-money expansion, which necessarily depends upon the existence of a state-determined reserve asset ratio (Pilbeam 2005). Yet, as Rochon has pointed out, this ratio has disappeared in a few western nation-states including the UK, and is minimal in others. This continued inaccuracy gives the impression that the state is still able to fully determine the overall level of credit-money expansion. There is a pressing need, therefore, for the textbooks to be rewritten (Rochon 2007). A notable exception is the Howells and Bain textbook. Here, there is an explanation, primarily for undergraduates, of the EMT with reference to double-entry bookkeeping. This is termed the flow of funds model, since money units are created in response to demand. The authors also note that the unreality of the alternative monetary-base multiplier model still persists in many textbook explanations (Howells 2002). However, since the state or central bank sets the short-term base interest rate in an exogenous sense, it could still be argued that they *are* still responsible for the overall level of monies created. Yet, this is ineffectual since they are not able to have accurate knowledge of the likely credit-consumer behavior and, therefore, no reliable indicator of the overall volume of credit money that will be established. The flow of funds model recognizes that money comes into being as a result of loans, and establishes a corresponding liability and asset on the balance sheet. The deposit, once created, becomes a bank liability, and the loan itself is an asset, since the principal plus interest needs to be repaid to the bank. The significant point here is that the bank has not lent preexisting funds, as is commonly thought, but represents a fresh money-issue in the form of an accounting entry. The credit-money has thus been created *ex nihilo* and then circulates as electronic bank account money until the loan is repaid. In the language of the French/Italian *circuitists*, this represents the creation and destruction of money. Money, therefore, really needs to be viewed as a flow across time as well as a static stock, depending on the specific purpose required for the data.

The balance sheets of the commercial banks at any point will consist of various assets and liabilities that are subject to any legal monitoring and audit that the modern state devises. The bank ratios of reserves, liquid assets, to their loan portfolios will necessarily change, as new lending takes place and deposits are drawn upon. A typical commercial bank balance sheet is represented in Table 7.1.

There is some PK debate, discussed in 4.2, between the structuralist and horizontalist view of endogenous money-issue, in response to demand at the short-term interest rate determined by the government or the independent central bank. In the horizontalist conception, the private banks expand credit completely in response to demand at a horizontal supply, whereas in the structuralist notion it is suggested that the banks require higher interest rates (compensation) at larger volumes of credit expansion (Wray 2004). It is assumed in both of these viewpoints that the government, or its delegated agency, sets the interest rate with regard to prevailing priorities. Yet, as Wray notes, even an exogenous interest rate has a measure of endogenous determination since, the policy-makers are responding to certain factors derived from the market (Wray 2004). In addition, the state has no responsibility for LIBOR (the federal funds rate in the US) in the UK system. The short-term

Table 7.1 Commercial Bank Balance Sheet

Assets	*Liabilities*
Notes and Coins	Capital Funds
Deposits at the National Bank	Shareholders Funds
Money Market Loans	Customer Retail Deposits
Investments	
Public Sector and Loans to Public	

(often overnight) interbank lending rates are instead determined by key decision-makers from a consortium of big banks, despite some state-influence, and private banks set their own rates for lending, albeit in an arguably competitive financial market (Ackrill 2001). So, according to the informed consensus, money is issued as debt, so-called credit-money, in response to consumer demand at a given short-term interest rate, regardless of who determines the actual level of the rate.

7.6 FINANCIAL INTERMEDIATION

Banks licensed to operate in capitalist nations thus provide all of the credit-monies in circulation.[2] In accordance with the EMT as stated, this credit creation is determined by demand and banking *supply* capabilities at the given interest rate(s). The processes of intermediation, matching any surplus agents with deficit ones is an important role that financial institutions perform in any advanced monetary system. They serve, as Buckle notes, to provide maturity transformation that is, lending long and borrowing short, risk transformation, and size transformation between counter-parties who deposit and borrow funds (Buckle 2004). Intermediaries reduce the costs and risks of lending by the provision of accumulated information and related procedures. The information costs, for example, could include credit—worthiness search, identity verification, monitoring and default enforcement costs and the risks include adverse selection that is, finding reliable borrowers (Buckle 2004).

Yet, despite the fact that banks and state are able to determine the allocation and level of credit, the *value* of *money*, in terms of purchasing power and exchange rates, is likely to be determined by a different set of state/market power relations. Prices, for instance, rise when market actors *choose* to raise them under normal competitive conditions. These choices, in turn, may be driven by random factors in conjunction with the normally cited forces of demand-pull, cost-push and overall money supply. However, while the approach of the book, identified in chapter 4, assumes that prices *generally* determine the money supply and circulation velocity, this is also deemed to be a reflexive relationship between variables. So, in other words, an exogenous increase in money supply *could* have an inflationary impact. In addition, floating exchange rates are driven by market forces and high volume trading, so these are, in turn, not always *fully* explained by changing market fundamentals such as the purchasing power parity between currencies. Currency markets are more often now driven by leveraged speculation, spread betting, derivative positions and political factors rather than the fundamentals. When assessing the state capability to influence money-*value* and the levels and allocation of credit-money, these monetary processes are all considered.

Financial intermediaries are also in close relations with the national banks. The national banks operate among the commercial bank network and, provide their daily need for reserves as required. However, this reserve requirement is usually satisfied through interbank lending these days. Table 7.2 represents a typical balance sheet of a national bank.

According to a widely sold and distributed textbook, the government, via the central bank, can determine or influence the money supply through three methods (Pilbeam 2005). First, by the buying and selling of treasury securities, known as open market operations, which then has a bearing on the LIBOR rate and, in turn, general lending volume. Yet, as Howells outlines, the overall determination of the money supply is *not* what the bank hopes to achieve when they engage in this activity in practice (Howells 2008: 260). They are simply aiming to target the interest rate. Secondly, by changing the reserve asset ratio the state can restrict or loosen any credit expansion, through the credit multiplier. However, since the reserve asset ratio no longer exists in the UK, multiplier explanations are fallacious. Thirdly, given the functioning of the central bank base rate, and its impact on general lending through its influence on market interest rates (Pilbeam 2005). Yet, private rates are only loosely based on the national bank for example, BOE monetary policy committee rates. Several studies have revealed, as Bain and Howells note, that these interest rate disparities can sometimes be substantial (Bain 2003). Nevertheless, there have been serious attempts from the state to monitor and determine the nominal amount of monetary growth at times but this has led to substantial difficulties in practice. In the UK in the 1970s, for example, the *corset* that is, special compulsory noninterest bearing deposits at the BOE to restrict credit expansion, cash ratios, strict reserve asset ratios and direct credit controls were all used by successive governments until finally abandoned in 1980. Most of these methods relied on monetary base (MB) control that is, the use of the level of liquid assets that banks have in relation to their overall lending—and this proved to be problematic (Howells 2008). Some of these difficulties are outlined here. First, when the state used to target the MB it often meant to target fluctuations in short-term interest rates, which led to undesirable macroeconomic instabilities. Secondly, since the MB is a liability of the central bank it can cause difficulties for the bank officials, because they do not always know what volumes they will need in

Table 7.2 National Bank Balance Sheet

Assets	*Liabilities*
Loans to Commercial Banks	Commercial Bank Reserve Accounts
Loans to Government	Government Deposits
Reserves of Foreign Exchange	Notes and Coins in Circulation
Government Debt Holdings	

their available "lender of last resort" capacity to the private banks. They tend to prefer more certainty in their *own* balance sheets in practice. Thirdly, even if the central bank knew exactly how to respond to reserve needs for example, through a precise value of bond-issue, they are not in practice able to respond *at will* to the relevant MB needs. It was this type of time lag, *inter alia,* that led the Thatcher administration to abandon monetary targets in the early 1980s. Fourthly, in some financial systems, there would need to be structural changes to the private banking system. In the UK, for instance, the clearing banks have overdraft facilities with one another, making it more difficult for the central bank to implement MB control by measuring private bank reserves. Fifthly, most of the assets of a typical bank consist of their nonmarketable loan portfolio.[3] It is not always possible for commercial banks to respond to reserve asset ratios, for example, since they cannot simply just sell parts of their nonliquid outstanding loan contracts, and the national banks needs to maintain systemic stability. Sixthly, private bank reserves at the national bank used to pay no interest, which amounted to a *de facto* tax on banks and this led to an increase in their spread between deposit and lending rates and, perhaps, a more detrimental impact on the general economy.[4] Finally, the "lender of the last resort" facility might be compromised when even solvent banks require reserves during times of tight MB control. The question could be asked, would the central bank still be able to offer convertibility in these circumstances? If they were not able, the stability of the entire system is undermined. As a consequence of this uncertainty, MB control in the UK was abandoned. Yet, as Wray identified the modern central bank still seeks to influence the short-term interest rate by adjusting overall liquidity and, in turn, affecting the *de facto* interbank rates. It is these historical motivations and processes that are later reviewed in the case studies to ascertain whether or not the state has experienced a diminished capacity to affect the overall volume and purchasing power of credit monies.

7.7 THE INTERNATIONAL FINANCIAL SYSTEM

In the absence of global government, historic monetary cooperation has relied upon interstate negotiation and trust. During the historical periods that gold and silver or convertible paper were accepted as international money, global trade could be expanded beyond that of barter since the commodity money transcended the financial boundaries of the nation-state. The gold standard of the nineteenth century, for example, had also benefited from the size and reach of the *Pax Britannica,* since confidence in the pound was instilled as a consequence of British international activity. In the era since WW2, exchange regimes such as the BW system, or the European Exchange

Rate Mechanism (ERM), have involved substantial collaboration and had significant implications for the monetary sovereignty of nation-states. During the BW fixed exchange rate system, for example, backed by central bank dollar to gold convertibility at $35 per ounce, capital controls were used to engender closer balance of payments equilibrium by virtually eliminating private speculation and member countries were expected to adjust their macroeconomic conditions to ensure trade balance. Monetary policy, open market currency operations and IMF occasional lending were needed to guide the member states toward this purpose. Yet, it was the reluctance of surplus countries to inflate for example, Japan and Germany, despite agreeing to restrict converting their surpluses to gold, which was one of the principal causes of the breakdown of the system in the seventies (Helleiner 2008: 222). When this was combined with the devaluation of the dollar, and oil price shocks, the BW system collapsed. During its operation, nation-states had needed to ensure that monetary policy adhered to the necessary conditions for balanced trade. The early period of the ERM, from 1979 to 1986, had also involved capital controls, and member states were restricted in their monetary sovereignty in the same manner. This erosion of financial capability was further accentuated when exchange controls were removed in 1986, as part of the Single European Act in Europe, and states needed to maintain market risk premiums. This meant keeping interest rates above the *strong* Deutschmark in practice, in order to prevent speculative attack and a breakdown of the system. In a nineties paper, Potts convincingly argued that, as a consequence, there would be more monetary sovereignty for the UK or any other EU member state in the Euro than could exist while remaining in the ERM (Potts 1997). Increased currency speculation, especially when leveraged, has served to recently erode the monetary sovereignty of nation-states, because individual state treasuries simply do not have enough funds to conduct effective open-market operations in comparison with colossal privately owned volumes a point highlighted by Griffith-Jones in her research on capital flows (Griffith-Jones 1998). Some critics have subsequently called for a "Tobin" tax to deter speculation and mitigate these harmful effects, restoring some sovereignty (Tobin 1978). Other forms of monetary regulation, however, which are a direct result of international cooperation, are likely to have an effect on monetary sovereignty. The BIS Basel accords, for example, have now led to the *de facto* reduction of state regulatory power since national reserve requirements have virtually disappeared. This contributed toward the 2008 financial crisis as a result of the greater self-regulation of security risk assessment. In response, Basel III has taken steps to remedy this. As several have noted, more in-house risk assessment creates conflicts of interest between financial agents (Pettifor 2006; Rochon 2007). These interstate or state regulatory matters will be explored further in the empirical chapters, since they directly impact the existence and operation of financial power.

It is interesting that, post-WW2, the use of the US dollar as main reserve currency has meant that other nation-state financial authorities have been, to a greater or lesser extent, affected by the vagaries of US domestic monetary policy. The US dollar is used as the denomination for multinational accounting, statistical measures, global commodity exchanges, multilateral institutions, capital markets, sovereign lending, commercial credit and as a vehicle currency for virtually all foreign exchange transactions. Fluctuations in the dollar exchange rate, and general reserve currency demand and supply conditions, therefore have a substantial impact on the global economy. Nation-states have found, in addition, that there are implications for their monetary sovereignty. Benjamin Cohen has identified that, as a consequence, there is interstate competition in order to harness the benefits that accrue to a nation-state when their currency is in more general use for example, cheaper borrowing and the US has certainly gained in this respect in the modern era (Cohen 1998). In a world of hard and soft currencies, and increasingly fewer currencies, the evolution of global monies is a constant activity with ramifications for sovereignty as financial power is eroded or indeed enhanced.

7.8 CONCLUSION

In this chapter, the general concepts of financial power and its exercise have been explored. This was then followed by a discussion of the manner in which the state has been viewed, in political theory, and outlined the monetary function of the state according to the conventional banking literature. Finally, the role of the state in the contemporary international-state system was discussed. The Gramsci-influenced Marxist theory of the state is considered valid, which is defined as a state that reflects the priority interests of capital and the expansion and accumulation of value.[5] An accurate perspective on the nature and function of the state, of course, is imperative for the appropriate design of policy for any future regulation of finance. In the precapitalist feudal era in the UK, and probably in all prior contexts, the authorities had more control over the money-issue and its purchasing power in comparison to today. The UK tally-stick money system, for example, was a successful monetary administration by the sovereign for several centuries and, afforded *seigniorage* that financed various state activities (Zarlenga 2002; Brown 2007). Also, in the early capitalist mercantilist era the monetary aim of the state had been to accumulate specie, for the purpose of the wielding of social power, and several states were able to exercise this power accordingly (De Brunhoff 1976). In the latter stage of capitalism, with the evolution of the credit system, however, the circumstances have changed and there has been, it is posited, a gradual decline in state financial capabilities. In this sense capitalism has shifted financial power away from the state. Yet, it is clearly not appropriate to view money-creation or money-function as determined entirely in response to market demand, in an endogenous sense, with minimal or nonexistent state involvement. Instead, the state and market still *both* have clear roles in the issue of money and its general functioning. In the next chapter, an amusing allegory of a steam train is presented to illustrate this complexity of money creation and operation, determined jointly by state and market, in relation to the real economy of production. The analogy helps to clarify the conception of money-issue and function that I have adopted here, that is, Marx and the EMT, which follows on from the review of historical monetary thought conducted in earlier chapters.

NOTES

1. In the modern era, the use of open market foreign currency transactions to influence the level of the exchange rate is ineffectual given the large volumes of private trading that take place.
2. There are also sterling credit monies that derive from offshore financial markets, such as the *europound,* in this statement but are not included in analysis. Alternative and complementary currencies are also not included. In addition, it is worth noting that state criteria for the licensing of banks did not appear until 1979.
3. The securitization revolution, with collateralized debt obligations, has (perhaps) further complicated this arena of government policy.
4. These days the Bank of England pays base rate interest to commercial banks with deposits.
5. This does not preclude, as Miliband noted, the possibility of certain state measures being pursued that were contrary to the key interests of capital from time to time (Miliband 1969).

Chapter 8

The Golden Age of Steam

8.1 INTRODUCTION

The purpose of this chapter is to illustrate the basic operation of the capitalist credit-money system, and its interaction with the real economy, by using a light-hearted analogy of a steam train. In addition, the analogy will illustrate how the EMT can be incorporated with Marx's understanding of production (and circulation) across periods. Any readers who are already comfortable with the combination of the two theories, or have less time, can skip the chapter. The chapter first outlines what the different parts of the analogy represent, and then describes the function of the credit system in response to money-demand. Next, there is a description of how financial crises can be illustrated by the steam train analogy. The chapter then considers how the mainstream, PK, Austrian and financialization approaches to the economy can be illustrated using the train. Finally, I use the analogy to illustrate one of the central themes of the book, that endogenous money can be incorporated with Marx's sequential production periods and law of value.

8.2 THE STEAM TRAIN ANALOGY

Figure 8.1 The EMT Steam Train.

In the illustration, our fictitious steam train travels from one station to the next and each separate journey (between stops) represents a single production/circulation period in the real economy. To simplify, the production of all output takes place while the train is at the station, and then its *movement* between stations represents the sales of all commodities (with no unsold stock). The steam locomotive itself (Figure 8.1) represents the commercial banks that provide the real economy with the quantity of credit-money units (cash is ignored for simplicity) that are required for transaction purposes.[1] The physical quantity of money used in each circulation period, the means of circulation, is represented by the *circumference* of the train's drive wheel (see Figure 8.2). Since the drive wheel actually *engages* with the track, this means that the track *length* represents the nominal value of total transactions. Marx used the phrase "means of circulation" to refer to the physical quantity of monies actually used for the circulation of commodities after production (Marx [1867] 1976: 213). In the train analogy, I employ a similar type of measure but rather than simply having enough monies to cover the commodity sales there is also enough monies to cover all other transactions. In the real economy, for example, purchases of goods from any secondary markets, or the transactions in financial securities, also need to be taken into consideration. To simplify, however, in the illustration it is imagined that total transactions consist of two categories, first those associated with real economic output, and secondly those associated with financial sector activity. Another consideration for the model, as Marx identified, is the velocity of circulation (Marx [1867] 1976: 216). In the illustration, if the train were to travel at a faster speed, then a greater nominal value of transactions can be covered with the same quantity of monies. This represents a faster velocity of (money) circulation.

As stated above, the track length represents transaction activity, but the actual *distance* to travel between stations (see Figure 8.3) as the crow flies,

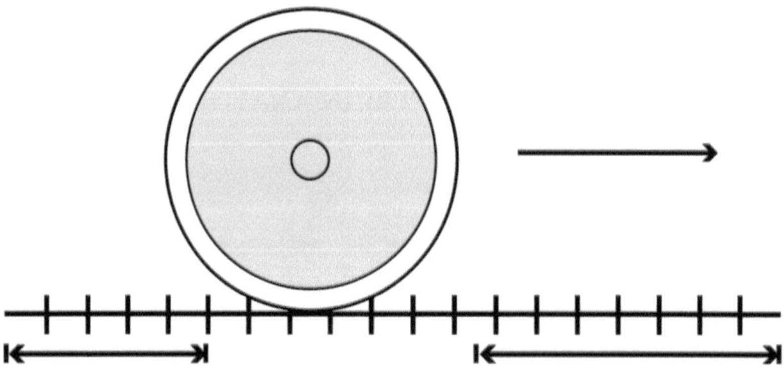

Figure 8.2 The Drive Wheel.

Figure 8.3 The Track Meandering or Rising.

represents the nominal transactions for the purchase of all *produced output.* This is measured in money but, following Marx, also represents value in abstract labor hours of output. If there are no transactions associated with fictitious capital, or any inflation from the last period, the track will be perfectly straight (see CD in Figure 8.3). Yet, importantly, if there are any fictitious capital transactions, these will cause the track to meander from side to side, thus lengthening the track and therefore the distance to travel, but not the measure of the distance between stops as the crow flies. Inflation will also cause the track to lengthen (represented by undulations in track height). In both instances there is greater nominal transaction volume but produced output in labor hours/money between stations remains the same (see AB in Figure 8.3).

8.3 THE CREDIT MONEY SYSTEM

In real steam travel there are different component parts of a locomotive that is, the coalbunker, water tank, firebox, boiler, boiler pipes, cylinder, piston, piston rods, etc. These (collectively) represent in the analogy the *resources* required by the money system in order to supply credit. They are analogous to the banks, bank assets, financial procedures, IT infrastructure, payment systems, clearing houses, interbank market, discount houses and national bank open-market operations, etc. Historically, as steam technology improved fuel efficiency improved. This was achieved through the introduction of newer technologies that included more aerodynamic locomotive designs, better valves and pipes, *compounding*—using multicylinder locomotives (using both high and low pressure cylinders to utilize spent steam before exhaustion from the blast pipe) and *superheating*—the practice of applying additional heat to saturated steam, since the latter creates water droplets when in contact with pipes and valves. Superheating involves gas formation that eliminates power loss through condensation. With a fixed level of technology, a locomotive can achieve higher speeds with extra strain on the system resources. Yet, with these stated improvements, greater speed is possible with the same level of resources, or similarly the same speed is achieved with use of lesser resources.

Similarly, banking system innovation has also led to a more efficient use of its resources. In the case of both steam locomotives and the credit system, the aggregate resources (and their ongoing development) represent the general *costs* of production. In the illustration, the train driver represents *decision-makers in the monetary system.* These are the agents that actually strategize, implement and organize commercial bank operations in order to respond to the demand for (planned) transactions. In my (admittedly unrealistic) analogy, the train driver is able to change the *size* (diameter and, hence, circumference) of the wheel before embarking on a new journey at each station stop. Clearly, with a larger wheel the train is able to cover a greater distance of track in a given time (at a given speed) during the next journey, thus economizing on resources required by the monetary system to supply credit.

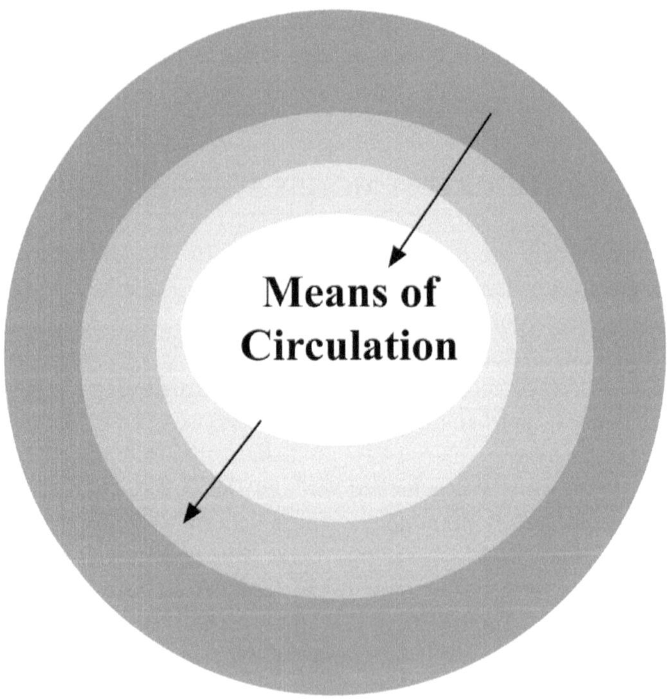

Figure 8.4 Means of Circulation.

Historically, steam engineers initially attempted to make larger wheels, but soon discovered that this compromised the stability of the locomotive since the boiler was situated too high. In the train illustration, whereas the drive wheel represents the means of circulation employed, there are also limits to the size of wheel that can be fitted. The drive wheel can be enlarged by one of two actions, dishoarding or fresh credit creation. The utilization of inactive balances, dishoarding, increases the means of circulation (money taken from time deposits for instance) although this is limited by the overall quantity of the broad money supply. Whenever commodity money has been in general circulation, this would have been a more important factor. Yet, I decided to ignore dishoarding in the illustration since credit-money almost exclusively now takes the form of bank deposits, and banks practice fractional reserve banking (discussed in chapter 4). This renders dishoarding as virtually irrelevant to the physical quantity of the means of circulation, since credit-money is created *ex nihilo* in response to demand by the banks. This is determined by factors such as interest rates, demand conditions, national bank open-market operations, bank balance sheets, risk factors, expectations and general credit policy. The primary concern for banks, of course, is their criteria for debt sustainability that is, the agent capability to meet principal and interest payments, which is limited by expected future income and credit-worthiness of

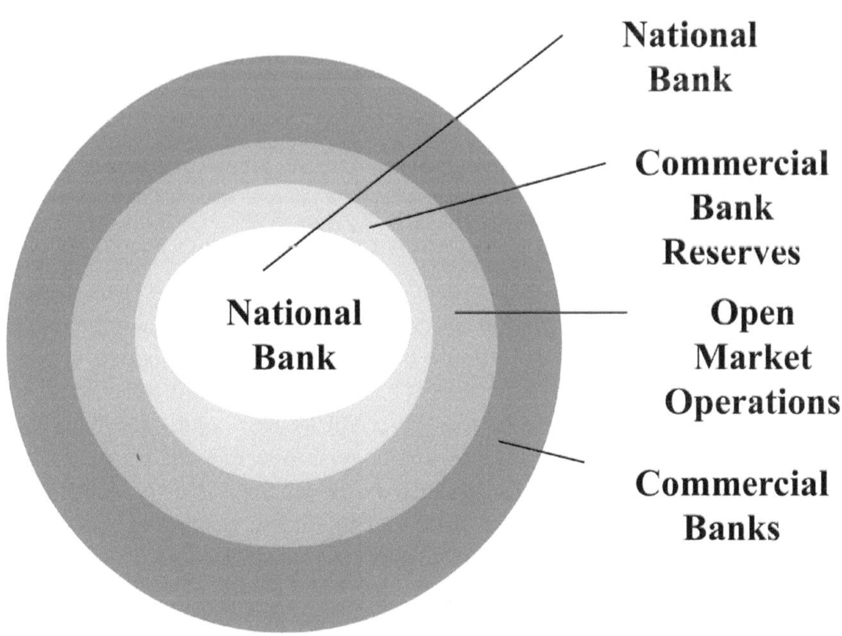

Figure 8.5 National Bank Open Market Operations.

the economic agents concerned. So, in the train illustration, the production of output takes place at the station and a certain quantity of means of circulation is then required for the next train journey. These monies are held in the form of bank deposits, and agents that require further credit then seek to obtain it. Given the assumptions of EMT (e.g., an accommodating national bank) it is then assumed in the illustration that the credit system dutifully supplies it at the given interest rate.

If we consider that C = newly created credit-money, V = the velocity of circulation, R = the reflux (i.e., debt settlement) and Q = the quantity of transaction demand for the real economy output in the period, F = financial securities demand for the period, and Z = total volume of money transactions if both categories are combined that is, Z = Q + F and M = the quantity of means of circulation. Means of circulation (ignoring dishoarding) for the period are therefore:

$$M_t = M_{t-1} - R_{t-1} + C_t$$

If the velocity of circulation in each circulation period is considered, then M can also be expressed as:

$$M_t = Z_t$$

The amount of credit-money that needs to be created is represented by:

$$C_t = Z_t - Z_{t-1} + R_t$$

The changing means of circulation across periods can be represented as:

$$M_t - M_{t-1} = Z_t - Z_{t-1}$$

It is worth noting that, as Marx identified, credit creation serves to economize on the means of circulation used and the commercial banking system is then rewarded by receiving a share of surplus value even though it does not create any value itself (Marx [1894] 1981, chap. 33). In order to meet the cash requirements of the period the credit system could, alternatively, increase the velocity of circulation of money. In the days of steam travel, the locomotive driver could use the piston stroke inlet valve (or cut-off) to increase (or decrease) the extent of the steam pressure entering the cylinder. A late cut-off is required from a stationary position, for instance, due to the additional torque needed to move the train's mass. This leads to the characteristic "chuff, chuff" sound of locomotives and, also uses more fuel. At faster speeds, the driver can allow for a reduced cut-off and save fuel.

The implication, therefore, is that in order to achieve a faster *speed*, a late cut-off and more fuel is required.

The demand for money (track length) in the economy (including fictitious capital transactions and inflation) triggers a response from banks. This means, importantly, that prices are driving money-demand (in line with Marx, as stated in chapter 6) rather than the opposite, as posited by the mainstream monetary theorists. The driver is then able to organize the suitable quantity of monies (in addition to any existing monies) by either increasing the velocity of circulation or through credit creation (or some combination of the two).[2] The Marx credit-locomotive is then expected to be able to complete the coming journey, which indicates that the circulation of commodities (and financial market transactions) is completed after price formation. A faster speed, and/or a larger drive wheel, can enable a steam locomotive to travel a greater distance in a given set journey time, although this places extra strain on banking system resources, and anyway it is more profitable to advance further credit.

In the train illustration, as stated above, it is *generally* assumed that expenditures *and* the necessary banking resources are sufficiently provided each period. Yet, interest rate changes (or other banking system supply conditions) during circulation will change the (expected) nominal volume of money available, leading to a possible shortfall of money-demand. The liquidity crisis will manifest in goods failing to sell in sufficient quantities and/or (in serious cases) defaults or the bursting of an asset bubble (falling prices next period). If such a serious credit crisis occurs, the train malfunctions. In the diagram (Figure 8.6) below, the steam train first heads toward a tunnel, say after speculative securities trading driven by low profitability mentioned in 5.9. In the tunnel, the crisis leads to a banking malfunction denoted by a stalled train. A new locomotive (or substantial repairs) are needed before the current journey and the next can be completed. In the next period, for instance, the banks may be unwilling to lend. In the days of real steam

Figure 8.6 Train Enters Tunnel.

travel, the danger of a *backdraft* (where engine gases could reverse direction, exploding the boiler) was at its highest level in a tunnel. If this occurred the steam train would inevitably break down, often killing the crew.

If there are extra credit requirements from any increased demand for money, this suggests that banking *costs* (e.g., computing infrastructure) will rise perhaps leading to higher interest rates in the next period, giving an upward sloping supply curve (across periods) for credit, in the manner suggested by the *structuralists*.[3] However, as stated above (following Moore), the illustration has assumed (except in crisis) that the supply of credit is horizontal, simply responding to credit demand at a given interest rate (Itoh 1999: 236).[4] It is also posited in the analogy that while finance creates no value (in line with Marx), the production costs of the actual means of circulation (credit-money) itself consume resources and thus *expresses* a certain quantity of abstract labor and, therefore, human effort. So, as stated above, the credit system operations during the train journey thus facilitate the necessary monies for the sales of the commodities produced, prior to and during the journey. These sales, in turn, become the next period's inputs and, as a consequence, create the preconditions for the next journey distance. Finally, in this new period, the distance traveled (as the crow flies) will not change even if there are fresh productivity increases. This is because, as outlined in chapter 6, productivity increases do *not* increase the value of the output they simply cheapen the per-unit value in terms of labor hours. When the train is finally ready to leave the station, the electronic train timetable can be adjusted in preparation for the pending passengers. Yet, it is posited that during the journey the *actual* distance traveled (track length) is determined by the nominal money-volumes of commodities traded (including any inflation from last period's circulation) in conjunction with any fictitious capital transactions.

In the theoretical scenarios considered next, a more *general* steam train analogy, rather than a Marx model presented here, is used to illustrate and contrast mainstream monetary views with the PK, Austrian, (Marxian) and financialization and TSSI of Marx schools of thought. In the TSSI section, there is a further discussion of the above stated mechanics.

8.4 THE MAINSTREAM VIEW

In the mainstream conception, money is neutral and, therefore, passively responds to any transaction need.[5] An entrepreneurial decision to invest, for instance, could lead to an expansion of credit that is motivated by expectations of demand, in conjunction with historic profit data, that is independent (at least directly) of financial system considerations other than the interest rate. This approach is consistent with many of the mainstream economists that tend to model money as neutral, in a *Ricardian* sense, and then (if needed) focus on business cycle theory to explain any fluctuations in monetary conditions. Rational expectations theory, for instance, maintains that there can be no endogenous business cycle at all, in the absence of shocks, since economic agents will be able to exploit arbitrage opportunities through their accurate prediction of future events.[6] It is generally recognized however, (e.g., the Friedman account of the Great Depression) that the money system may *not* provide enough liquidity unexpectedly, and this can be denoted (as in Figure 8.6) by the steam train malfunction (Friedman 1993). Yet, this is, in turn, attributed to random exogenous factors. It is, therefore, the productive agents, market conditions and resource allocation that together determine the transaction output demand for the next period. Furthermore, since supply is assumed to create its own (income) demand, all is presumed harmonious in usual circumstances regardless of credit. Our mainstream train, therefore, simply travels from station to station providing that there is no train malfunction. The mainstream Keynesian synthesis (discussed in 4.2) also still assumes a harmonious economic system across periods (train journeys), providing that the IS/LM equilibrium interest rate (equating production with financial sectors) has been established, which is itself derived from simultaneous method.

8.5 THE POST-KEYNESIAN VIEW

The PK's using Keynes's notion of aggregate demand (C + I + G + [X – M]), and assuming that G + C are stable and ignoring trade for simplicity, would posit that investment is key to the volume of sales in the circulation period. Interest rates, derived by liquidity preference, have sequentially determined this *investment* demand according to marginal efficiency at the level of expectation.[7] Aggregate demand for the period, with multiplier impact assumed complete then determines the output's transaction needs.[8] The variables that constitute Z are thus established, at the given *market* rate(s) of interest, and assuming that other monetary factors impacting demand for example, firms economizing on money with barter, remain fixed during the period. In addition, the exogenous interest rate is driven by the state but is influenced by the market in varying proportions.[9] The transactions may not, however, be settled in full if there are changed credit *supply* conditions, such as collateral requirements or sudden interest rate changes *during* the circulation. This allows for the illustration to demonstrate a disruption to transaction activity during the period as a direct result of the credit system. The bursting of an asset bubble, for example, could be illustrated by the malfunction of the steam train.

The journey(s) between stations, and the output sales that is represented by this does not have to correspond to the full employment level. Yet, it is assumed that targeted state policy can remedy this across periods. If, during a single train journey, there are unrealistic (optimistic) expectations this raises the likelihood of future debt defaults, asset bubbles and reduced returns. During the next journey, in turn, expenditures may not be met as the credit system fails to respond and the train malfunctions at the so-called Minsky moment and limps on (see Figure 8.6) to the next station. The next period, with credit squeeze and higher interest rates, has reduced transaction demand. In the PK conception, as Tily notes, it is ideal if investors have an understanding of the "correct" MEC schedule that will deliver the *realistic* return on capital employed (Tily 2007: 235). Appropriate (national) debt-management strategies are recommended, in order to stabilize low interest rates (and expectations) between the short and long term. The economy can then achieve a steady state and, the PK train happily travels between stations ad infinitum.

In terms of the business cycle *per se*, as Tily notes, Keynes came from the school of thought that identified the credit cycle and its monetary drivers, based on respect for the work of Hawtrey and Fisher (Fisher 1993; Hawtrey 1919, Tily 2007: 233). *Excessive* credit expansion in booms is responsible for creating *unsustainable* economic activity and asset bubbles, as the expectancy of reduced returns and default (raising interest rates) looms (the Minsky moment) so credit tightens, instigating a deflation and output decline or worse crisis. In this scenario, as Tily notes, *cheap* money has *facilitated* the business cycle, but *dear* money *caused* it (Tily 2007: 233). Tily further argues that this explains why, in order to stabilize the cycle, Keynes had a specific view of the *correct* (underlying and, therefore, long-term) marginal efficiency schedule, against which short-term aggregate demand (whim-driven) could be appropriately evaluated (Tily 2007: 234). Tily writes:

> The real dimension concerns the trajectory of investment during the economic cycle, and the associated forces dictating that trajectory. In the short period, investment demand may be dominated by animal spirits. But there are underlying forces related to the potential yield of an investment at each rate of interest that define whether any investment demand will be sustainable in a timeframe that looks beyond the short period. The discussion shows that to boost short period demand without taking into account these considerations can lead to instability.
>
> (Tily 2007: 234)

The new credit simply meets the demands of short-term aggregate demand. Yet, according to Keynes, when the marginal efficiency of capital fluctuates in conjunction with other variables, the trade cycle is determined as this passage (p. 235) indicates (Tily 2007):

> I suggest that more typical, and often the predominant, explanation of the crisis is, not primarily a rise in the rate of interest, but a sudden collapse in the marginal efficiency of capital (*CW VII, p. 315*)

Keynes is thus indicating that the short-term expectations determining the MEC were not always synchronized with the underlying *correct* expectation, leading to an *excessive* expansion of credit. This is a really important insight since it suggests that Keynes is actually citing *productive* sector factors as *drivers*, which in turn lead to the *financial* factors that are normally identified by debt deflation theory. In this respect the PK and Marx approaches are similar.[10] It is also *this* analysis that led Keynes to his policy position of a comprehensive state debt-management strategy for short- and long-term securities, in order to stabilize the short- and long-run interest rates and expectations of future rates, in order for the authorities to *steer* the economy toward the (cheap money) *correct* marginal efficiency reference position.[11] Keynes, therefore, has provided a plausible explanation of underlying production factors that were impacting economic trends, in the form of expectations, despite these being somewhat subjective, subject to time lags and shy of measurement. It is also interesting to note that Tily argues that there is also no guarantee that cheap money policies would not experience big shifts in the MEC schedule, thus leading to debt deflation and crises. He contends, however, that excessive expectations are less likely in an economy operating at capacity that is also without unpredictable interest rate policies instigated by the state authorities (Tily 2007: 245).

There is no doubt, however, that this PK analysis gives us valuable insight into the working of a capitalist integrated monetary economy, and proffers policy prescriptions in a political environment that is intent on maintaining the capitalist production mode. Yet, this is predicated on the assumption that capitalism can work, indeed that it is possible (in the words of Tily) to reach *a state of tranquillity* with high and sustainable output (Tily 2007: 244). Marx, on the other hand, is cynical in his remarks about those who simply advocate cheap or completely interest-free credit, as the passage below suggests, since the inherent exploitative contradictions, private property in this case, of the capitalist economic system will still remain unscathed. Marx writes:

> The notion of *credit gratuit,* incidentally, is only a hypocritical, philistine and anxiety-ridden form of the saying: property is theft. Instead of the workers *taking* the capitalists' capital, the capitalists are supposed to be compelled to *give* it to them.
>
> (Marx [1858] 1973: 123)

Government cheap (or free) money policies, as Marx suggests, are likely to be resisted by the capitalist class. Yet, even if is impossible to prevent the endogenous regularity of capitalist crisis, it could be argued that PK policies have *real* value in modern economies that have no critical mass in favor of systemic change and, these can lead to favorable outcomes in these circumstances. The heterodox Austrian school, in contrast, is also concerned with interest rates in the banking system and their impact on the business and credit cycle, yet with a different perspective from the PK's.

8.6 THE AUSTRIAN SCHOOL

In the Austrian view the credit cycle, and business cycle, is seen as endogenous. Yet, if the state intervenes with a *cheap* money policy, they posit that credit expansion will be excessive, leading to inflation, leveraged speculation and asset bubbles. The planned expansion of financial activity then leads to a *meandering* track for the next train journey, with greater nominal transaction volume but still the same level of output. This later journey, in turn, sets the preconditions (in the illustration) for a downturn in output and other transactions for the next trip. Austrian economists argue that an appropriate *market* rate of interest will prevent this across periods and that a steady-state economy can ensue. Their other policy proposal involves the elimination of fractional reserve banking (FRB), and monetary diversity to replace monetary monopoly. In terms of the latter idea, a single (credit-money) currency monopoly creates a monetary dependence that often becomes the focus of the problem in a financial crisis (Mouatt 2010). This idea draws on the work of Hayek *et al.* who had posited the dangers of centralized planning in general, suggesting that inefficiency and information deficiency hindered effective decision-making. Hayek extended this idea to the fragile functioning of a single currency (credit-money) system and, consequently, recommended *free banking*, which encourages currency diversity from the market instead. He argued that the greater competition would lead to the more appropriate and trusted currencies becoming established and sustained. Austrian monetary thinking tends to prefer commodity money and backed currency, at a community or business level use (Hayek 1990).[12] In the following passage, when referring to the greater use of bank deposits as money, and the society dependence on credit in single currency-units from banks that need to ensure their adequacy of reserves, he pointed out that this would lead to liquidity fluctuations and a disturbed business cycle revealing its fragility:

> The consequent dilution of what was still believed to be a government monopoly of the issue of all money resulted in the control of the total circulation of money being divided between a central bank and a large number of

> commercial banks whose creation of credit it could influence only indirectly. Not till much later did it come to be understood that the 'instability of credit' [R.G.Hawtrey] under that system was a necessary outcome of this feature; that liquid means was mostly supplied by institutions which themselves had to keep liquid in terms of another form of money, so that they had to *reduce* their outstanding obligations precisely when everyone else desired to be *more* liquid. By the time this kind of structure had become so firmly established that, in spite of the 'perverse elasticity of the supply of credit' [L.Currie] it produced, it came to be regarded as unalterable. Walter Bagehot had clearly seen this dilemma a hundred years ago but despaired of the possibility of remedying this defect of the firmly established banking structure. And Wicksell and later von Mises made it clear that this arrangement must lead to violent recurring fluctuations of business activity—the so-called 'trade-cycle' . . . not the least advantage of the proposed abolition of the government monopoly of the issue of money is that it would provide an opportunity to extricate ourselves from the *impasse*.
>
> (Hayek 1990)

If monetary diversity were pursued this would undermine the financial role of the state, which has centralized control of the currency in conjunction with the commercial banks. However, particularly in the incidence of acute liquidity crises, as Lietaer has noted in his analogy of sustainable ecosystems, effective currency competition should lead to a monetary *resilience* in the face of instability (Mouatt 2010). Yet, ironically, the FRB proposals of the Austrian school for 100% reserve banking, which is shared by parts of the monetary reform movement, will certainly strengthen the state's financial role while having a mixed impact on efficiency in the real economy. This is due, in part, to the state-maintained *fiat* nature of *money* that would be required, in contrast to the normal demand-responsive availability of credit-money in the current era. If there was an entirely debt-free fiat money supply, for instance, that remains in circulation, this may lead to *planning* in credit allocation with its associated *political* implications and bureaucratic costs. Yet, this practice would be the exact opposite of the recommendations that derive from Austrian school ideology. There could also be an increase of moral hazard for the state, thus encouraging profligate public spending, and the inefficient use of resources. In addition, there may be circulation blockages as economic agents hoard monies, or form inward thinking plutocratic money-elites wielding social power derived from their cartelization of the monetary entity. This is, arguably, less likely to occur in the current credit-money system that has evolved for the capitalist nation-states over several centuries. Notwithstanding, the Austrian school of thought argues that their proposals would be a less exploitative alternative and would also facilitate a stable monetary system for the real economy.

In the steam locomotive illustration, it is likely that financial sector *speculative* activity will be reduced, leading to a straighter train track, if Austrian proposals were adopted. Yet, the level of production output may be less, since (arguably) a 100% fractional reserve implies that credit will be more difficult to obtain and be subject to certain circulation inefficiencies. In the case of monetary diversity, if an alternative currency from the market is formed then this could be represented in the illustration by a *separate* new train and parallel track. In contrast, a different locomotive that is able to travel on the same track could represent any complementary currency created by the market.

8.7 THE FINANCIALIZATION SCHOOL

In the Marxian *financialization* view, the productive sector and/or the financial sector have an endogenous propensity to crisis, albeit with no *direct* reference to the (objective) falling rate of profit. The train can malfunction, therefore, as a result of monetary factors during the journey. It was also posited by Toporowski, that capital *accumulation* can be "depressed" by financial sector activity (Toporowski 2010). This view implies that capital migrates to higher returns and/or marginal productive investments are, therefore, abandoned given certain conditions in the financial sector. This would manifest, in the illustration, in the form of a decreased ground distance (real output) with an increased track meander. Yet, noted in 5.9, the rate of accumulation has consistently tracked the profit rate in the US, and is therefore likely to be the same in the UK (Kliman 2010).[13] This suggests that Marx's *law of value* is a *more* significant driver of events than financial factors. It is recognized, however, as Lapavitsas notes, that the securitization revolution has created more opportunities for the plutocratic classes to extract a surplus from society and needs to be noted (Lapavitsas 2009). In addition, monetary factors in credit markets can, as Marx commented, disrupt production "in the most dangerous manner" and all manner of crises can occur (Marx [1894] 1981: 678). Yet, Marx was dismissive of those thinkers that *solely* focused on financial matters to derive a panacea for the economic system. In his critique of Proudhon, for instance, Marx ridiculed those that presumed that the contradictory and exploitative elements of capitalism could be overcome by reforming finance. Marx argued instead that monetary sector reform, while beneficial, was a false hope to those that felt oppressed by capitalism and would simply leave surplus value from labor, falling profit rates and *rentier* incomes from property intact. In some cases the ruling elites might even advocate monetary reform in order to distract attention from other exploitation within the system—to scapegoat the bankers. Marx writes:

> It is equally clear, on the other side, that to the degree to which opposition against the ruling relations of production grows, and these latter themselves push even more forcibly to cast off their old skin—to that degree polemics are directed against metallic money or money in general, as the most striking, most contradictory and hardest phenomenon which is presented by the system in palpable form. One or another kind of artful tinkering with money is then supposed to overcome the contradictions of which money is merely the perceptible appearance.
>
> (Marx 1993: 240)

Since the financialization school argued that financial factors, rather than low profitability, were solely responsible for the 2007–2008 crisis, their policy recommendations are unlikely to be successful in preventing a crisis from occurring. In a crisis, with general financial uncertainty, people also tend to hoard their monies. This means that over production takes place, as goods fail to sell in sufficient quantities. Marx had scoffed, as Harvey notes, at those vulgar thinkers who claimed "supply creates its own demand" (Say's law), since the capitalist frequently does not realize surplus value in such instances (Harvey 2010: 66). There is no guarantee that all commodities will sell and capitalist losses will be experienced. Yet, paradoxically, many authors have sought to *explain* the existence of financial crises with reference to this lack of aggregate demand as a precursor to crisis. Kliman, for instance, has argued that the so-called *under-consumptionists* use circular (tautological) reasoning, since their explanation of crises seems to simply describe the *manifestations* of the various crises in question rather than the causes (Kliman 1999).[14] Marx, conversely, identified that the law of the tendency for the profit rate to fall was underlying albeit indirect cause of the overproduction. The falling profit rate, via its impact on the credit system and speculation, then leads to the financial instability and any shortfall of demand. The vagaries of market forces, driven by *animal spirits*, are still important, as we would expect, and Marx recognized this. However, they do not, as it is claimed in this book, occur in a vacuum driven by random subjectivities, but instead occur as a general consequence of the law of value in operation. This is the key distinctive, as identified in this chapter, between the PK and Marx perspectives of political economy. It is accepted, for instance, that if economic agents experience stable expectations of low interest rates, this will to some extent compensate for falling returns on capital advanced. Yet, the mechanics of successive periods of production will tend toward falling profitability and, therefore, the *imperative* of counter-tendencies and/or crisis in order to sustain capitalism is of paramount importance.

8.8 THE TEMPORAL SINGLE SYSTEM INTERPRETATION OF MARX

The TSSI of Marx approach, in contrast, notes a tendency for the profit rate to fall that, in turn, leads to a *decreased* rate of accumulation manifested in output transactions in the next train (ground-distance) journey.[15] Also, since the computation of real output value uses the MELT, *separating* output transactions from fictitious/secondary ones, it is not necessary for financial sector activity to be *directly* determined by the profit rate. Instead, as argued in chapter 5, the falling rate of profit *indirectly* impacts the financial sector activity through the migration of surplus capital toward fictitious capital and/or credit creation in the financial sector for purposes of speculation and swindles. Track length varies, therefore, as fictitious capital creates a meandering during the period. In line with Marx, the commodity real output prices are formed at the *end* of production prior to the circulation where the *realization of exchange-value* takes place (Marx [1858] 1973: 196). The distance to travel between stations that is, the next journey, therefore, is determined by these *realized* values. The MELT/inflation changes (from the previous period), as commodity prices are formed at the end of production, are also taken into account and are subject to their own fluctuations across successive periods.

The LTFRP as stated, manifested in price formation, thus impacts the rate of accumulation for the next period. Yet, as illustrated in Table 5.3, an increasing mass of surplus value still occurs as productivity increases (with rising physical profit rate), as a consequence of the devalued means of subsistence, despite the falling value profit rate. The rising surplus value is likely to encourage rising share dividends/prices, and hence surplus capital migration to the fictitious capital and credit creation in the financial sector. This will also be fueled by lower interest rates as a consequence of falling productive investment. This can collectively lead to the build-up of excessive debt and asset inflation that then leads to the onset of financial crisis manifested in default(s), unsold goods and burst bubbles. The LTFRP and impact can be illustrated in successive train journeys by decreasing rates of growth of the track, but with increased meandering from the speculative fictitious capital

Figure 8.7 The Tendency for the Rate of Profit to Fall.

activity eventually culminating in a train malfunction. In normal conditions, it can be expected that the credit system will *accommodate* the credit demand. Yet, the panic among financial agents can lead to raised interest rates and crisis. The LTFRP *inter alia* can also instigate a sudden investment fright by production agents, conscious of the falling profit per pound advanced and fictitious capital problems. This illustrates the reflexive influence of the productive *and* financial agents on agent behavior. The track distance, as a consequence, will be reduced in the next period as capitalists cut back investment leading to stagnation across periods. The restoration of the profit rate in the ensuing crisis, as the means of production are marked down, following Marx, is then imperative for the survival of the capitalist system. The government, in the circumstances described above, can also impact productive and financial sector agent behavior through monetary and fiscal policies. A low interest-rate policy, for instance, will restore profitability for productive investment but may also encourage fictitious capital trading. Yet, since production creates new value, and financial trading does not, there is less systemic risk in the short term. Speculative activity, therefore, should be mitigated. In the long term, however, as I argued in chapter 5, Marx's law of value will still exert its influence on the general economy with its propensity to engender crises.

In this TSSI train analogy, therefore, financial factors can be seen to disrupt production while production factors, that is, the LTFRP, *remain* as the key drivers of the capitalist trajectory. In addition, since prices and values reciprocally determine each other in successive periods of production (in TSSI models), the *reflexive* interaction between the real and financial sectors *form* the preconditions for output in the next period. It is claimed in this book, therefore, that in contrast to the first four approaches, in the TSSI, the human *and* the monetary costs are reflected in the economic analysis and, the *law of value* has been restored to prime position in political economy without ignoring the disruptive (to production) and usurious nature of financial sector exploitation. This is also conducted with the use of EMT credit money units.

It should be noted that the plutocratic classes in capitalism gain from these exploitative credit system practices that, as a consequence, perhaps need to be reformed in some way. Indeed, our steam locomotive consists of *private* bankers and investors that clearly benefit from interest, fees, commissions, bonuses and charges. Yet, the state can and may choose to regulate the credit system differently. Cheaper credit, for instance, would mitigate the *impact* of the falling rate of profit by increasing the capitalist share of surplus value. Marx, however, while recognizing the predatory, disruptive and lucrative tendencies of banking firmly posited that the ultimate driver of real outcomes derives primarily from production. Monetary system reform on its own would not be sufficient to eliminate the many contradictions of capitalism. It is the socialization of private capital itself that would be required to eliminate contradictions. Marx, therefore, sees the capitalist state, as the extension and defender of the interests of the capitalist classes. In reality, this includes the owners of financial *and* nonfinancial corporations and their various beneficiaries.

8.9 CONCLUSION

The EMT, it is argued, is a clearer reflection of the reality of modern money in the capitalist nations. The train illustration is able to demonstrate transaction activity and the operation of EMT *ex nihilo* money-creation, in conjunction with the exertion of Marx's *law of value* on the monetary economy. Each train journey, between stations, represents a separate production and circulation period in order to reflect the sequential nature of Marx's analysis. Credit creation in any period, in response to credit demand, can be expressed as a *proportion* of the *means of circulation*. The means of circulation, in turn, are a proportion of the overall money supply that is, money supply minus inactive balances. It was argued earlier in the book that the EMT can be synthesized with Marx's political economy and it has been illustrated here in the steam train analogy. Human effort involved in the production of credit-money, that is, the costs of circulation, can thus be measured in units of abstract labor. Yet, since the banking system consumes a share of surplus value and is *not* considered by Marx to *add* value in production, as stated above, these particular circulation costs merely *express* an abstract labor value, the banking does not *embody* labor value.

In assessing how credit works, this train illustration concludes that mainstream views of money attribute business and credit cycle fluctuation to exogenous factors, rather than an integrated and reflexive monetary economy. This conclusion also extends to the theoretical framework of the Keynesian synthesis. Secondly, the dominant view, especially after the recent financial crisis, spans the ideological spectrum and identifies varying financial factors as determinants of credit fluctuation. Post-Keynesian monetary theory, in contrast, reveals a much richer analysis that notably identifies productive factors, that is, changing marginal efficiency, as independent variables driving the normally cited financial factors determining output. Yet, it is concluded here that these factors were predicated on subjective notions of expectation, and a *correct* MEC schedule, that is difficult to quantify in practice. In addition, the assumption that the capitalist process can be harmonious ignores the contradictions identified by Marx. The Austrian school idea, similarly, has no predisposition to question capitalism *per se*, and assumes that if FRB and cheap money can be eradicated, the economic system will obtain a steady state. In its consideration of Marx, the book dismisses the *simultaneous* method and the *financialization* school, since these have tended to lead, in clear opposition to Marx, to *financial* sector explanations of business and credit cycles. Instead, the book has accepted the TSSI of Marx, which it argues most closely resembles Marx's own approach to political economy. In this regard, the LTFRP, and investment contraction, lead indirectly to financial sector activity and to output fluctuation. This serves to position profitability considerations at the heart of the analysis. The policy implication, therefore, is that the survival of capitalism depends upon a restored profit rate achieved through the destruction of capital or reduction of *real* wages in crisis, and/or the increasing *commodification* (creating new markets) of the natural world. It is difficult to conceive of these responses as being anything other than detrimental to people and planet. It appears there are, therefore, some difficult choices for policy-makers ahead.

NOTES

1. Other financial institutions that create credit are ignored for the purposes of the steam train analogy.
2. Credit creation is considered endogenous, at an exogenously determined interest rate (Wray 2004).
3. Rousseas suggested, for example, that increases in the demand for money "need not be accommodated fully by the central banks" due to dishoarding, economizing on transaction balances (e.g., a more efficient interbank market) and financial innovation, leading to raised costs (Itoh 1999: 238)
4. The central bank, following Moore, will simply "accommodate" demand for reserves since banks cannot quickly sell or reduce their loan assets in order to achieve the desired level of liquidity. Failure to do this would undermine the efficiency and operation of the real economy (Itoh 1999: 236).
5. The intricacies of the credit system are largely ignored and the money supply is assumed to be exogenous. The classical view of interest posits that more (pre-existing) money is supplied at higher rates of interest. The neoclassical/Keynesian *loanable funds* approach, in contrast, recognizes *ex nihilo* credit creation (and dishoarding) but, higher economic activity still requires higher interest rates, suggesting an upward sloping supply curve for credit money (Tily 2007).
6. The *efficient market hypothesis* assumes that the arbitrage (and, therefore, the reliable pricing) is dependent on the level and quality of information pertaining to the asset (Fama 1970).
7. In the TSSI (and this model) conception, profit rates are the key determinant of investment for next period.
8. To simplify, these processes occur during the production period (when the train is stationary) but the output was determined in the last circulation. The transaction demand is then established for the period of circulation.

9. Changing interest rates, from the last period, will impact the demand (Q) variables differently. Commodities for consumption, for example, may be inversely impacted, higher rates reducing demand, whereas the bond market (which constitutes part of the demand for fictitious capital) is likely to be positively affected.

10. The expectations of entrepreneurs, driving investment demand, will inevitably consider profitability.

11. These interest rates then, in turn, influence the other rates of interest across the spectrum.

12. Bernard Lietaer also argues that currency diversity will lead to a more resilient financial order since there will be "slack" in the system that enables it to cope with random shocks more appropriately (Lietaer 2011).

13. The *financialization* school has also posited that a decline in the wage proportion of income (in favor of profit) has taken place in the post-WW2 period, serving to sustain capitalism during the neo-liberal era. Kliman disputes this and claims that the worker share has remained consistent. This is backed with empirical evidence from the US economy (Kliman 2012: 68).

14. Robert Brenner, noted by Kliman, suggests that firms expand "faster than demand will permit." Yet, if the crisis (which involves insufficient demand) is solely explained (in terms of causality) with reference to the lack of demand this is indeed tautological (Kliman 1999: 3).

15. In the absence of counter-tendencies (e.g., falling real wages or commodification), therefore, the rising organic composition of capital means that steady-state capitalism is not possible.

Chapter 9

German Monetary Policy

9.1 INTRODUCTION

In this first empirical chapter, I explore the monetary policy environment of Germany since the 1930s, to examine if an erosion of state capability to influence money-creation and value can be identified. First, there is a discussion of the interwar years, where the monetary ideas that shaped the case-study period were formed. Next, there is an investigation of the period from 1945 to 1957 when certain institutional and monetary events laid the foundations of the post-WW2 German economy. This section reveals some interesting aspects of post-WW2 financial sovereignty in Germany. The main, and final, section of the chapter evaluates the Federal Republic of Germany's (FRG) monetary policy effectiveness, from the BW period post-WW2 to the neo-liberal era (since 1973), in terms of the state's ability to influence credit levels and currency value (internally and externally). It is concluded that, notwithstanding the proactive monetary policy of the German state, the FRG has indeed conceded sovereignty in the arena of financial power across the period.

The state has various monetary policy instruments at its disposal, in order to achieve price stability and other objectives, and these will differ in their specific context. The state can instigate, for example, reserve requirements, open market operations, national bank lending criteria, base interest rates, direct credit controls and foreign exchange reserve trades.[1] The finance ministry and/or the national bank as agent of the state, depending on the specific arrangements and protocols that exist between the two institutions, can also adjust these policy variables. As perhaps expected, the monetary policy of the capitalist nations following WW2 was predicated on the prevailing (and evolving) underlying economic and political philosophies. In the BW period

1945–1973, for instance, the fiscal pursuit of full employment and growth inspired by Keynes was combined with a monetary policy stance that prioritized the maintenance of the BW exchange rate regime. Central banks, as Mishkin notes, simply focused on nominal interest rates, capital controls, bank advances and so-called free bank reserves (excess reserves after borrowings) during this early period, in order to guide credit relations and macroeconomic stability (Mishkin 2007).

In the immediate post-WW2 era, Germany experienced severe economic hardship and the jurisdiction of an American, British, Soviet and French occupation. Initially, the Reichsbank and Reichsmark continued to function, before they were replaced by the Bank Deutscher Lander (BDL) and the Deutchsmark in 1948, in preparation for the new Federal Republic of West Germany (FRG), formed in May 1949. The Bundesbank was formed in 1957 and remained the national bank of FRG (and Germany after 1990) until the creation of the European Central Bank (ECB) and the Euro in 1999, for the purposes of European Union monetary integration established during the Maastricht Treaty negotiations. Yet, despite these changes, many of the German prewar monetary traditions survived intact and, therefore, the interwar years are first briefly discussed in order to provide context for the chapter.

9.2 THE WEIMAR REPUBLIC AND THIRD REICH

The monetary history of the Weimar Republic 1919–1933, and Third Reich 1933–1945, had influenced the state thinking toward the post-WW2 financial system structure and policy, in terms of its constituent form(s) and mode of operation.[2] The fear of inflation and economic instability from the aftermath of hyperinflation in 1923, for example, was manifested in the tight monetary policies of the BDL and Bundesbank, wage/price constraint and the reluctance to revalue exchange rates during the BW period. The inflation and exchange rate collapse that culminated in November 1923 had been truly devastating. The usual view of these occurrences in German financial history is that excessive reparation demands had led to a *state-driven* excess issue of currency and subsequent inflation (Zarlenga 1999).[3] The first reparations in 1920, for example, had been made in US dollars with freshly minted marks so the international community anticipated German devaluation (Marsh 1993). Keynes had famously warned in 1919 that reparations set at Versailles were unsustainable and would lead to economic strife of some description, and this had certainly manifested (Keynes 1919). The Reichsbank, formed in 1875, was privately owned but was considered part of the state since the president and directorate were under the "supervision and direction" of the Reich and were fully expected to "follow at all times the rulings and directions of the chancellor" (Marsh 1993: 93).[4] Gold convertibility had been suspended in 1918, as spending rose, and post-WW1 deficits were made worse by reparations that needed to be financed. The Bundesbank records that the Weimar state was not able to raise taxation and, therefore, the Reichsbank discounted government bills to meet the shortfall. Yet, it is interesting to note, the Reichbank was not overly concerned with inflation prior to 1922, since this relieved the aggregate state debt burden (James 1999: 18). In addition, *private* firms with preferential access to the Reichsbank were able to discount their corporate bonds at negative real interest rates creating distorting market effects and fostering inflationary pressure (James 1999: 19).

Schacht became Reichsbank chief in 1923 and was soon credited with the stabilization of the new Reichsmark, set at a conversion rate of 1:1 trillion marks. The international banking connections of Schacht, combined with prudent budget cuts from the finance minister Hans Luther, served to create confidence among the German people in the new currency. Schacht then criminalized the massive volumes of alternative currencies (*Notgeld*) that had been created by corporate and municipalities to overcome the devaluing mark. In addition he established a gold discount facility that had the power to create credit in sterling, thus helping to mobilize credit in foreign currency (Marsh 1993). This strategy was further boosted by the Dawes plan, negotiated with the allies that reduced the reparation payments and led to a short period of economic growth. Yet, by the latter half of the twenties Schacht had become increasingly concerned about monetary laxity and appealed for stabilitatspolitik, that is, stability policy, a phrase that soon became a buzzword in the post-WW2 German financial system. Dollars were being borrowed from US financial institutions, repaid to France and Britain in reparations and recycled back to the US for allied war debt repayments (Guinnane, 2004: 12). It was later default on reparation payments that contributed to the onset of the Anglo Saxon Depression as this recycling was stunted. The Young Plan in 1929 had sought to alleviate the payment difficulties, after the default with the Dawes plan, but to no avail, leading to the resignation of Schacht in 1930. In the following three years, the deflationary policies of Hans Luther contributed toward deteriorating economic conditions, preparing the way for the Reichstag transfer of absolute power to Hitler in 1933 (Marsh 1993). Meanwhile, the Great Depression was now firmly established in the US and the UK.

At the outset, the Hitler regime borrowed externally from international financial institutions, but later began to issue its own debt. Schacht was reappointed at the Reichsbank and a full-employment strategy, wage (and price) constraint and sovereign debt issue served to facilitate powerful real economic growth. The impact of these policies transformed Germany from the weakest economy in Europe in to the strongest in just four years, even without the later substantial state rearmament spending (Overy 1982,

Williamson 1982, Liu 2005).[5] This *wirtschaftswunder*, or economic miracle, was even more remarkable if we consider that in 1933 Germany also had no prospects of inward foreign direct investment, or any credit rating with international financial institutions, thus forcing the German state to adopt a distinctly *national* monetary strategy. Economic growth 1933–1938 averaged 9.5%, a much more favorable performance than the UK and US economies (Preparata 2002). Sovereign debt involved the *arbeitsheshaffungswechseln,* so-called Work Creation Bills (WCB's), following the inspiration of the Reich finance minister Fritz Reinhardt in 1932 in order to circumvent rules imposed on the Reichsbank by the allied at Versailles. These stipulations included national bank decision-making autonomy from the state (1923), a 40% minimum reserve against banknotes, held in gold or foreign currency, and a ceiling on the discount of treasury bills (Silverman 1998). The WCB's were distributed to participating government agencies and credit institutions, such as the *Deutsche Gesellschaft fur offentliche Arbeiten AG* (Offa). The institutions were now able, despite allied rulings, to discount the bills at the Reichsbank and pay contractors in Reichsmarks.[6] The state also undertook to retire a proportion of the bills, up to 30% per year, financed from the expansion of taxation. These Offa Bills became the forerunner of the later MEFO bills introduced by Schacht. These latter promissory notes were drawn by approved armaments contractors and were accepted by the *Metallurgische Ferschungsgesellschaft* (MEFO), set up by the Reich (with minimal capital) as a dummy company in 1934. The contractors could then discount the bills for Reichsmarks at any bank who, in turn, could discount the bills at the Reichsbank. The state was essentially procuring armaments on credit but via the MEFO as named debtor. The scheme lasted until 1938, when Schacht felt that the money-creation and rearmament had reached appropriate levels (International Military Tribunal, 1948).

As the tensions leading to WW2 intensified, Hitler sought more control of the Reichsbank and disagreements emerged with Schacht. This was partly due to Schacht's international banking connections, and Hitler's increasingly hostility toward them, and Walter Funk subsequently replaced him in 1939.[7] Ironically, through an attempt to increase the powers of the state, or rather political incumbents, over the financial system, the Third Reich lost all state capability to the allies following defeat in WW2. In turn, the allied occupying postwar powers insisted on autonomy for national bank decision-making, albeit subject to approval from the allies, to protect the nascent state from ambitious politicians.[8] As a result, the peculiarity of German national bank autonomy was established that later became the hallmark of the FRG monetary culture (Bibow 2009). The year 1948 is therefore an important point in the empirical investigation since it was the year that the BDL was established, currency reform was enacted and the Deutsche Mark was introduced to replace the Reichsmark, in preparation for the inauguration of the FRG in 1949. This formulation of the BDL thus established the German national bank as a *semi-state* institution, a conception that is adopted here[9]. If the national bank exercises monetary policy autonomy this may reflect the interests of private banks or prevailing politicians (or both), but in all circumstances the central bank represents, for the theoretical purposes of this book at least, the interests of state.

9.3 BANK DEUTSCHER LANDER 1948–1957

As stated earlier, the 1945–1948 period involved substantial economic hardship for FRG people, under the three occupation zones administered by the French, Americans and British. Price controls were in place, unemployment was rising, international trade was managed through bilateral negotiation with rising trade deficits and the domestic monetary arrangements were conducted through the Lander regional banking system using an inflated Reichsmark. The key monetary objective for the allied powers, despite their disagreements, was the prevention of a return to centralized banking with strong links to large corporations and politicians (Hetzel 2002).[10] Thus Article 3 of the law establishing the BDL, for instance, stated that the institution "shall not be subject to the instructions of any political body or public non-judicial agency" (Marsh 1993: 145). The BDL's mandate, therefore, was limited to the stewarding of monetary resources, issuing the new currency banknotes, monitoring the financial system and coordinating the Lander banks. The new bank was owned by the Lander Banks and was not permitted to directly lend to corporations, unlike the Reichsbank, had no initial responsibility prior to 1949 for foreign currency and had strict limits placed on its ability to bridge the deficits of the zone's economic administration (Marsh 1993). The decision-making process of the new BDL was conducted by the *Zentralbankrat* council, derived from the heads of the eleven *Landeszentralbanken* (LZB), with executive functions performed by a nonvoting directorate appointed by the council.[11] Yet, despite the necessity of approval from the Allied Banking Commission (ABC) for important decisions, the new bank managed to achieve substantial autonomy as they grew less dependent on the allies, and seized the opportunity to extend this to independence when the FRG government was established in Bonn in 1949. In June 1948, for instance, the allies had wanted a discount rate of 8% but the BDL resisted and set the rate at 5% instead (Marsh 1993).[12] In the event, this monetary policy action facilitated a 14% rise in inflation between June and October, once price controls had been removed (Hetzel 2002). Yet, the interest-rate *exogeneity* had been established. Notwithstanding, between 1948 and 1950, although the BDL was not particularly successful in taming inflation, and this reflected in the worsening trade deficits during this period, at least the bank could respond as they saw fit.[13] The currency reforms of 1948, imposed by the allies, also accompanied the formation of the Deutsche Mark (Dm) and were particularly harsh on owners of Reichsmark balances.[14] The West Germans were able, under the policy, to exchange sixty Reichsmarks on a 1:1 basis, but larger balances were exchanged at a ratio of 10:1 (Hetzel 2002: 22). Many Germans subsequently suffered losses (except those who had ownership title to assets), especially those that had financed the Nazi regime, and this extraordinary yet, arguably, necessary policy represented a clear act of state financial sovereignty over the level of circulating currency right at the outset of the case-study period.[15] The currency reform has real significance for the key argument of this book, since for many asset-holders this amounted to a *de facto* 90% reduction in their debt obligations and, therefore, delivered a substantial boost for the restoration of profitability. Profitability is the *sine qua non* of a sustainable capitalism and is discussed in chapter 11 in relation to falling rates of profit.

After currency reform, it soon became apparent that the neutralization of wealth held in the form of Reichsmarks, and the general impact of the financial claims on the Third Reich, had also left the German banking system with a serious undercapitalization. In order to deal with the problem the BDL, with ABC approval, created an artificial financial instrument entitled an *equalization claim*, with the government as debtor, to restore solvency on the bank balance sheets. The new claims were to be financed over many years from central bank profits, and were backed by government guarantees (Pontzen 2008: 148).[16] The potential future danger of *moral hazard* for the banks, that is, the incentivization of risky overexposure, was overlooked. Yet, following the subsequent Herstatt Bank crisis in 1974, or the crash of investment bank Schroder, Munchmeyer, Hengst and Co in 1983, when the financial authorities chose not to provide a similar facility, it was clear that the FRG authorities had viewed the 1948 recapitalization as a one-off policy due to the particular post-WW2 conditions that prevailed (Pontzen 2008: 152).

A key instrument of monetary policy at the disposal of the new BDL was the imposition of minimum reserve requirements.[17] This enabled the *Zentralbankrat* to have a measure of control over *market* interest rates in combination with their use of the discount and Lombard rates.[18] The supply of credit would be reduced if they tightened monetary requirements, and vice versa. This depended, however, on the extent and level of development of any interbank money markets that existed. This book posits that a greater quantity of bank deposit monies, in relative proportion to base money, is *prima facie* indication of a reduced state ability to influence *market* interest rates. It is argued that this is a consequence of setting the discount/Lombard rates, which are assumed to involve a reflexive decision-making process and, therefore, the market sentiment(s) is of greater significance for state economic management in such a scenario. Finally, unlike the Reichsbank where the Lander regional banks had some role, the BDL was also given *sole* issuing rights for the Dm banknotes, enhancing state sovereignty. In addition, the BDL also gained the ability to conduct open market operations and the operation of a financial clearinghouse for the Lander banks. Through the design of this new bank structure and function the allies hoped that:

> Unlike the Reichsbank, the bank of the German *Lander* will not compete directly with the other banks for private funds, and will not be subject to domination by the state politicians. On the other hand, it will have even greater influence over general monetary conditions, by virtue of its power to influence reserve ratios. It is felt it will therefore be possible to avoid many of the undesirable monetary and credit policies followed by the German central banks in the past.
> (Marsh 1993: 147).

In terms of the capability to determine the exchange rate of the Dm, however, the capabilities of the BDL were somewhat restricted, at least at the outset of the BW N-1 exchange system.[19] The zone authorities without BDL consultation implemented the German BW involvement in April 1948, in line with the concluding agreement that was established at the monetary conference in 1944, and maintained an exchange rate of 3.33 Reichsmarks/USD while retaining control of foreign currency reserves (Marsh 1993). In September 1949, following the UK devaluation of the pound, the Dm was devalued by 20% to DM4.2/$. This time the three victor powers did consult the BDL, and the Bonn government, but still established (against the wishes of Bonn) their desired rate anyway (Marsh 1993). Yet, by 1950 the influence of the ABC had waned and in 1951 the BDL law was changed that phased out their role. The national bank autonomy and culture, however, remained intact. In the time leading to the Bundesbank law this was vociferously defended by Vocke (BDL Directorate President).[20] Chancellor Adenauer, for example, had sought more political central bank control and failed to achieve it. The new Deutsche Bundesbank law of 1957 then established the Bonn, now transferred to Berlin, government practice of the appointment of the directorate, but monetary policy was *not* to be subjected to political whim, and this policy has never been seriously challenged since.

9.4 THE BRETTON WOODS ERA TO THE NEO-LIBERAL ERA

The Deutsche Bundesbank (DB) was created in 1957 and was given responsibility for the stability of the German currency and unique banking system.

The German financial system had evolved into three distinct sectors, constituted of private banks such as Deutsche Bank, the cooperative banks such as Volksbanken or Raiffeisenbanken and the regulated public bank networks such as Sparkasse and Landesbanken (Hufner 2010: 8).[21] In 2009, a total of 82% of the financial institutions in Germany, representing 44% of total assets, are now nonprofit maximizing institutions (Hufner 2010: 8).[22] In addition, 97% of German banks are so-called *universal* banks that combine investment and retail (and other) functions together in servicing the real economy. This can lead, as Franke noted, to conflicts of interest and the concentration of financial power, impairing the efficiency of capital markets, which weakens the ability of investors to control corporations (Franke 1999: 222). Yet, it has been commonly suggested, most notably by Gerschenkron, that universal banking, with its close working relationship with capital interests, has played a key role in Germany's post-WW2 economic development (Gerschenkron 1962).[23] In addition, public-banking credit provision can perhaps be considered to have a *counter-cyclical* impact on the economy, in comparison to private banking, since the bank decision-makers are less driven by the profit imperative during any deflationary conditions. These credit decisions are, in turn, of paramount importance to the level of money-creation that circulates as currency in Germany. Figure 9.1 illustrates the growth in the volume of credit-money, in the form of bank deposits, in proportion to the quantity of base money across the period. This is *prima facie* evidence of the *loss* of financial sovereignty over the level of credit creation, particularly from the

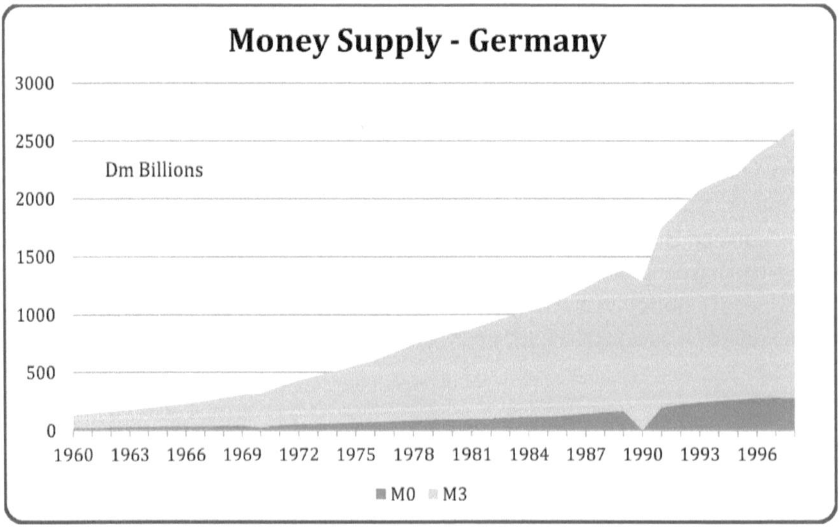

Figure 9.1 German Money Supply.

1980s. This is first because the state determines the issue-conditions and the allocation of base money in the system, and, secondly, as private credit volumes increase there is *more* scope for cheaper interbank lending which in turn decreases the dependence on DB discount refinancing and Lombard lending, forcing DB rates to be driven more by market sentiment. If there is less base money, more *private* decision-making is involved in money-issue, and the spectrum of market interest rates that track money market lending is therefore more likely to be driven by market sentiments (i.e., interbank rates) than DB policy, if the interbank market is larger. During the later BW period (1960s), as Franke notes, the DB continued to regulate interest rates but banks increasingly found ways to circumvent the control. Thus the effective interest rates diverged from the official ones (Franke 2013).

It was the control of inflation (see Figure 9.2) that was the main priority for the new FRG state. In general, as Holtfrerich notes, the Central Bank Council (CBC) of the DB was more successful in achieving price stability during the BW era than during the neo-liberal era that followed (Holtfrerich 1999: 308). This was due in part to the fiscal policy stance of the FRG, and their incomes policy, in addition to monetary measures (Holtfrerich 1999: 308). The key instruments of monetary policy during the period involved the control of *free liquid reserves* (liquidity in the interbank system) achieved by the conduct of open market operations (OMO), discount rates/refinancing quotas and minimum reserve requirements (Holtfrerich 1999: 319).[24] However, as Franke noted, the DB rarely engaged in large open market operations, and reserve requirements have also been revised downward, leaving discount and Lombard rates/quotas as the main policy instruments (Franke 1999: 233). The influence of this interest rate control, as stated above, waned

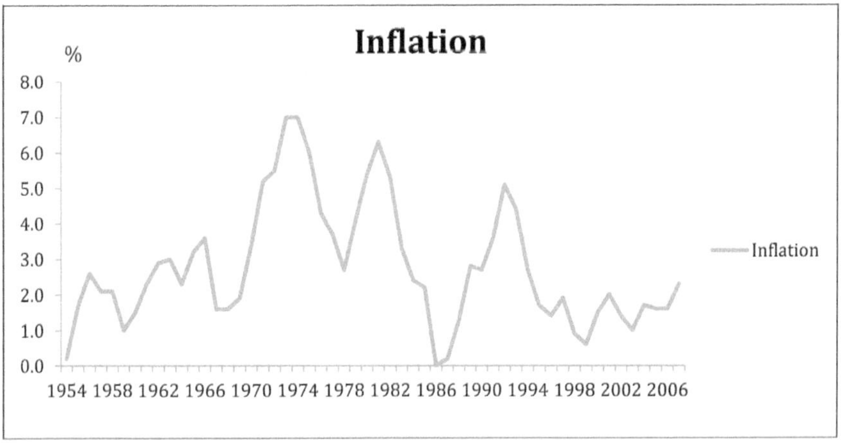

Figure 9.2 German Inflation

in the later BW period. Nevertheless, the CBC had a measure of control over the level of credit creation in the banking system and, implicitly, the control of inflationary pressures.

DB open market operations in the money market, as Baltensperger noted, changed substantially at the end of the 1970s with the introduction of securities repurchase agreements. This development also indicated a de facto *decline*, during the case-study period, of the *ability* of the authorities discount and Lombard rates to influence credit creation via interbank rates in the private credit markets (Baltensperger 1999: 453).[25] Yet, this could simply have represented, arguably, a *change* in the monetary instruments used for fine-tuning with no loss of sovereignty at all. The increased use of repurchase transactions where rates are more variable, as Franke noted, then gave a better indication than discount rates of the interest-rate policy of the DB that the market reacted to (Franke 1999: 234). Efficient financial markets, Franke further notes, react to *expected* and *unexpected* interest-rate policy measures differently (Franke 1999: 234). If the DB announces a closely defined measure for the future, for instance, the markets will respond to the *announcement* rather than any change, whereas if the change is unexpected the market agents will respond to the *implementation.*

So, since changes to the discount rate were more retrospective, simply responding to conditions, the markets responded less. In addition, it is also important to note that the *relation* between interest rate-setting (decision-making) for discount (and Lombard) rates and money market (interbank) rates is a *reflexive* one. In other words, market conditions influence DB decisions and *vice versa.* The key question is whether the *relative* power relation has changed. Since the repo rate is partly dependent on market sentiment, in conjunction with DB decisions on OMO, the *greater* involvement of market agents suggests *prima facie* that financial sovereignty over interest-rate determination and therefore the entire spectrum of market rates has been marginally lost since the BW era.[26] In Figure 9.3, the discount interest rate is compared with the money market rate across the case-study period. The discount rate, as Franke notes, is usually *below* the market rate, having a mitigating impact on money market activity (Franke 1999: 234). This, interestingly, is in direct contrast to the UK where the opposite case is the norm, which suggests a greater measure of state financial sovereignty in Germany generally. In the BW era, in the low inflation environment, discount and market rates remained close together. The rates during this period were predominantly adjusted in response to the fluctuations in GDP (Franke 1999: 237). During the rising prices of the late 1960s and 1970s, however, the inflation factor became a key driver of interest-rate decisions. During the neo-liberal era as Franke notes, conversely, the discount interest-rate fluctuations can be best explained as *driven* by the average overnight and one-month rates (Franke 1999: 238).

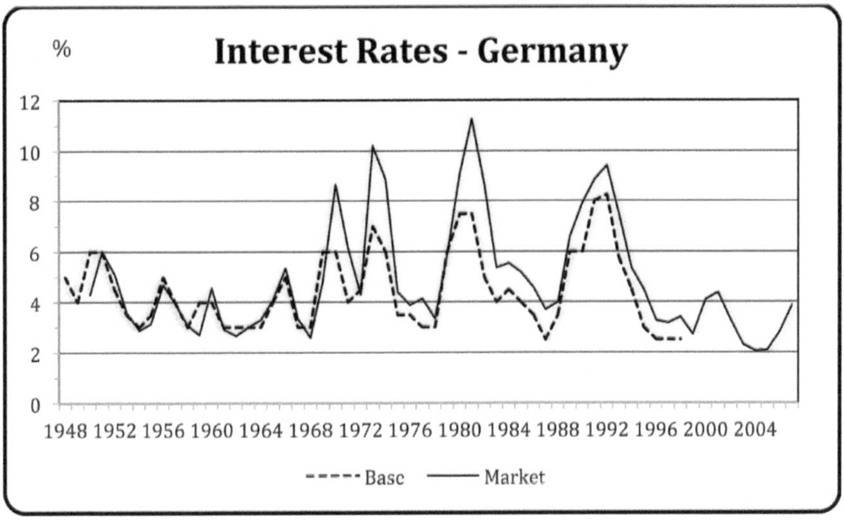

Figure 9.3 German Interest Rates

This is significant because it represents an increase of market influence and, a decline in the financial sovereignty of the DB over interest rates.

The financial sovereignty in respect of inflation of the DB is also evident, since 1974, with their monetary aggregate targeting. Germany, as Mishkin and Posen pointed out, did not necessarily need to adopt monetary targets after the breakdown of BW, given the price stability and strong Dm (Mishkin 1997: 21).[27] Yet, Mishkin later argues, that the DB wanted to reassert a measure of control over monetary policy in an overt manner that had been non-existent during the course of the BW era due to exchange-rate requirements (Mishkin 2007: 7). In this perspective, monetary targeting *communicates* to the financial markets the general objectives of the authorities and, therefore, is likely to have a mitigating impact on inflationary *expectations* and thus behavior of market agents.[28] Monetary target policy had been derived from monetarist (e.g., Friedman and Phelps) doctrine that claimed there was no long-term trade-off between unemployment and inflation (Mishkin 2007: 2). Money, therefore, was seen to have a neutral effect. This was supported by the rational expectations proposition, which stated, assuming flexible wages and prices, that monetary policy would be ineffective if it is *expected* as market agents adjust their positions (Mishkin 2007: 3). The trouble is that if money is *not* neutral, the logic is undermined. Mishkin notes that, in the late 1970s, the observed relationship between monetary aggregates and inflation (nominal income was also a goal variable) was seriously weakened (Mishkin 2007: 6). The UK (and North America), for instance, subsequently abandoned targeting in the early 1980s. Yet, the DB, conversely, continued with their policy of using a monetary target, first base money and then M3 from 1988, as a nominal anchor until the onset of the euro in 1999 with arguably greater success than other countries (Mishkin 1997: 23).[29]

The capability of the state authorities to influence the Dm/$ exchange rate during the BW era is also evident (see Figure 9.4), despite the fact that German stability-orientated policies were at odds with more expansionary monetary and fiscal policies in the anchor currency of the US (Pontzen 2008: 154). The necessary parity with the dollar was achieved through the sales of Dm for dollar reserves, in DB open market operations, to counter their successful restriction of real wage growth (and other price inflation) during the BW era. It is usual for economic historians to cite the inflation differentials as an explanation of the increasing pressure for exchange-rate adjustment during the BW period yet, as Pontzen and Schobert noted, the substantial relative growth in German productivity (1950–1970) was a key and related factor that also needs to be taken into consideration (Pontzen 2008: 155).

Since capital controls existed in continental Europe until 1986, German international transactions in foreign exchange were mainly restricted to payments related to trade in goods and services.[30] The consistent current account surpluses, therefore, placed continual pressure on the Dm to appreciate during the BW era. Yet, as several authors have noted, the German state was often reluctant to revalue their official fixed rate, fearing a loss of competitiveness, and inflationary policies were certainly ruled out by the prevailing DB

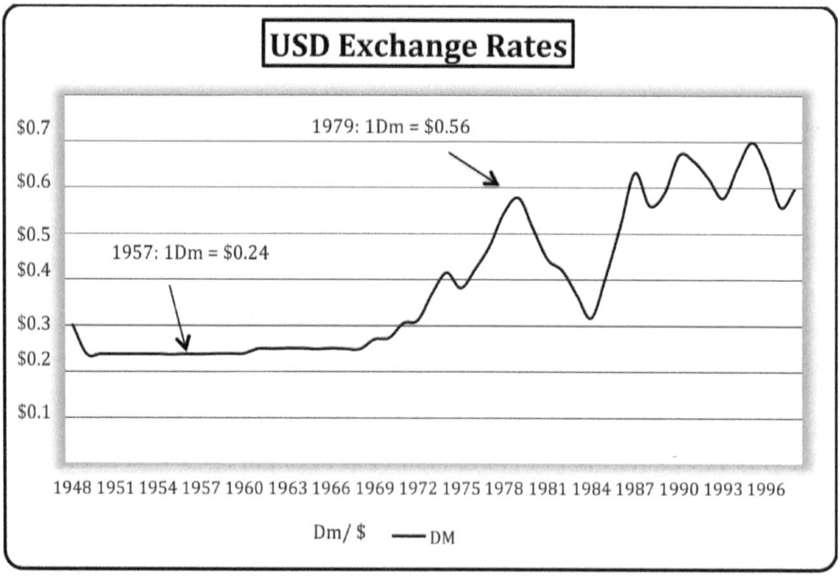

Figure 9.4 Deutsche Mark Dollar Exchange Rate.

political culture (Holtfrerich 1999; Owen-Smith 1994; Eichengreen 2011).[31] The DB simply focused on the restriction of capital inflows and OMO in foreign exchange. In terms of the capital inflow measures there was a ban on the payment of interest on foreign deposits in domestic banks, a ban on the sale of money market paper to nonresidents, a ban on repo securities transactions between residents and nonresidents (from 1960) and a tax (from 1965) on coupon interest received by nonresidents on domestic bonds. In addition, in 1968, domestic banks accepting deposits from nonresidents had to seek state authorization and, from 1972, borrowings from abroad were subject to cash deposit requirement (Pontzen 2008: 158). Capital controls were removed (in 1986) with the EC Single European Act.

The level of USD reserves (see Figure 9.5), in relation to GDP, illustrates the potential ability of the DB authority to influence Dm exchange rate across the case-study period, through the engagement of open market operations in foreign exchange. In the BW era, as Pontzen and Schobert note, the build-up of reserves support the argument that the DB intervened heavily to prevent the revaluation of the Dm (Pontzen 2008: 157). In the late 1960s, however, it is clear that the interventions were even more substantial with a rapid increase of reserves as the BW system verged on collapse.

Yet, after 1984, there is a sustained *decline* in dollar reserves that is perhaps indicator of the universal increasing *inability* of central bank intervention to affect exchange-rate value in the face of growing volumes of privately controlled monies on the foreign exchange market.[32] The growth in foreign exchange volumes is illustrated in chapter 11. Notwithstanding,

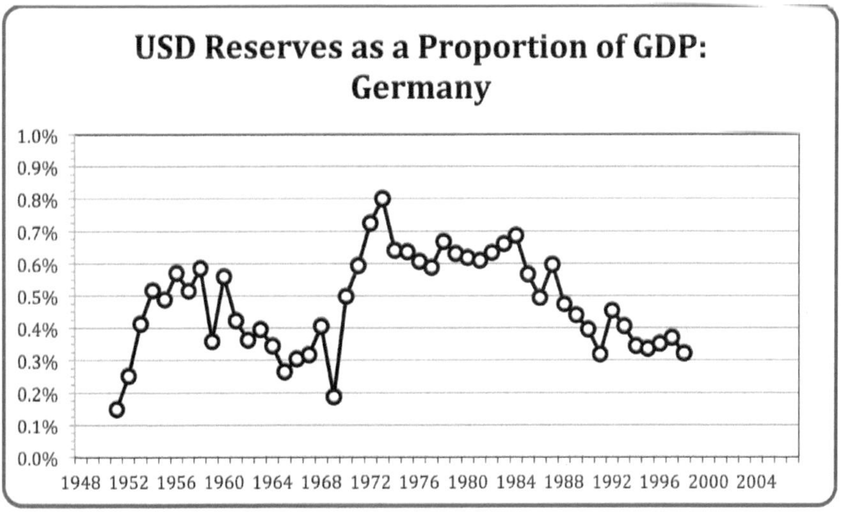

Figure 9.5 German USD Reserves as % of GDP.

in the neo-liberal era, the DB arguably still exhibited ability to influence exchange rates, in comparison to other states, albeit diminished by liberal and growing capital flows and the increasing phenomena of leveraged currency speculation.[33]

9.5 CONCLUSION

Inflation was a primary concern of the FRG state and during the Weimar Republic after 1923. After WW2, under the jurisdiction of the BDL and allied control, price stability had been maintained through the continuation of price controls. Once these had been removed however, following currency reform in 1948, the first two years were marked by rising prices. Yet, this simply illustrated the immediate post-WW2 economic development needs rather than the lack of financial *capability* of the monetary authorities. After 1950, however, the rapid FRG economic recovery was underway and the stable Dm became its hallmark. This was achieved through a combination of monetary, fiscal and industrial policies. Yet, with greater quantities of credit-money in circulation in the neo-liberal era, and with the more market-driven interest rate determination, financial sovereignty appears to have been eroded. In terms of FRG exchange-rate variability, it is much clearer to illustrate the diminishing state sovereignty, evidenced by the increase of leveraged capital flows and ineffectual central bank intervention capability that is, their relative inability to manipulate exchange-rate values through the sale/purchase of their own currency in open market operations.

The regulated public banking dimension of the German financial system has indicated that the FRG state has manifested a greater historical capability to influence credit creation (and allocation), in contrast to nation-states with a more private system such as the UK.[34] It has been noted (e.g., Helleiner), however, that the private commercial banks in the West have lobbied the state, during the BW era, for increased financial liberalization in order to enhance their profitability (Helleiner 1994).[35] In Germany too, there are some driving forces of *market*-orientated change in the banking world. Rolf-E Breuer, for instance, from Deutsche Bank, has been a key driver of *Finanzplatz Deutschland* (promoting Germany as a notable financial center) and he has been seeking more Anglo-Saxon-style market reforms (Herdt 2002: 14). Breuer has further suggested that the financial markets can potentially form a beneficial source of social power, collectively serving as a check on governments and firms (Hengsbach 2002: 163). The quintessential German financial culture remains intact, however, but there arguably appears to be more evidence of a gradual erosion of the public banking stakeholder ideology. This suggests a gradual erosion of the state's capability to influence credit and currency value, in particular its exchange rate.[36]

NOTES

1. In addition, the state is able, through its prudential regulation of the financial system, to establish principles of operation for banks (and engage in *persuasion*) in order to determine behaviors of various financial agents.

2. Many central bank key staff from the Weimar and Third Reich administrations continued in office after WW2. Thirty-nine percent of Bank deutscher Lander and Bundesbank financiers had served the Hitler regime (Marsh 1993).

3. The view that this illustrates the profligacy of the state has been challenged, since the overissue of monies derived from a *privately* owned *Reichsbank* and the currency instability had been exacerbated by private leveraged short-sellers (Zarlenga 1999). However, it is more realistic that both state and market were complicit.

4. Private shareholders were represented by a relatively weak *Zentralaus-schuss* committee that had the power to veto central bank financing of state needs, clearly ineffective in 1920–1923 (Marsh 1993).

5. Rearmament spending was only 1.9% in 1934 and 4% in 1935 (Silverman 1998)

6. The circumvention of allied rules was overcome by the semipublic nature of the agencies used and the real economic activity nature of WCB's issued (Preparata 2002). Schacht also imposed a (cheap money) interest rate ceiling of 4% on the discounting, down from 5.21% in 1932 (Preparata 2002).

7. Prior to this, Hitler had given Goring jurisdiction over foreign exchange in 1938, weakening Schacht's capabilities at the bank. Yet, these disagreements most probably saved Schacht's life since he was one of only three Nazis not executed following the Nuremberg trials on account of his later opposition to the Nazis.

8. In line with the discourse in chapter 7, the National Bank is regarded as a semi-state institution for purposes of the case studies of Germany and the UK.

9. Marx used the phrase semi-state institution to depict the Bank of England (Marx [1894] 1981: 675).

10. The Americans preferred a decentralized model whereas the British were in favor of a centralized one. Yet, either way, the new BDL was not permitted to lend to business directly unlike the Reichsbank and the monies to be provided for zone government deficit purposes were subject to strict limitations (Marsh 1993).

11. Karl Bernard was appointed as president of the *Zentralbankrat* and Wilhelm Vocke was appointed as president of the directorate. Both men served until the establishment of the Bundesbank in 1957 (Marsh 1993)

12. They reduced it again to 4% in 1949 (Marsh 1993)

13. In 1950, following the Korean War increased domestic spending also led to a large balance of payment deficit and Germany reached its credit quota within the European Payments Union (established with $350 million Marshall Plan money in 1950 for European trade payments). The BDL responded by increasing the discount

rate from 4% to 6% and by 1952 the *Wirtschaftswunder* of trade surpluses had begun (Ishizaka 1999).

14. Currency reform, as Buchheim explained, was unlikely to have occurred without the German authorities being able to distance themselves from the decision by claiming it was imposed (Buchheim 1999: 80).

15. Some of Third Reich and interbank financial obligations were simply canceled (Pontzen 2008: 149).

16. The policy was also used at the time of German reunification in 1990 (Pontzen 2008: 152).

17. The Americans wanted the BDL to have more control over credit creation in the bank system (Marsh 1993).

18. The discount rate is the cheaper form of refinancing for the banking sector, but subject to quantitative restriction, whereas the Lombard rate (with security) is higher but without a limit on issues (Baltensperger 1999: 452). The Lombard rate acts as a "cap" on the interbank money market rates that exist and, is normally 0.5% higher than the discount rate (Kaen 1997: 3).

19. The national banks of member countries were able to exchange any dollar reserve currency for gold at a set rate of $35 per ounce and, had a responsibility to maintain fixed exchange rates with other members (within a 1% band), except in situations of severe imbalances. In such instances, revaluation/devaluation could be negotiated among BW members. Although the BW regime restricted the BDL (and the ABC), the exchange-rate system still represented a *state*-managed multilateral agreement and was, therefore, evidence of *state* financial sovereignty (albeit in an interstate sense) over the exchange-value of the currency.

20. In the meantime (1953) the London Debt Agreement had also marked down 50% of the interwar reparations due and rescheduled the remainder (Guinnane 2004).

21. The public bank networks manage 40% of total assets in the German financial system (Hufner 2010: 7).

22. The figures are for 2010 (Hufner 2010). The impact on credit allocation decisions, therefore, will be different to that of profit-making financial institutions.

23. Still others, such as Fohlin, suggest that this has been overestimated (Fohlin 2007).

24. The reserve requirement deposits attract no interest.

25. In 1980 repurchase agreements represented 6% of central bank money, rising to 60% by 1989 and over 70% in the 1990s (Baltensperger 1999: 453).

26. The particular nature of the weekly tender (and bid) process for repurchase agreements in Germany implies a measure of market involvement with the setting of repo rates (Franke 1999: 242).

27. Since it took Germany three years to develop monetary targeting they were clearly not in haste (Mishkin 1997: 21).

28. This was particularly evident in a general *culture* of wage restraint that existed in post-WW2 Germany.

29. The key to DB monetary-target longevity was their flexibility of implementation, allowing for big overshootings and undershootings of target, for instance, when

prioritising short-term policy considerations. Mishkin and Posen also note that targets were useful in restraining prices (Mishkin 1997: 31).

30. Germany had introduced the convertibility of the Dm in 1958, and their exchange controls, as Pontzen and Schobert note, were not *too* restrictive since they were keen to engage in trade and wanted scope for capital outflows (Pontzen 2008: 158).

31. The Dm was, however, revalued by 5% in 1961 (Pontzen 2008: 156). The alternative inflationary policies were not acceptable to the DB given the experience of the 1923 inflation.

32. The reality of this loss of financial sovereignty, in terms of currency value, was experienced by the UK during the exchange rate mechanism crisis of 1992 (Potts 1997).

33. The exchange-rate stability was aided, by a culture of wage restraint and relatively lower inflation.

34. It is worth noting that the payment and information systems operated by the DB, in conjunction with decision-making autonomy established by the allies, have all contributed toward the general state capabilities.

35. Lavoie has also pointed out that the commercial banks, during the neo-liberal era, have also lobbied the state for the virtual removal of all reserve requirements for the same profit motive (Lavoie 2012).

36. The recent global financial, and Eurozone national debt, crises are likely to have strengthened arguments supporting the traditional German philosophy toward finance and public banking in general.

Chapter 10

UK Monetary Policy

10.1 INTRODUCTION

This chapter reviews the operation of UK monetary policy 1931–2007. The aim is to explore the extent to which the state has lost sovereignty in the exercise and capability of impacting money-creation and its purchasing power. In the opening section there is a review of the historical foundations of UK state monetary policy, from the mercantilist capitalist era to WW2. In the next section the procedures, institutions and protocols of UK monetary policy operation in the period are presented. Next, there is an outline of the ideological foundations that have underpinned decision-making in UK monetary policy. This is followed by a section that examines the BW era until 1973, in terms of the UK state's capability to impact credit creation and inflation levels, followed by a section that considers the relative proportions of narrow and broad money and their effect on state financial sovereignty. Next, there is a review of the neo-liberal era from 1974 to 2007, in terms of state capability to impact credit and inflation. In the final section, there is an exploration of the ability of the state to impact exchange-rate values. During the years studied there was substantial change in the UK financial system, in terms of intermediation and the growth of securitization. Banks are now much larger, offer a greater range of services to consumers and nonfinancial corporations (so-called nonbanks) also provide retail banking services. In addition, the deregulation process has facilitated a blurred distinction between retail and investment banking. Financial innovation, especially complex derivatives, has also complicated the finance sector to the extent that many financial markets appear remote from the monies that actually engage with the real economy. Recent IT growth has also greatly transformed the whole financial sector.

After the abandonment of the gold standard in 1931, as Collins noted, a closer cooperation between the UK Treasury and BOE had developed (Collins 2012). In the BW era, 1945–1973, direct UK state controls on financial institution's lending were implemented. These included limits on overall credit levels and rationing of mortgages and hire purchase. Governments relied heavily on the persuasion of the financial sector and, capital/exchange controls were also applied in order to comply with the international BW regime.[1] In the 1970s, more attention was paid to monetary policy and in 1971, with the Competition and Credit Control Act, a more *market*-related approach was adopted. Quantitative lending limits were removed and (exogenous) interest base rates were given prominence. In 1973, however, driven by inflation concerns, the Supplementary Special Deposit Scheme (Corset) was used to restrict excessive credit creation. In 1979, broad monetary targets were set, according to a medium term financial strategy (MTFS). This was abandoned in 1983, due to operational difficulties, in favor of narrow-money targeting. In the 1990s the policy emphasis shifted toward inflation targeting, which defined UK monetary policy until the end of the case-study period. Internationally, the dollar became established as the principal reserve currency existing during the case-study period, thus affecting the operation of UK monetary policy.[2] In addition, European monetary *et al.* integration has also been a significant influence on UK policy. The chapter begins with a brief historical, legal and ideological review, in order to establish the UK financial system context; these abovementioned policies *inter alia* are then reviewed in order to explore the questions under investigation in the book.

10.2 HISTORICAL CONTEXT

Britain was the first of the current industrialized nations to move away from silver-backed currencies, to establish a *de facto* gold (specie) standard, when Sir Isaac Newton changed the silver-gold mint ratio, effectively devaluing silver, in 1717. In 1821, the UK state formalized its (state) acceptance of this gold specie standard, following the production of the gold sovereign in 1816 (Cooper 1982). In 1833, the BOE's convertible notes were established as *legal tender*, with the discouragement of note-issuance from other banks. Finally, in 1844, the BOE was given sole responsibility for note issue and, their notes were *fully* backed by gold stored in the vaults. At this juncture, the state had consolidated its jurisdiction over the creation and, therefore, the level of the circulating medium and, by implication, was able to influence its domestic value albeit dependent on reserves.[3] Internationally, the gold exchange standard mechanisms ensured, albeit imperfectly, that parities were maintained by specie flows and relative price changes.[4] The global influence of sterling was enhanced with the growth of the British Empire and its trading relations, and this continued until WW1 when *de facto* convertibility was suspended.[5] The war financing needs, as Hawtrey noted, were simply too large to sustain convertibility (Hawtrey 1919: 431). Simultaneously, the US dollar began to achieve preeminence as the new twentieth century progressed.[6] After the war, Britain returned unsuccessfully to gold convertibility with the British Gold Standard Act 1925 (Cooper 1982). This differed from the specie standard since gold coins were not circulated and, convertibility (at the fixed rate) was only possible in exchange for gold bars containing at least 400 ounces.[7] Winston Churchill, as chancellor, had insisted, arguably in error, to set the gold-sterling ratio at its overvalued pre-WW1 level. This placed stress on the ability of Britain to maintain international competitiveness and, with the onset of the depression, led to declining shares of global trade, deficits and an outflow of gold. As a consequence, the gold standard was abandoned in 1931. During WW2, Britain continued to experience an outflow of gold, and increased US debt obligations, in order to finance the resource needs of the war. At the BW negotiations, therefore, America emerged as international creditor, with 59% of *official* gold reserves, with substantial political capital to achieve their objectives (Cooper 1982: 21). In some sense, therefore, UK state autonomous financial power was limited at the outset of our case-study period, since Britain had insufficient gold to be able to restore its own gold standard. In addition, the BOE, despite the 1946 Nationalization Act, remained autonomous. Notwithstanding, the BW era (1945–1973) represented a time of economic management for the *nation-state* in monetary matters and the general economy, inspired by Keynes, though some financial sovereignty over exchange rates and to some extent inflation was also shared between BW members.

10.3 UK MONETARY JURISDICTION

The formalized structure for UK monetary policy decision-making, from the BW to neo-liberal era, was somewhat ambiguous and is outlined in this section. The creation and value-management of *money*, as stated in chapter 1, has historically been determined by state *and* market in varying proportions, depending on context, although the UK capitalist state and its economy has been predominantly served by a *private* banking system since the feudal tally-stick system, albeit tempered by the state jurisdiction.[8] The BOE can be considered as a state (or semi-state) institution that, since it is charged with authority to make executive decisions regarding monetary policy, interacts with and presides over a private grouping of licensed banks. Yet, under the 1946 BOE Act, any BOE recommendations to the banks were subject to Treasury approval (Burnham 2007: 399). In addition, as Burnham notes the

Treasury held (at least in theory) powers to "direct" the BOE, after "consultation" with the Governor (Clause 4 [1] BOE Act 1946), even though it was clear that *both* of these executive function powers, in terms of decision-making and implementation, resided with the BOE in practice (Burnham 2007: 399).[9] This was contrary to the original policy objective of the Ramsey Macdonald government for BOE nationalization and the 1945 Labour Party manifesto, which intended that "the Bank of England, with its financial powers, must be brought under public ownership, and the operation of other banks harmonized with industrial needs" (Burnham 2007: 397). It is ironic therefore, as Burnham further notes, that when the BOE was granted independence in monetary policy in 1998 (BOE Act), one of the main rationales posited was the need to "end [the virtually non-existent] *my emphasis* political interference" in monetary policy-making (Burnham 2007: 396). Treasury/BOE relations are crucial to appreciating the operation of UK *state* financial capabilities in the case study. The separate vested interests of different parts of the state for example, BOE officials, Treasury officials, and political incumbents, collectively termed the *state* financial authorities, may converge or not at any particular point in time, and relations may be strained or harmonious. However, in the consideration of the any loss of state financial power in this book I have assumed for simplicity that internal political struggles are completed. In other words, the BOE is viewed as in receipt of authority to conduct the affairs of state, with their privileged relations with the private banks, in *conjunction* with the Treasury that, in turn, is viewed as the financial arm of the prevailing government as executor of state affairs. The specific Treasury/BOE relations can be compared with ministerial relations with departmental officials, as transient politicians and permanent career bureaucrats respectively. One group represents the current driver of state affairs and the other simply represents their continuity. Yet, together they constituted the elements of the UK state regulatory and monetary policy operations in the financial sector.

10.4 IDEOLOGICAL ENVIRONMENT

The monetary policies pursued during the case-study period had political/ideological underpinnings and these are now outlined. The classical view of the QTM (i.e., $MV = PQ$) as stated by Fisher, with a stable Q determined by supply-side factors such as technology or labor force size and a stable V leaving independent variable M to directly impact P, remained dominant in the 1930s before being superseded by the hybrid *Keynesian* synthesis at the outset of the post-WW2 period.[10] It was no longer accepted that the economy would equilibrate at the full employment level and, since (as Dimsdale noted) wealth-holders would have liquidity preference if they expected interest rates to rise, with capital losses to bondholders, this speculation would make it more difficult to adjust interest rates to impact investment levels (Dimsdale 1991: 90).[11] Keynes had advocated, therefore, fiscal measures to supplement his monetary debt-management proposals in order to stimulate the economy. The *synthesis* followers, however (as Dimsdale noted), took this one stage further, in contrast to Keynes, and argued that investment was unresponsive to interest rates as a general rule (Dimsdale 1991: 91).

The monetarist challenge, in the form of Friedman, appeared in the late sixties and argued for a return to an emphasis on monetary policy. This was predicated on the belief that the demand for money, thus the velocity of circulation, was stable and that causation ran from money to price rather than vice versa. In addition, fiscal policy was seen to increase public expenditure financed by bonds, raising interest rates, and "crowding out" private investment (Dimsdale 1991). This assumes that the bond market influences market interest rates. As a consequence, instead of focusing on nominal interest rates, Friedman argued for monitoring the monetary aggregates and increasing the money supply in tandem with real output growth. In the seventies, these ideas were further advanced with the neoclassical school notion of *rational expectations.* With the assumption of flexible wages and prices, an increase of aggregate demand would, after a temporary increase in output, simply be reflected in higher prices. These ideas, as Dimsdale notes, were the major influence on monetary policies adopted in the 1970s and 1980s (Dimsdale 1991: 92). Neoclassical ideas continued to dominate monetary policy for the remainder of the case-study period, although the emphasis turned from monetary aggregates to narrow money considerations and then, in the 1990s, toward the use of interest rates to target inflation.[12]

Internationally, the state-driven BW regime, negotiated in 1944, required a monetary policy that was conducive to the maintenance of agreed exchange rate parities.[13] As the BW system collapsed and floating exchange rates were adopted in 1973, monetary policy *per se* became more effective. Lower interest rates could devalue the currency and lead to export growth, thus raising output providing that inflation was avoided. Yet, as Dimsdale noted, monetarists and then neoclassicals argued that such action would lower exchange rates but leave *real* rates unchanged, as rates adjusted with inflation (Dimsdale 1991: 92). These latter ideas persisted in policy-making circles throughout the neo-liberal era.

10.5 THE BRETTON WOODS ERA

In the BW regime, exchange-rate parity requirements meant that capital/exchange controls were employed to maintain monetary policy effectiveness.[14] In addition, a complex array of exchange controls on the pound existed in the *Sterling Area*. The area instigated in 1939 consisted of mainly colonial sterling users, or countries pegged to sterling, holding balances in London. In the 1960s, as increased capital mobility for example, the Eurodollar market began to emerge, capital/exchange controls became problematic. If the BOE practiced open market operations, and expanded the money supply, this would lead to lower interest rates than other countries and capital outflow. The reduction in reserves would then be necessary, to purchase domestic currency, in order to maintain exchange parities. Subsequently, interest rates would need to rise to protect the level of reserves (Dimsdale 1991).

In order to appreciate the changing financial role of the UK state at this time, in terms of the creation and management of sterling, it is necessary to examine the operation of the sterling money markets. In this early BW period (prior to 1971) the financial authorities were responsible for setting the *Bank Rate* when lending to members of the discount market, and they also bought and issued treasury bills and gilts with the same market in open market operations to ensure balance in the system. Since the interbank market did not develop until the 1960s, the *Bank Rate*, lent to the discount market against security, was the *de facto* reference point used by the London Clearing Banks for the rate paid on deposits and charged on advances. This was instrumental in the level of credit creation (Bank of England 2012). This, as a consequence, gave the BOE a measure of control over the level of credit creation overall and, by extension, a measure of control over the *value* of money.

So, in the late 1940s and 1950s, the state sought to control the level and direction of bank advances (Bank of England 2012). The policy of guiding credit allocation permits the financial authorities to promote the development of sectors that is considered to be in the national interest.[15] This was viewed as particularly important during the immediate reconstruction post-WW2. In addition, during the 1950s, the British government sought to limit bank credit, as a form of demand management, through *appealing* to the banking sector for restraint. This action avoided the necessity of raising interest rates to combat inflationary pressures (Ross 1992).[16] Since the key economic concerns for the state in these years were inflation, trade deficits and the maintenance of fixed exchange rates this was perhaps an appropriate policy. In 1945, the National Debt Enquiry Committee had, following Keynes, led to a UK state cheap money policy that maintained the *Bank Rate* at 2% and long-term rates at 3% (Dimsdale 1991: 98).[17] In 1951, the new Conservative administration adopted a monetary strategy to raise short-term interest rates, discontinue the wartime practice of BOE willingness to provide cash to discount houses at 0.5% interest, and impose restrictions on hire-purchase companies.[18] In addition, they issued statements that expressed the need of banks to restrict credit (Ross 1992: 200). They repeated these persuasions in 1955, culminating with Macmillan as Chancellor, in July 1956, calling the bank decision-makers to a meeting.[19] The previous Atlee government, conversely, had failed to achieve credit ceilings on advances in 1948–1949, due to opposition from BOE officials. Notwithstanding, the evidence taken from British Bankers Association data reveals a successful reduction in advances on both occasions in the 1950s (Ross 1992: 201). In addition, the Association of British Chamber of Commerce report to the Radcliffe committee observed that banks were also allocating credit in the directions desired by the government (Ross 1992: 203).[20] Figures 10.1 and 10.2 illustrate these findings. This is *prima facie* evidence, I argue here, of the UK state capability to influence inflationary or deflationary conditions through the regulation of the credit-money supply. In Figure 10.1, immediately following the government interventions of 1951 and 1955, the level of bank advances fell. The UK inflation levels were also noticeably reduced (see Figure 10.6) after the same interventions. In Figure 10.2 the government approved advances, such as activities favored by government for example, manufacturing, are contrasted as percentages of overall lending with advances for purposes deemed as either inflationary or harmful to the balance of payments for example, retail. The remaining credit was viewed to have a neutral impact (Ross 1992: 202).

The UK government also sought to limit the issue of banknotes during the period, in order to secure a measure of control of narrow money and subsequent credit advances, since the banks needed to ensure adequate

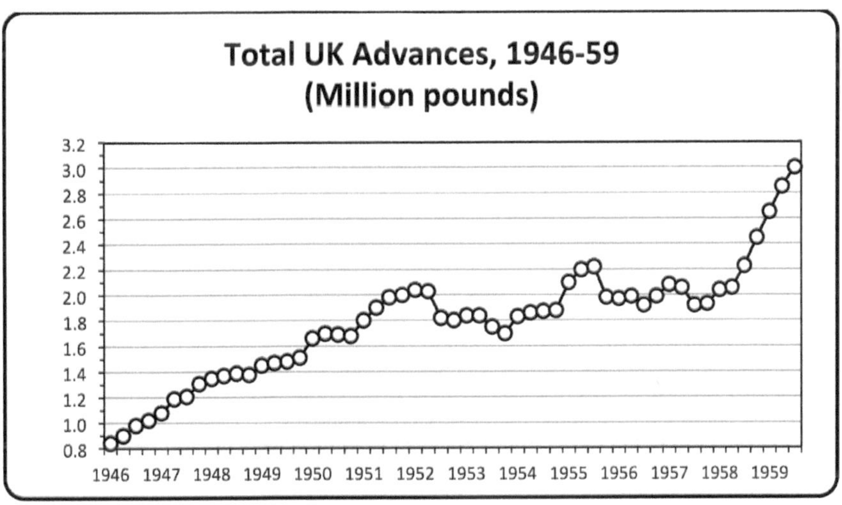

Figure 10.1 UK Total Advances.

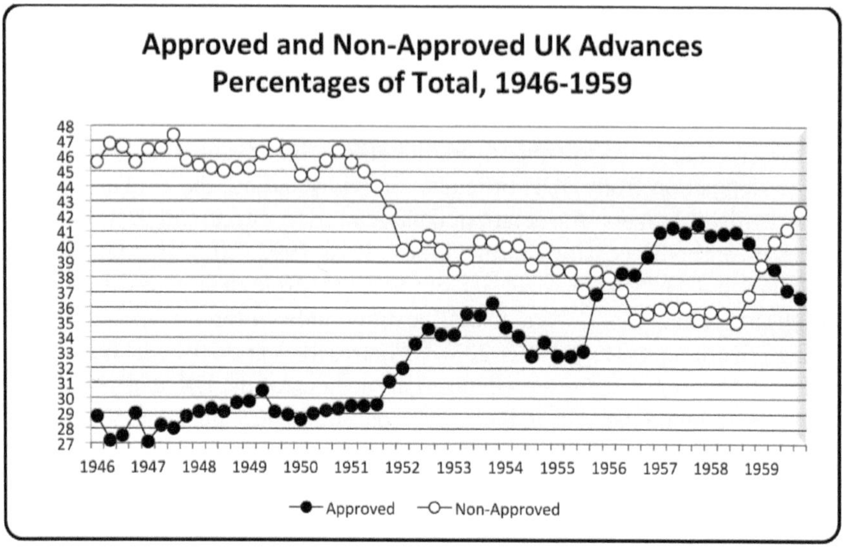

Figure 10.2 UK Approved Advances.

liquidity and cash. The Currency and Bank Notes Act 1939 had limited notes to £300 million and, the later Currency and Bank Notes Act 1954 increased this to £1575 million with some flexibility (Capie 2010: 60). In addition, the Capital Issues Committee, that monitored the raising of business capital until 1967, also afforded the state some measure of control over the creation of credit volumes (Wadsworth 1973: 205).[21] Though, this depended on the extent to which investments in shares or corporate bonds were financed by the provision of credit.

The state also exerted control of credit creation with the existence of the liquidity ratio, in the form of notes, coins, money at call, treasury bills and reserve balances as a proportion of their loan book. There was also a cash reserve ratio, which private banks were obliged to maintain. The cash ratio was mandatory and had been set at 8% in 1946, and the liquidity ratio was set at 25% (Dimsdale 1991: 98).[22] This liquidity ratio was now less than the wartime 30% since the authorities were keen to reduce the amount of liquidity in the system that had resulted from the war. They introduced so-called *Treasury Deposit Receipts* (TDR's) in 1945, paying 0.5% interest, in order to absorb the excess liquidity that were not counted as part of a bank's liquid assets. In 1946, these constituted 29% of total bank deposits in contrast to the 17.4% of deposits advanced as credit (Dimsdale 1991: 98). The banks had hoped to reduce these less profitable TDR's, in favor of expanding advances, but were compliant with the wishes of government for constraint. In order to mitigate the need for credit ceilings, the government also introduced *Special*

Deposits held at the BOE in 1958, called at their discretion, which earned interest but did not count as liquid reserves. This further regulated lending levels. So, during the 1940s and 1950s, the UK state manifested a considerable amount of financial sovereignty over the issue and value of money, through a range of measures that regulated the banking system's ability to create credit monies.

In terms of the exchange rate of the pound during this period, it is important to note that Britain remained the main reserve currency at the outset. In 1950, for example, more than 55% of the world's reserves were still held in sterling (Mushin 2012).[23] The international monetary order had been established at Bretton Woods, with the intention to prevent a repeat of the collapse of trade and competitive devaluation of the 1930s. The dollar, as the anchor currency, was convertible to gold at a fixed $35 per ounce by member national banks and, member states had a fixed (albeit adjustable under certain conditions) exchange rate with the dollar. Capital and exchange controls, combined with open market operations, were expected to ensure that individual member states were able to maintain their dollar parities. The existence of the Sterling Area and BW arrangements *per se*, are *prima facie* examples of a strong financial state through the *effective* regulation of exchange rates. Figure 10.3 is a cursory indicator of the (albeit latent) capability of the UK state to conduct open market operations and, therefore, impact exchange-value during the case-study period. In the early BW years, for instance, there was a dollar shortage reflected in the lower reserves, mitigated in part by the Marshall Plan and the dollar pool within the Sterling Area. The shortage was due *inter alia* to the current account surplus of the US, prior to 1958, and the

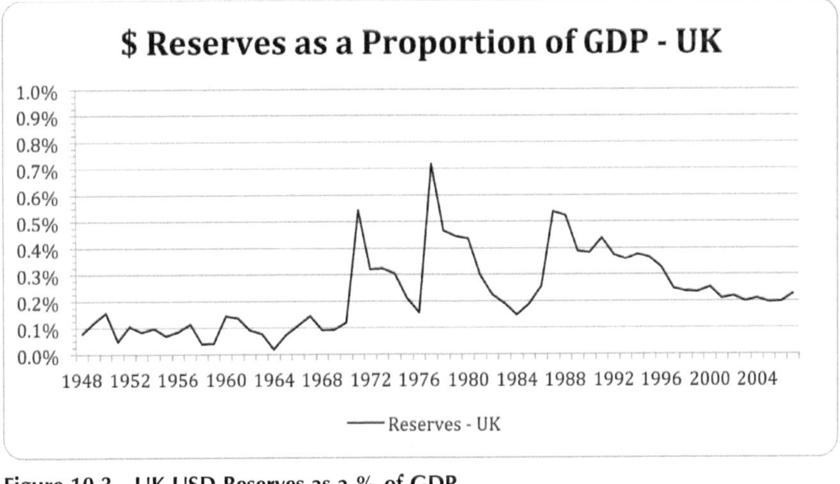

Figure 10.3 UK USD Reserves as a % of GDP.

increasing dollar denomination of internationally traded commodities. Yet, notwithstanding the two devaluations in 1949 and 1967, the UK state managed to maintain BW dollar parity (see later Figure 10.7) reasonably well.

The failure of the so-called *Robot* plan in 1952 further illustrated the capabilities of the state, or at least international power relations, in blocking the proposal to extend the financial power of the market, even though the plan had been originally hatched by state Treasury and BOE officials, albeit with strong market links. Their aim had been to immediately restore sterling convertibility, though not extended to individuals, restrict sterling balances held in London and allow the currency to float (Cairncross 1995: 122). The plan instigators feared another devaluation of sterling, after the experience of 1949, since the UK state might have insufficient reserves to defend the currency and this would mean loss of competitiveness for UK manufacturing exporters in the meantime.[24] It is most likely that the need to maintain the US-driven BW monetary order was a key factor in the plan's rejection and, also that the BW fixed rate regime was much more consistent with the Keynesian synthesis thinking that had become established in UK policy-making circles.[25] The later Radcliffe committee on UK monetary policy practice, appointed in 1957, had also advocated these synthesis ideas, despite some of their policy prescriptions being ignored at the outset of the report findings.[26]

During the early 1960s the financial markets grew in volume and, many international banks were established in London (Buckle 2004: 204). The rising size of the interbank market as a market for loanable funds, in particular, had implications for the financial capability of the state since market interest rates and thus the market now increasingly determined lending levels.[27] Banks with new deposits that were not facing an immediate demand for a loan could place a deposit on the interbank market and earn interest. Interest rates (note Figure 10.4) were, in general, lower than base rates and these represented efficiency savings for the banks. In addition, new forms of financial intermediaries, so-called nonbanks, appeared. These nonbanks, without settlement accounts at the BOE, were able to access finance from the money markets and did not have to conform to the regulatory requirements imposed on the traditional banks. These financial intermediaries then became substantial contributors to overall credit-money levels. Yet, as a result of an overvalued pound in the mid-1960s the authorities exerted monetary restraint, prior to the 1967 devaluation, through the use of Special Deposit requirements, overall credit ceilings and hire purchase constraints (Dimsdale 1991: 110). The Keynes synthesis still prevailed, Capie notes, since the state assumed that restricting the money supply would alter the structure of interest rates but have minimal impact on investment (Capie 2010). The higher rates would simply strengthen the currency.

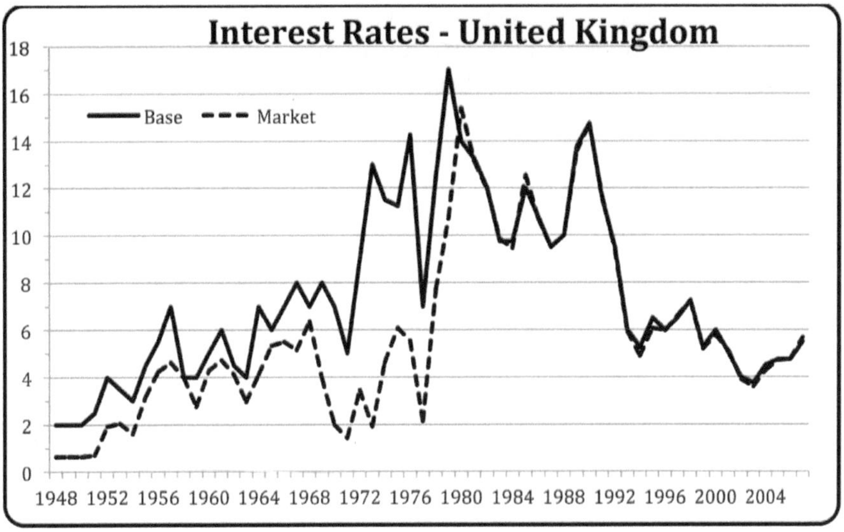

Figure 10.4 UK Interest Rates.

As the 1960s drew to a close the BW system was also experiencing strain as the US current account deficits grew, surplus countries such as Germany and Japan were often reluctant to revalue, and the *market* confidence in the dollar waned.[28] The pressures were exacerbated by the growth of the Eurodollar market and the enhanced opportunities for currency speculation, which circumnavigated capital controls of BW members, following full sterling convertibility in 1958. Eurodollars, USD's held in Europe, had emerged in the 1950s after the Russians had deposited large quantities of USD's in the UK.[29] International banks with wholesale dollars soon found that their gains in intermediation efficiency, such as no reserve or retail deposit insurance requirements, enabled them to lend and take deposits with lower and higher interest rates respectively.[30] The necessary adjustment of BW exchange rates became increasingly problematic as capital flows, speculation, inflation and current account differentials continued. These culminated in the Nixon-instigated end of USD gold convertibility to gold in 1971 and, finally, the end of the BW fixed exchange rates in 1973. Notwithstanding the measures taken by the UK state in monitoring credit levels from 1965 to 1971, therefore, the collapse of BW represented a waning of state financial sovereignty over exchange-rate value at least, and the start of new era.

In the period from 1948 to the late 1960s, as stated earlier, the bank rate was more deterministic in respect of any interbank rates that existed, supporting the earlier discussion of the UK state capability to guide credit levels. Yet, from the late 1960s onward, a divergence between the rates emerged reflects a loss of state sovereignty over money-creation and overall supply. The reaction to inflation in the 1970s, it is posited in the book, is the likely cause of the divergence between base and market rates during this period. At the end of the 1970s, however, with monetary aggregate and later interest rate and/or MB control, the rates began to converge. Yet, while this might, at first glance, indicate an *increase* in state manifested capability to affect market rates, the monetary policy ideology that existed since 1971 had instead emphasized the significance of *observing* market rates of interest as a guide for policy-making. Open market operations to regulate commercial bank liquidity, therefore, are likely to have been directed toward an interest rate target largely determined by market forces. In any case, the growth of the M3/M4 money supply since 1971 (see Figure 10.5) indicates an enhanced market capability to provide for an expansion of credit that was, in turn, fully accommodated by the state and banking system.

10.6 NARROW AND BROAD MONEY

The size of the monetary base, in comparison to the level of overall credit monies, is also an indication of the extent to which the state is able to influence the issue of currency *per se* and, implicitly, the value of money. This is predicated on the idea that the state determines the *conditions* under which changes in the composition and volume of narrow money are provided through their intervention in the money markets, supply of banknotes and

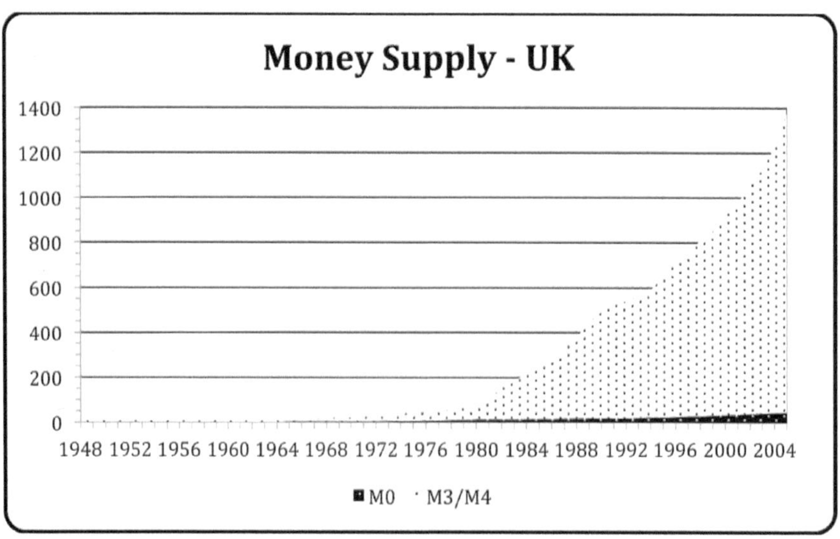

Figure 10.5 UK Money Supply.

the regulation of settlement bank reserve accounts. Figure 10.5 illustrates that, during the case-study period, the supply of credit monies has been substantially increased in the post-BW era (the measures are exaggerated from 1982 onward, since the data utilized switches from M3 to M4 monetary aggregates). M3 is inclusive of narrow money, sight/time deposits, repurchase agreements and debt securities of less than two years maturity. The M4 monetary aggregate is the same but includes foreign currency deposits held by the private sector in the UK banking system, and the sterling and foreign currency deposits of UK public corporations held in the UK. In the tables that precede Figure 10.5 (Tables 10.1 and 10.2) the ratio of narrow money

Table 10.1 UK Ratio of M0 to M3

1948	0.23	1965	0.25
1949	0.22	1966	0.25
1950	0.21	1967	0.25
1951	0.21	1968	0.25
1952	0.22	1969	0.26
1953	0.22	1970	0.27
1954	0.23	1971	0.25
1955	0.23	1972	0.21
1956	0.25	1973	0.21
1957	0.25	1974	0.20
1958	0.26	1975	0.21
1959	0.26	1976	0.21
1960	0.26	1977	0.23
1961	0.26	1978	0.22
1962	0.26	1979	0.22
1963	0.25	1980	0.21
1964	0.25	1981	0.18

Author's Calculations based on data from Capie and Webber (1985).

Table 10.2 UK Ratio of Narrow Money M0 to M4

1982	0.08	1994	0.04
1983	0.08	1995	0.04
1984	0.07	1996	0.04
1985	0.07	1997	0.04
1986	0.06	1998	0.04
1987	0.05	1999	0.04
1988	0.05	2000	0.04
1989	0.04	2001	0.04
1990	0.04	2002	0.04
1991	0.04	2003	0.04
1992	0.04	2004	0.04
1993	0.04	2005	0.04

Author's Calculations Based on Data From IMF *International Financial Statistics* (2015a), IFS tables 19MC-ZF (M0) and 59MD-ZF (M4).

to M3/M4 is presented. The base money ratio remains reasonably consistent during the BW era, whereas in the post-BW period a distinct fall in the proportion of base money to credit deposit monies has taken place (mitigated by the use of the M4 measure) suggesting that since BW there has been a clear erosion of state sovereignty.

10.7 THE POST-BRETTON WOODS ERA

The year 1971 marked a distinct change in the direction of UK monetary policy, with the introduction of reforms known as *Competition and Credit Control*. The BOE had relied too heavily on the restriction of bank lending (then being criticized) that was imposed on the *settlement* banks in the 1960s, thus encouraging the growth of unregulated nonbank financial intermediation. One of the other concerns for the authorities, as the Radcliffe committee had noted was the BOE needed to regain some state control over the credit creation process that had been lost, as a result of the recent ineffectiveness of the liquid asset and cash ratio (Dimsdale 1991: 115).[31] The ratio, alongside the bank rate, was the means by which assuming credit could be restrained by the BOE, assuming there are no direct controls.[32] Some success was achieved in the 1960s by the BOE funding the short-term debt (treasury bills) and increasing the long-term gilts thus reducing liquidity but, as private bank holdings of *commercial* bills *increased* in the sector as a whole, the liquid assets simply contained a higher proportion of private bills. This was problematic since, in addition to the growth of unregulated financial intermediation, settlement bank liquidity remained high and the level of bank advances remained unrestricted by the liquidity ratio. In response to this, from the mid-1960s onward, as stated, credit ceilings had been introduced. The year 1971 thus marked a divergence from the policy-culture, noted by Hodgman, of "informal but binding" regulation of credit levels, credit allocation and interest rates, which had prevailed between the state, private banks and discount houses in the 1950s and early 1960s (Hodgman 1973: 143). The traditional influence of the UK monetary authorities, that had extended to deposit/lending interest rates, call money (between banks and the discount houses) rates, commercial paper discount rates and Treasury bill bids, was beginning to wane, as the state was now less able to determine *market* interest rates.

The 1971 reforms were predicated on the view that the instruments of monetary policy required an overhaul and, that any policies should be extended to all financial intermediaries. One of the ideas driving this shift in thinking was the perceived need to foster more competition between banks. A *de facto* private cartel for setting interest rates and charges, albeit correlated to the BOE bank rate, had existed since the time of WW1 that was now considered to be detrimental to the efficiency of the marketplace (Dimsdale 1991: 118).[33] Competition between banks for deposits, and between their interest rates offered, was therefore to be encouraged. The raft of new policies introduced also included the elimination of credit ceilings replacing the 28% liquidity ratio with a 12.5% *reserve asset* ratio of bank liabilities, where eligible assets utilized were clearly defined by the BOE, for *all* banks and (in 1972) the formation of a new *Minimum Lending Rate* (MLR) which varied with the Treasury bill rate (Cairncross 1995: 190).[34] This meant, in practice, that the MLR was now *more* driven by *market* forces instead of the more political considerations that underpinned the bank rate, representing a loss of financial sovereignty.[35] This was mitigated, however, by the monetary authority's requirement for the clearing banks to maintain 1.5% of their eligible liabilities in non-interest bearing deposits at the BOE, the *continued* use of special deposits, that could now be called from all banks, and a 10% reserve asset ratio that was given to the hire purchase finance houses to maintain balance sheet health.

Yet, despite these measures the new market-based policies, perhaps expectedly, soon led to a sharp expansion of credit and *less* state control over credit creation in spite of the good intentions of the instigators. Cairncross noted, for example, that while between 1963 and 1972, bank lending grew at approximately 12% per annum while, in 1972, it increased by 37% and, in 1973, by 43% (Cairncross 1995: 191). Banks had become competitive in attracting deposits, and were successful, which enabled easier attainment of reserve targets and thus advances continued unabated. An immediately observed feature of this increase of money supply was its correlation to the inflation of the early 1970s, thus adding weight to the emerging (albeit latent) monetarist doctrine.[36] As the decade progressed, inflation worsened and, consequently, interest rates began to soar. The state authorities responded with calls for special deposits and eventually, in 1973, with quantitative credit restrictions. In addition, in 1973, the so-called *corset* was introduced (Supplementary Special Deposit Scheme) that imposed penalties on banks whenever their liabilities expanded faster than the authority-determined desired rate and remained in force until 1980 (Dimsdale 1991: 24).[37] Yet, there was mixed success in the control of credit creation by the authorities. Banks avoided the restriction of the corset by the process of disintermediation, this involved accepting bills and then selling them on to the nonbanks, that was off balance sheet (Argy 1994: 490).[38] The interbank money market had also substantially grown in size since its appearance in the 1960s and was increasingly constituted from deposits by commercial enterprises. This gave the banking system more scope to be able to manage liquidity and provide credit on demand.

After 1973, the authorities increasingly turned their attention toward monetary aggregate control due, in part, to persistent inflation, the failure to contain union pay demands and the rise of monetarist ideology. The notion of *rational expectations*, for instance, with its proposition that attempts to reduce unemployment would simply raise inflation and leave employment unchanged questioning the Phillips curve, had been gaining ground (Mishkin 2007: 3).[39] These monetarist policies, later advocated by proponents such as Walters, Pepper and Griffiths *et al.*, were predicated on the QTM and mainstream money-multiplier theory, where credit-induced deposits are extended by a multiplication of the inverse of the reserve asset ratio (Hotson 2010: 19).[40] In response, the UK authorities reasoned that the adoption of a monetary target would serve to create lower inflation expectations and achieve price stability, even without any sanctions. The Wilson government first adopted informal targets for M3 in 1973 (Mishkin 2007: 4). Yet, it was the onset of the sterling crisis in 1976 with its $3.9 billion IMF loan that led Healey to *publish* a monetary target that was intended to not exceed nominal income, though there was no predetermined monetary policy to be activated in the event of an overshoot (Hotson 2010: 14). In later years, Denis Healey, though recognizing his growing awareness of the significance of monetary factors at the time, was keen to distance himself from the monetarist doctrine claiming he had simply aimed to "placate the financial markets" with the publication of aggregate monetary targets (Hotson 2010: 9). The aim to reduce money supply growth in relation to nominal income was a clear part of the Labor administration's strategy to reduce inflation from 1976. Their flexible and somewhat indifferent approach to monetary targets continued until 1979.

In 1979, conversely, the new Thatcher government adopted a more proactive and strict MTFS for money targets, based on the ideas of Friedman. However, as a policy instrument in the UK, strict money-aggregate targeting was short lived, ending in 1981.[41] The key problem was the dependency on the belief in a strong correlation between money supply and inflation and (as noted in chapter 2), that the direction of causation ran from money to price. In practice (in 1979–1981), the relation between the two variables became increasingly difficult to identify even if the mainstream conception of causation was accepted. This may have been due to time lags or, as Mishkin noted, the tendency for the BOE to *change* the initial starting point for calculation when it suited them (Mishkin 2007: 5). Notwithstanding, the monetarist experiment was perhaps evidence of the *intention* of the state to determine the credit-money supply, in response to the inflation of the 1979. Yet, the post-BW era had a different set of monetary conditions. In reality this manifested, as discussed above, in a 1970s (financial) marketplace that was *more* able to circumnavigate monetary-reserve regulation and issue credit in response to demand in the manner described by the EMT in chapter 4. However, while 1973–1981 ostensibly represented a period of inadequate inflation and credit control by the authorities, this is mitigated by the prevalence of externally driven primary product inflation, especially oil in 1973 and 1979, which was simply coincidental. It is also important to recognize the significance of imported inflation even though it makes the task of identifying the erosion of sovereignty difficult.

The 1981–1987 period, which followed this era, was marked, conversely, by a more flexible approach to multiple monetary targets (Hotson 2010: 26). The initial enthusiasm for targets had waned and the authorities (in 1983) began to focus on narrow-money targeting, in order to control the overall level of credit and inflation.[42] In the UK, most probably as a consequence of the early 1980s recession rather than monetary constraint *per se*, inflation had now been tamed. It is apparent, however, that many factors contributed to this, not least of which was the abolition of national collective bargaining in the UK. In addition, policies based on the notion of the non-accelerating rate of unemployment (NAIRU), or so-called *natural rate*, meant that expected unemployment fears also had a mitigating effect on wage claims. In the early Thatcher years, the authorities also reduced the PSBR in order to check monetary growth, further creating deflationary conditions.[43] Yet, toward the end of the 1980s, the extension of credit-fueled asset bubbles in private housing and equity suggested that the state ability to regulate money-growth, and hence money-value, had a limited life span. The UK Stock Market *Big Bang* innovation in 1986, which removed fixed commissions, the separation of jobbers/brokers and introduced an electronic platform, had further contributed, combined with a weakening dollar, toward this more virile trading that culminated in the market crash on *Black Monday* in 1987. It seemed that to consistently regulate both credit levels and inflation was an elusive objective for the authorities.

In response, the Treasury/BOE adopted the position that they were able to influence credit levels *or* interest rates in order to combat inflation, but not both, a view that remained until the end of the case-study period. They decided, therefore, to focus on the *market* interest rate(s) through the setting of BOE base rates and specific open-market operations.[44] This aim was, in turn, predicated on the responsiveness of variables to changes in interest rates. While, this confidence in interest rate policy-effectiveness has waned in some circles, the inflation performance during the neo-liberal era *was* markedly better than the 1970s.[45] In Figure 10.6, for instance, the inflation measures reveal the severity of the inflation in 1973–1981 (with peaks in 1973 and 1979 after the oil price hikes) and the low levels attained since.

In the latter period of the case study, the 1990s and 2000s, mainstream ideas on money were still prevalent in the policy-making of the state although, more emphasis was given to the recent developments in monetary theory. In the BOE macroeconomic model set out at the end of the 1990s, for instance, the *neutrality* of money was assumed (see chap. 2), based on

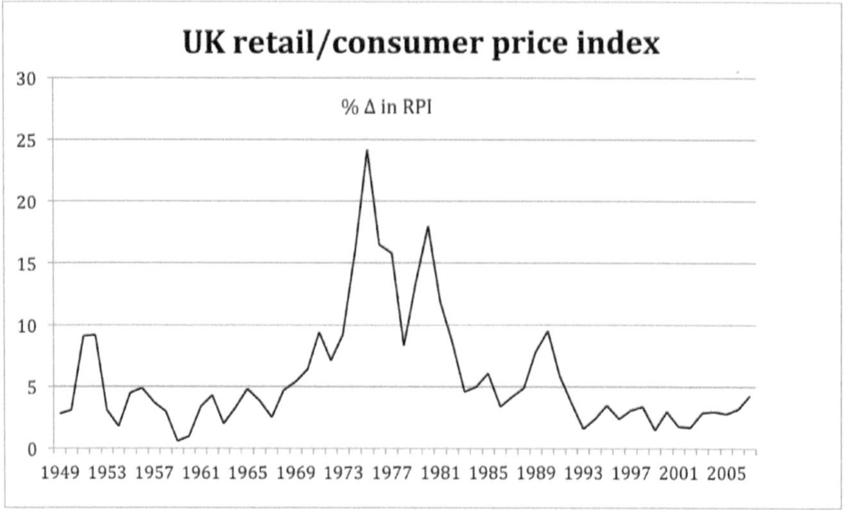

Figure 10.6 UK Inflation.

the perhaps ideological notion of a vertical Philipps curve (Arestis 2002: 2). In addition, the setting of key interest rates in the model responded to the *target* rate of inflation set by the state, the money stock was seen to correlate with the price level and the sluggish adjustment of nominal and real variables was assumed (Arestis 2002). They did recognize, however, that prices drove money stocks. The BOE, as a consequence, contended that if markets *clear* in a neutral-money sense, which the BOE argued did occur, then it is longer term. This represented a continued adherence to neoclassical rather than monetarist ideas. It is interesting to note, however, that these adapted monetary ideas still arguably do not reflect conditions in the *real* world even if they represent an improved level of reality.

In recent years there has been much analysis and discourse, particularly among PK's, on the *mechanics* of state open market operations in the interbank market that *actually* occur, rather than what is espoused in textbook theory. The aim has been to analyze, in an exogenous sense, the target interest rate(s) that, in turn, determine(s) the spectrum of market interest rates offered to businesses and consumers (Lavoie 2010; Rochon 2007; Gaspar, Quiros *et al.* 2004; Jurgilas, Zikes 2012). This, in turn, has a direct impact on the level of credit creation. It has been posited by Palley, for example, that financial innovation for example, derivatives and banking disintermediation, in the form of securitization, have made it more difficult for the state to affect the interbank rate since there is a *reduced* demand for the liabilities (narrow money) of the central bank for final settlements (Palley 2003b: 67).[46] This may explain the recent adoption of the so-called *corridor* system in many capitalist nations, where the central banks *target* an overnight rate that is set in the middle of a band between the credit and deposit rates for reserves (Lavoie 2010; Rochon 2007).[47] The *payment* of interest on reserve deposits is thus used to serve as a disincentive to the interbank settlement of imbalances taking place outside of national bank control. The BOE, for instance, adopted a policy of paying interest on positive balances in bank reserve accounts in 2009 (Bank of England. 2009). The likely rationale, as Wray posited, for private banks to have sought such innovation was profit, driven by the demands of equity return (Wray 2007). While the *corridor* system operation appears, *prima facie,* to indicate an *increase* in financial sovereignty over the level of credit-money via market interest rates, it could also be argued that the new policies are simply an attempt to reclaim capabilities *lost* through the processes of disintermediation and innovation. This could perhaps be described as a knee-jerk response. Furthermore, the idea of an exogenous short-term interest rate *per se* has been questioned. Wray, for example, distinguishes between the authority-control sense of exogenous money, where they choose the interest rate but are influenced by market factors, and the theoretical or causal sense (Wray 2004). A strongly exogenous variable, in a causal sense, is one that is autonomous of all endogenous variables including lagged ones. A target interest rate for the interbank market and/or base rate, therefore, may be exogenous in a control sense but the choice may be more or less dependent on the values of endogenous variables (Wray 2004). If we consider the close correlation between base rates and interbank rates during the neo-liberal era (see Figure 4), for instance, this may provide *prima facie* evidence of increased state capability but actually be driven by strong market-driven signals instead. It is also perhaps likely that these market signals have driven authority decisions in a reflexive manner *more* so than during the BW era with its stronger ideology of an interventionist state. In addition, as has been posited by Moore, the demand for reserves in the system is always fully *accommodated* by the central bank (Wray 2004). This is because the quick portfolio adjustment for banks is not easy, the national bank operates as a lender of last resort, an orderly payment system is important and the demand for reserves is inelastic which would lead to instable interest rates without reserve accommodation.

10.8 EXCHANGE RATE MONETARY VALUE

In many respects, the contrast between the state capability to determine the *exchange rate* of the pound during the BW era and the financial sovereignty of the post-BW period is clearer to identify. In the first instance, the neo-liberal era has been characterized by increasing financial globalization, deregulation of international financial transaction restriction that has greatly increased the volume of cross-border flows (Germain 1998; Cohen 1998; Griffith-Jones 1998). During the BW era, virtually all cross-border flows were directly related to trade, whereas now a very small proportion of flows are current account transactions. Since the vast bulk of these flows are constituted from *privately* owned monies, the ability of foreign exchange markets, and the private agents that inhabit them, to determine currency value in contrast to the state has been enhanced. The existence of exchange controls (prior to 1979) had given the state some measure of control over exchange rates. The liberalization of finance was, as several authors have identified, the consequence of a concerted political project rather than a market imperative, driven by free-market ideology that was applied internationally (Cerny 1998: 355). Notwithstanding, as Helleiner posited, the banks as market agents consistently lobbied the state during the post-WW2 era for the industry privileges associated with liberalization (Helleiner 1994). In addition, as Filipovic has noted, markets and private transnational forces, such as the International Securities Market Association, were also at work (Filipovic 1997). These latter points may, it could be suggested, be *prima facie* evidence of the Miliband notion of the state in capitalist society, furthering the interests and objectives of financial (plus industrial) capital (Miliband 1969).

The composition of capital flows had now radically changed in the neoliberal era with the proliferation of speculation, foreign direct investment, portfolio investments, capital and derivative markets. As a consequence, it had become increasingly difficult for the state to be effective in foreign exchange open market operations (OMO). This was more pronounced

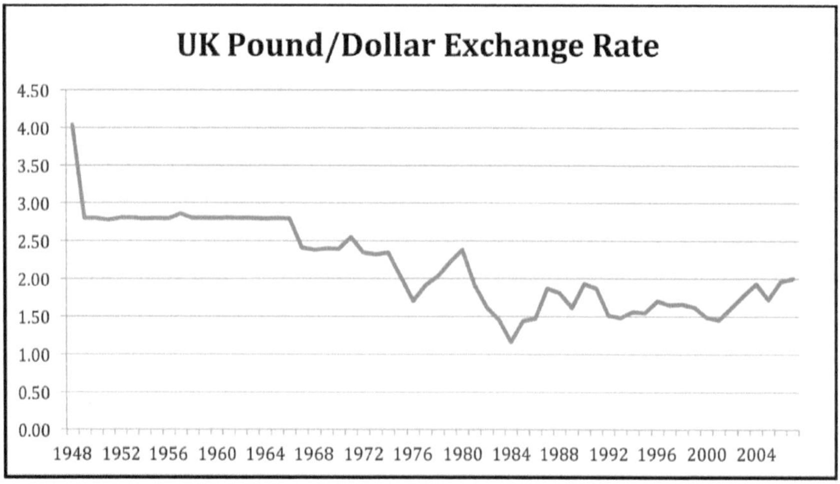

Figure 10.7 UK USD Exchange Rate.

following the removal of capital controls in 1979. During the BW fixed exchange rate era (see Figure 10.3), for example, the quantity of dollar reserves in proportion to GDP was steady, reflecting relative price stability and exchange control, whereas during the 1970s following the end of dollar convertibility and floating rates the need for greater reserves for OMO was apparent. In contrast, during the neo-liberal era, the need for reserves starts to taper off after the futility of OMO is realized, following the UK ERM crisis in September 1992. The Chancellor Lamont initially, at great expense to reserves, had tried to support the pound against the deutschmark and failed since the volume of private trades in the opposite direction more than countered the action (Potts 1997). The difficulty for the capitalist authorities to regulate the exchange rates is also exacerbated by the *leverage* that currency speculators with collateral are able to obtain from the financial system. The demand and supply conditions, affecting the foreign exchange marketplace (now electronic), are thus magnified as a consequence.[48] In addition, currency derivatives contribute toward the increased volatility of currency markets, through leverage, and the mitigation of any state capability to regulate exchange rates. Finally, offshore financial markets, such as *eurosterling*, are also responsible for the mitigation of state financial capability to determine exchange rates in the neo-liberal era, since wholesale credit facilities impact credit-money volumes in circulation. This, in turn, impacts inflationary pressure and the foreign exchange trading conditions. Cohen, for instance, has identified that these *blurred* boundaries for territorial currencies, since liberalization, have also led to an enhanced *currency competition* between states to obtain seigniorage (Cohen 1998). Cohen, however, had also posited that the policy-goal of maintaining a competitive exchange rate, which serves the needs of *private* sector actors, is of primary importance to states and, for some for example, Japan, this had been achieved by avoiding floating rates. Yet, he argued, they have since realized the inevitability of liberalization (Lukauskas 1999: 281). The feature of the new monetary geography, Cohen continued, is that the authorities *increasingly* share power with private agents, manifested in policy-choices, representing an erosion of financial sovereignty (Lukauskas 1999: 282). The balance of power, between state and market, has clearly shifted in the period studied.

10.9 CONCLUSION

This chapter has presented evidence suggesting that UK financial sovereignty has been lost. It was identified, for instance, that in the 1950s the authorities were able to determine credit levels, inflation measures and exchange rates better, in comparison to the period since BW. Yet there are some people, as Lukauskas noted, that have suggested the erosion of UK sovereignty has been exaggerated (Lukauskas 1999). Notwithstanding, it certainly appears that the empirical evidence from the UK case study supports the erosion proposition overall. Another objection that could be argued is that, during the BW system, the state was *unable* to pursue inflation or exchange rate policies that differed from or threatened the BW regime, thus *undermining* the capabilities of the state for autonomous action. It has also been suggested that neo-liberal floating exchange rates afforded national monetary policy a more effective role. Yet, the BW regime, and Sterling Area, clearly represented the *strength* of the interventionist state and interstate relations during the era, as well as the *restrictions* placed on private agents in the financial system. This suggests a strong financial state. Furthermore, the interests of market agents have also found *more* expression in the neo-liberal financial order that has followed, despite the effectiveness of monetary policy. So, in summary, in the 1950s, the Bank Rate, cash/liquidity ratios, exchange controls and the persuasion of the commercial banks had enabled the BOE to exert a reasonable amount of capability to determine the levels of credit and the value of UK currency. In contrast, in modern times, it was identified that capital mobility, financial liberalization as well as the growth of financial markets have reduced this state capability. The question that now remains to be asked is what has been the driver of this transformation of financial activity identified and, by implication, the driver of the subsequent erosion of financial sovereignty? This forms the subject of the next chapter, capitalist development.

NOTES

1. Exchange controls are defined in the study as controls and/or taxes on foreign currency exchanges, where capital controls refer to controls and/or taxes on certain cross-border portfolio and foreign direct investments.

2. At the G5 Plaza accord (1985), for instance, countries agreed to engage in open-market operations in order to weaken and then stabilize the US$ following a strong period for the dollar, and later at the Louvre accord meeting (1987) nation-state signatories aimed to strengthen and then stabilize the US$ after it had devalued.

3. Private stocks of specie represented latent financial power to determine values and, the fluctuations of gold mining supplies also had the capacity to disrupt state monetary arrangements.

4. The gold exchange standard for international trade existed between 1870 and 1914, after countries had established official gold convertibility, before it was suspended during WW1 with the need for public spending.

5. The gold specie standard still existed legally, however, but convertibility was discouraged by the state.

6. The German reparation payments, following WW1, were denominated in dollars. This was the first time that the dollar achieved significance as a *reserve* currency. Sterling remained significant, however, through the interwar years and even now stands with the yen, euro and dollar in determining IMF Special Drawing Rights.

7. The policy-makers favored this convertibility arrangement at the time (Cooper 1982: 437).

8. The banks are private in the sense of ownership and control, with their shareholder capital and dividends.

9. This was particularly evident during a well-reported incident with Thorneycroft in 1957, the Chancellor under Harold Macmillan, when he tried to instruct the banks to restrict credit. The BOE Governor refused and, after consultation with the Treasury solicitor, Thorneycroft found that he could neither force compliance nor dismiss the BOE Court of Directors according to the BOE 1946 Act (Burnham 2007: 405).

10. It is worth noting, as Collins has observed, the UK authorities pursued a cheap money policy in the 1930s (Collins 2012, chap. 4). This marked a gradual move toward the ideas of Keynes in the period.

11. Liquidity preference theory, developed by Keynes, had been instrumental in informing these ideas.

12. The narrow money targets followed the practical difficulty of monetary aggregate control, in 1983, and the shift to interest rate targets came as a consequence of the gradual decrease in reserve requirements (noted by Rochon) and the subsequent irrelevance of credit multiplier theory (Rochon 2007). The banks had lobbied for the reduction in reserve requirements, since any nonperforming assets affected their profitability (Lavoie 2012).

13. While this restricts domestic monetary policy it does not denote, it is argued, a mitigation of state financial sovereignty. This is because the BW regime represented

14. Mundell and Fleming had famously provided the analytical foundation for this (in the early 1960s) through their explanation of the impossibility of pursuing more than two of either free capital flows, fixed exchange rates and/or an independent monetary policy (Obstfeld 2004).

15. Industrial sectors likely to promote exports, and defense, were particularly seen as important in the 1950s.

16. Lower interest rates were needed for the British economy, in order to minimize UK state debt-servicing costs after the build-up of wartime debt and to also encourage business investment.

17. Keynes had considered that stability in interest rates was beneficial, a key theme of Tily's book (Tily 2007).

18. Although the bank rate (for banks) had been set at 2%, in wartime and the late 1940s the London Discount Market Association financial intermediaries had been able to borrow at this lower rate (Ross 1992: 200). The discount houses, as Batten noted were underwriters of the weekly UK Treasury bill tenders (Batten 1990: 21). Since public debt (in relation to GDP) was high at this time, the state was more dependent on the LDMA.

19. It is likely that this annoyed the BOE officials, which may have accounted for the humiliation of Thorneycroft in 1957 that was mentioned earlier.

20. It is worth mentioning, as Cairncross noted, that this *politicization* of credit provision, level and allocation created uncertainties in the banking sector that (arguably) led to less business investment in the 1950s than would otherwise have occurred (Cairncross 1995).

21. In 1956, the state limited the amount of capital that could be raised, without reference to the Capital Issues Committee, to £10,000 (Wadsworth 1973: 205).

22. Although, as Dimsdale notes, the Radcliffe committee revealed that the liquidity ratio was losing significance as a credit control mechanism, since banks were able to call money from the discount houses who were able to borrow at will from the BOE. This was because the government valued the London Discount Market for their underwriting of Treasury bill issues. If the BOE wanted to restrict credit advances, therefore, they overissued Treasury bills thus forcing the discount houses to borrow at an increased penal bank rate (Dimsdale 1991). This had diminished to 2% by 2011 (Mushin 2012). Eden, as Fforde noted, had been decisive in the cabinet rejection of the proposals (Fforde 1992: 440).

23. This had diminished to 2% by 2011 (Mushin 2012).

24. Eden, as Fforde noted, had been decisive in the cabinet rejection of the proposals (Fforde 1992: 440).

25. Keynes advocated the stabilizing of exchange rates and, perhaps more importantly (albeit not accepted at BW by the Americans), an international *clearing union* that would penalize through charges *excessive* deficit *and* surplus trading countries to foster incentives for agents to balance trade in the long term (Williamson 1985: 92).

26. The Radcliffe committee concluded, for instance, that monetary policy should play a subordinate role to fiscal policy in the context of demand management, that the velocity of circulation was changeable, that direct credit and hire purchase controls had longer-term market-distorting effects and that while (base) interest rates helped with the management of sterling, business investment was less responsive to base rate changes. The UK government finally removed the credit control regulations in 1971 (Dimsdale 1991: 108).

27. The international banks in London extended their foreign currency (interbank) lending to sterling transfers and the money markets grew (Buckle 2004: 204). However, as BOE open market operations developed, the UK state managed to regulate the interbank interest rate, and hence impact the level of credit, through the monitoring of overall excesses or shortages of liquidity in the banking system.

28. Some countries made the problem worse, particularly France, draining the US of gold reserves.

29. The Russians had initially deposited their dollars in France. The Russian government motive was to avoid the potential freezing of assets during periods of particularly tense international relations.

30. The US government approved of the development of Eurodollar markets since this relieved the pressure on the dollar from capital exports from domestic financial institutions. This also served to meet the emerging interests of US multinational corporations seeking foreign direct investments in Europe.

31. The banks were able to increase advances by reducing their holdings of liquid assets.

32. If the BOE wanted to restrict credit in the 1950s, they increased the sales of treasury bills thus reducing bank reserves, this put pressure on the discount houses who returned cash demanded (at call) to the banks. Since the BOE determined the (penal) Bank rate paid by the discount houses, this impacted the market rates. Yet, since the private banks had access to this call money, however, advances were often not reduced. It was only, therefore, the liquidity and cash ratio that could be used by the BOE to enforce credit restraint (Dimsdale 1991: 109). The BOE also determined the terms under which cash requirements could be met.

33. The Crowther committee had also criticized the inefficiency of consumer credit restrictions that had existed (Dimsdale 1991: 118).

34. The eligible liabilities did not include deposits with a maturity of more than two years (Dimsdale 1991: 118).

35. The cash ratio was retained, however, which gave the authorities some measure of control over the Treasury bill rate and therefore, as stated above, the bank rate decision.

36. The 1970s became known as the *Great Inflation* in more recent years.

37. The *Corset*, involved further non-interest bearing deposits placed at the Bank of England on request. Although this first appears to strengthen financial capability it was (arguably) a response to an erosion of sovereignty with respect to the market anyway *and*, furthermore was circumnavigated by the banking system.

38. The banks also were able to find new ways to circumnavigate the *corset* when exchange controls were removed in 1979 and Eurocurrency markets were more developed (Argy 1994: 490).

39. The theory depended on the flexibility of wages and prices (Mishkin 2007: 3).

40. The theory is remarkably enduring despite the (virtual) nonexistence of statutory reserve ratios in most of the modern capitalist economies (Rochon 2007). The Pilbeam textbook, for instance, still provides a worked example of the money-multiplier (Pilbeam 2005: 202).

41. It is interesting to note that Germany pursued monetary targeting for much longer, and with greater success, as a consequence of a more flexible implementation (Mishkin 2007: 5).

42. Reducing base money, for instance, was considered to reduce the banking system's ability to create the multiplication of deposits by credit advances.

43. These policies may be *prima facie* evidence of the *imperative* of the capitalist class, through the medium of the state, to restore *profitability* as an essential ingredient of accumulation and thus ensuring the sustainability of the economic system.

44. Open market operations of the authorities are designed to regulate the inter-banks interest rates (Wray 2004).

45. Professor Werner, for instance, has emphasized the (relatively) ineffectual role of interest rates in the macroeconomy (Werner 2005). By the early 1980s the BOE had also concluded that credit demand was relatively price-inelastic (Dimsdale 1991: 135). Notwithstanding, state interest-rate targeting has continued to exist. The authorities usually base this on some form of Taylor Rule where rates are raised by a greater proportion than the increase of the price level and output (Taylor 1993: 202).

46. This is quoted in Rochon and Rossi (Rochon 2007: 2).

47. In the US, the use of the *corridor* to target the Federal Funds rate was made possible after Congress granted the Federal Reserve the right to *pay* interest on reserve deposits in 2008 (Lavoie 2010: 10). There has also been the further development of the so-called *floor* system in the US, which deliberately sets the target Federal Fund rate at the (low) level of the deposit rate paid on reserves. The only time that interbank rates are likely to fall below this is when there is a particularly large volume of interbank transaction activity between *non-settlement* banks (Lavoie 2010).

48. Foreign exchange trading is also impacted by *high frequency trading* with the (increasing) use of sophisticated computer models to generate trades.

Chapter 11

Capitalist Development

11.1 INTRODUCTION

In this chapter, the intention is to consider the mechanics of the capitalist mode of production, according to Marx, in order to predict the future system transformation and, account for its development during the case-study period. I claim that this will offer plausible explanation(s) of the erosion of financial sovereignty that was identified in the last two chapters. It was stated earlier in the book that the key theoretical contribution to political economy, from Marx, suggests that there will be a tendency for the profit rate to fall (LTFRP) across periods that may be held back by counter-tendencies, but only temporarily, as accumulation proceeds. As a consequence, this serves as a *driver*, albeit an indirect one, of other developments and agent behavior in the economy.

Kliman, as developed in 5.9, has argued that in the modern global economy this tendency for profitability to fall, and persistent low profitability, has led to economic stagnation through successive governments, using expansionary policies to limit recession. Consequently, the restoration of the profit rate that is required to return to boom has not occurred (Kliman 2012). Kliman, in his specific study of the US, has also demonstrated, using a range of profit measures, that this *has* taken place since the Great Depression. His findings illustrate that while sufficient destruction of capital value occurred during the depression years, to restore profitability, this has *failed* to take place since and, falling profit rates can also explain the build-up of debt and financialization.[1] Kliman contends, therefore, that low profitability is the "crucial, though *indirect*, cause of the latest economic crisis" (Kliman 2010: 7). This argument is considered to be a valid one, and therefore, forms the basis for the empirical study of the UK and Germany presented in this chapter.

The key aim, therefore, is to ascertain whether the profit rate has fallen in the relevant case studies, and then discuss any correlation with the growth of fictitious financial markets and debt. If this exists it should provide *prima facie* evidence to support the view that production factors are the key underlying drivers of any transformation of money and banking and, by implication, any observed decline of state financial sovereignty. In addition, other trends that are relevant to Marx's prediction of the tendential behavior of capitalist economies are discussed. These ideas will directly contrast, it is contended, with the view that neo-liberalism has led to rising profitability, partly as a result of increased labor exploitation, and the position that the recent crisis was purely *financially* driven (Lapavitsas 2009; Moseley 2009). These popular views are significant since they imply that government policies could be devised to tame finance in the hope that capitalist crises can be eliminated. Kliman notes that these finance-sector explanations are usually based on two methodological approaches. First, by *cherry-picking* trough to peak years in the data studied and, secondly, by using *current cost* profit rates that is, valuing fixed assets by their current replacement cost (Kliman 2010: 9). Yet, paradoxically, as Kliman discovered in his US case study, when the latter method is chosen the current cost profit rate can at times be *rising* simultaneously with a *falling* rate of accumulation that is, ratio of new investment to advanced capital (Kliman 2010: 49). This finding can then be cited, by above advocates of financialization, as a justification for positing financial factors as drivers of crises since they cannot point to a falling profit rate due to their method of analysis. Kliman, in response, challenges the validity of using current cost measures in theory since they are not used by businesses or investors, who generally aim to maximize net present value estimated returns, and because current cost profits do not represent the *actual* returns to advanced capital anyway (Kliman 2010: 41).

Kliman points out instead, that since the rate of accumulation has tracked the historic cost profit rate very closely in the US case study, the historic cost profit rate is therefore a more appropriate measure to use since it measures what was actually spent (Kliman 2010: 49).[2] In addition, his empirical work has revealed that post-WW2 *changes* to the profit and employee-compensation *share* of income have not been *sustained*, with the exception of a notable fall in the profit share at the end of the sixties (Kliman 2010: 53). The US evidence, arguably similar for the UK, suggests that if explanations of rising profitability are founded on increasing labor exploitation, they are likely to be problematic. It is often expressed that the neo-liberal era has increased labor exploitation, leading to a rise in profitability, but the evidence in the US does not support the view. Finally, Kliman has also taken account of the increasing rate of depreciation due to obsolescence, moral depreciation, which occurred during the information age. If this is taken into account appropriately, the actual profit rates are much lower than official estimates would suggest (Kliman 2010).

In response to these considerations this book, following Kliman, has chosen to observe the longer-term profit-rate trends and utilize historic cost profit rates, which are then compared with current cost calculations. In order to estimate data for UK historic fixed assets for each year (to calculate a historic profit rate), the study uses reported UK *current* cost values and then adjusts them according to the commensurate proportion of US historic rates to current ones as a proxy:[3] This is because historic cost data for fixed assets is unavailable in the UK.

$$\mathrm{HC}^{\mathrm{UK}} = \frac{HC(US)}{CC(US)}\mathrm{CC}^{\mathrm{UK}}$$

In addition, to adjust for inflation using Marx's own procedure, the historic rates are deflated by an approximation of the MELT changes, using Kliman's method, where the GDP measure is divided by employment. This estimate enables us to have some idea of the changing value, in monetary terms (the MELT), of an abstract hour of labour.

11.2 DIFFERENT RATES OF PROFIT

A profit *rate* is always, by definition, a ratio of profit in terms of the capital advanced at the start of the production period. Yet, this can be calculated in different ways according to the intentions of the researcher. In the real world, as Kliman posits the most important investment consideration for the entrepreneur is the *anticipated* profit rate, though it is difficult to measure this *expectation* objectively (Kliman 2010: 13). The entrepreneur will be driven by many factors, not least of which are the recent profit rates and interest rates. If we wish to measure historical profit rate trends, conversely, then we need to observe the actual *realized* rates achieved. Kliman points out, for instance, that if we are measuring profit in comparison to other forms of investment return for example, shares then we need a narrow measure such as profits after tax. Yet, Kliman's favored method is the *property income* measure which does not deduct rents, profits and interest, since this identifies the impact of class-based income distribution changes on the rate of profit (Kliman 2010: 18). Finally, if we wish to analyze fluctuations in *observed* profit rates it will help to adjust the figures for inflation, using Marx's method or as a comparison the RPI, in order to gage real returns. These real returns are an important consideration for the level of business investment.

The calculation of a *Marxian* rate of profit is also problematic. Kliman, for instance, has identified that in Marx's work, Marx employed several different measures of profit in order to explain different things (Kliman 2010: 14). He generally used, for instance, the labor rate of profit, and one with a constant MELT, when he was discussing theory. Sometimes Marx used surplus value in the numerator and, on other occasions, he used realized profit in nominal terms, which is equal in the aggregate to surplus value but not at the level of the individual firm or industry. He also employed all parts of surplus value in the numerator that is, profit, interest and rent and, at times, just industrial profit in the numerator. It is also practically difficult to calculate a truly Marxian profit rate. This is because Marx's notion of total social capital involves the whole world, and reliable data is not available. Also, official recorded data in the capitalist nations does not separate moral depreciation from wear and tear, the statistics reduce asset measures by the combined sum, which is a prerequisite for Marx's method to be followed perfectly. In addition, his measurement of fixed assets was rather unusual, in comparison to modern practices. He includes for instance, some (but not all) stocks in his calculations, wage payments, land purchases and financial instruments. Yet, even if a calculation was possible it might not be desirable anyway since our primary aim is to identify the *actual* rates of return that *concern* investors, and thus influence decision-making of entrepreneurs, rather than any theoretical construct per se (Kliman 2010: 14).

The calculations pursued, following Kliman, have chosen to focus on the corporate sector alone for its data series, although in contrast to Kliman one section of data contains a deliberate *separation* of nonfinancial corporations from financial ones for the purposes of illustrating relative changes in profit rates. These changes reveal issues that are pertinent to the primary objective of the book. The rationale for this corporate focus is that corporations arguably best illustrate the returns to advanced capital since they represent more than two-thirds of national income. In addition, as Kliman notes in the US study, few non-corporations generate enough property income to support their owners *without* their remuneration for their personal contribution to the firm. This means that despite the large number of small businesses, most do not operate in the same way that large capitalist firms do.

11.3 FIXED ASSET MEASURES

The net investment of any particular year is the difference between the gross investment that year and the depreciation, the ONS uses a straight-line depreciation method, which occurred during the same year.[4] The historic cost calculations measure this depreciation as a proportion of the nominal sums originally extended for the fixed assets. Using the symbol I to denote the net investment that occurred in year *y* we can ascertain that the value of fixed assets (i.e., advanced capital) in historical cost terms (H) is:

$$C_y^H = I_0 + I_1 + I_2 + \dots I_{y-1} = \sum_{y=0}^{y-1} I_y$$

In order to adjust for inflation following Marx's concept of value, each yearly measure for net investment is divided by the MELT for that particular year to achieve a deflated measure of the value of fixed assets:[5]

$$C_y^L = \frac{I_0}{M_0} + \frac{I_1}{M_1} + \frac{I_2}{M_2} + \dots \frac{I_{y-1}}{M_{y-1}} = \sum_{y=0}^{y-1} \left[\frac{I_y}{M_y} \right]$$

Fixed assets as advanced capital in current cost terms C^C have been *revalued* in order to approximate their *replacement* cost at the end of the year. The net investment data is the same as those used above, though the depreciation is measured at current rather than historic cost. First, each year's net investment figure is deflated by the same year's price index for fixed assets in order to get the *real* cost of the net stock of assets. Next, in order to get the current cost measure of the advanced capital, this net stock of fixed assets is then reflated by the particular year's fixed assets index (F):

$$C_y^C = F_y \left(\frac{I_0}{F_0} + \frac{I_1}{F_1} + \dots \frac{I_{y-1}}{F_{y-1}} + \frac{I_y}{F_y} \right) = F_y \sum_{y=0}^{y} \left(\frac{I_t}{F_t} \right)$$

11.4 PROFIT RATES

The historical cost profit rate (R_y) is thus profit (P_y) divided by the net fixed assets (C_y^{HC}):

$$R_y^H = \frac{P_y}{C_y(H)}$$

The MELT deflated labor rate of profit (R_y^L) is thus profit divided by the adjusted net fixed assets (C_y^L) as follows:

$$R_y^L = \frac{P_y / M_y}{C_y(L)}$$

Finally, the current cost rate of profit is profit divided by the current cost net fixed assets:

$$R_y^C = \frac{P_y}{C_y(C)}$$

In Figure 11.1, the *historic* profit rate of the UK is illustrated. It is interesting to note that a *clear* secular decline, a 29.4% reduction, is identified between 1948 and 2007. In addition, in the Kliman US study it was also evident that, since the prices of fixed assets were marked down during the depression years that is, the destruction of capital discussed in chapter 5, an even higher profit rate existed during the later depression years and WW2 (Kliman 2010). This means that, if we assume arguably there was a similar scenario in the UK, 1934–1948, there were even higher rates. In addition, the period immediately following the case study was also marked by a financial and real economy crisis where the UK profit rate is likely to have been lowered. If these trends were added to the graph, therefore, the *fall* in the profit rate would have been even more marked. There have been times of partial restoration for the profit rate, however, notably the mid-1970s and early 1990s, but this has not been sustained.

The profit measure that has been used as a numerator in this profit rate calculation is *net operating surplus* reported by the ONS, which has been used as a proxy (it excludes net producer subsidies/taxes) for Kliman's *property income* measure (Kliman 2010: 26). The measures both give a closer representation of the actual profit (surplus value) generated by production, since they *include* the gross surplus accruing to the capitalist class in the form of interest, rent and profits.[6] Kliman, in his study, also calculated the US historic profit rate using profits before tax data and including stocks in the denominator and found that the resulting profit rate trends are very closely correlated (Kliman 2010: 26).[7]

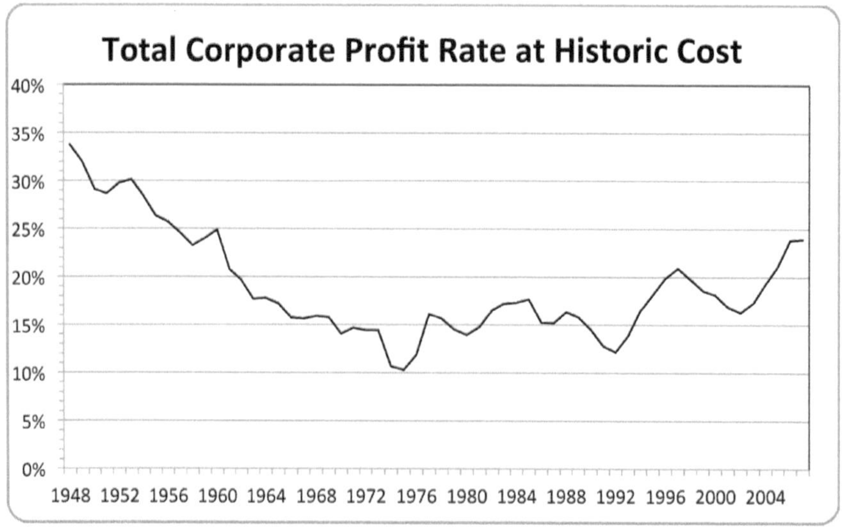

Figure 11.1 UK Historic Corporate Profit Rate.

In Figure 11.2, the *current cost* calculation of the profit-rate 1948–2007 is illustrated. It is interesting to note that, if you were to consider the neo-liberal era, a distinct increase of the profit rate can easily be identified. This arguably accounts for the popularity of current account calculation and the practice of *cherry-picking* the data from trough to peak, identified by Kliman, to claim restored profit rates (Kliman 2007: 132).

Yet, even with current (replacement) cost calculation, a *fall* in the rate of profit in the UK of 12.5% can be identified from 1948 to 2007 and it fails to recover sufficiently prior to the 2007 crisis.[8] The likely higher rate from WW2, and lower rate post-2007, also needs to be taken into consideration. Yet, the current-cost calculation cannot really be considered a profit-rate *proper*, while useful, because it does not measure the *nominal* profit value unlike historic cost, in relation to the nominal value of the capital actually advanced.[9] It is these actual returns that entrepreneurs use to service their debt obligations and dividends and formulate their *perception* of general business profitability, and actual resources, that guides their future investment plans. Notwithstanding, current costs are still an integral part of the investment considerations, since they equate to the actual monies that need to be expended.

In Figure 11.3, the historic and current cost profit rates are compared. In addition, the constant MELT historic profit rate is represented, in order to account for the rising monetary expression of an hour of labor-time in the manner that Marx intended. This measure illustrates the *equivalent* prices

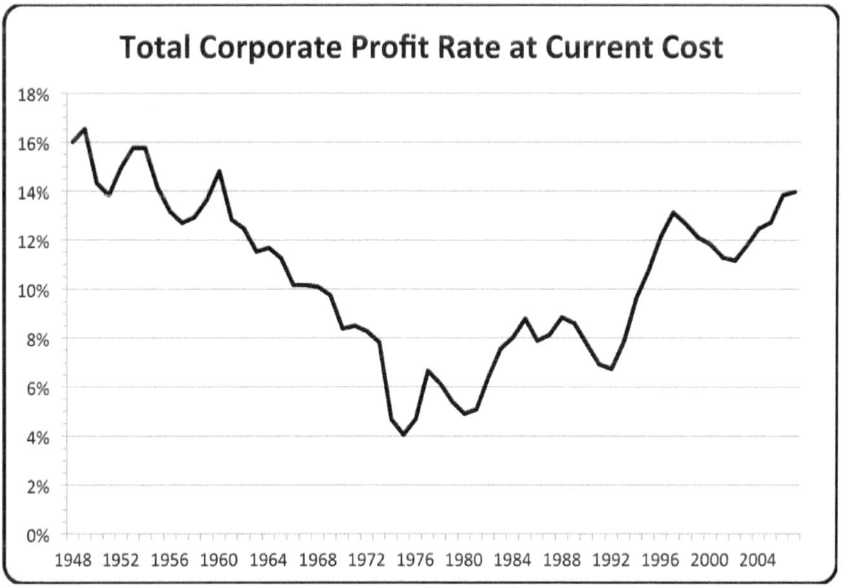

Figure 11.2 UK Current Cost Corporate Profit Rate.

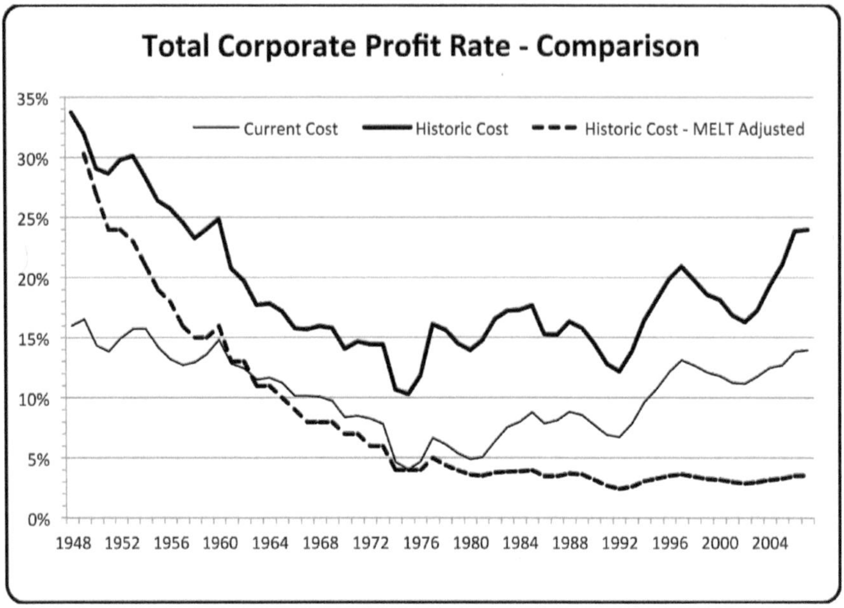

Figure 11.3 UK Profit Rate Comparison with MELT.

of the relevant fixed assets, if paid today, by deflating the historic prices by the MELT.[10] The net operating surplus, of the relevant year, is also deflated. This MELT graph reveals, interestingly, a clear fall in the profit rate and, most importantly, a distinct lack of recovery.[11] In addition, it is interesting to note that if the historic profit rate is deflated by the inflation index (see Figure 11.4) the results are the same.

These graphs illustrate, in a general sense, the *law of value* in operation and suggest that individual capitals are receiving *less* profit per pound advanced. UK capitalists have therefore needed to find some way to compensate themselves, manifested in a variety of particular behaviors. They may, for instance, have sought to increase the rate of exploitation of labor, compete more intensely with rival firms, incorporate smaller capitals through acquisition or engage in their own financial sector activity or, most notably, asset speculations. In short, as argued in chapter 5, the falling rate of profit engenders a range of profit-seeking activities, in the absence of sufficient countertendencies or a crisis that sufficiently marks down the values of advanced capital. The factors derived from production, it is therefore argued, can then be seen to be driving the more general UK systemic change that indirectly impacts the financial sector.

In Germany, profitability has been higher but a decline is still evident. This study takes the position that Germany (importantly) has been a lead producer. In chapter 5 it was identified that while profit equalization

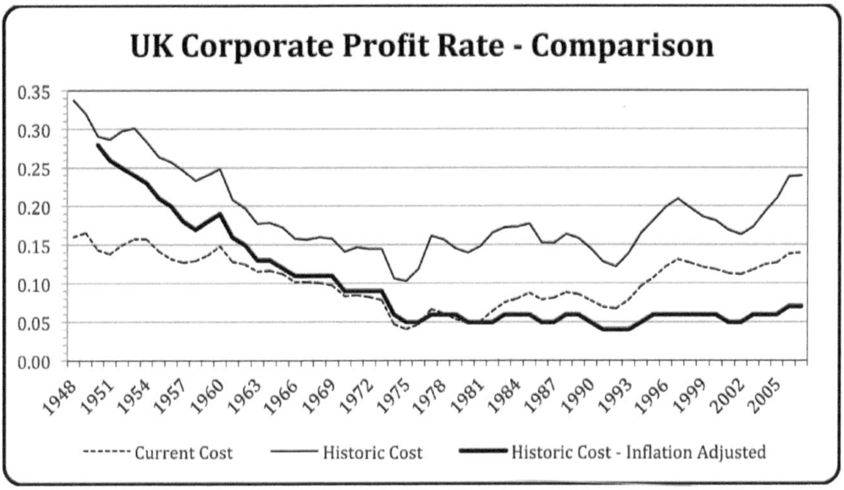

Figure 11.4 UK Profit Rate Comparison with Inflation.

between sectors is expected to tendentially occur across periods, this is not likely though possible within sectors. It was also identified that the persistence of rents hinders the profit equalization process. In Germany these are likely to have taken the form of technology rents.[12] In the following diagram, Figure 11.5, the current and historic cost profit rate measures for Germany are illustrated from 1970 to 2007.[13] The figures reveal a *higher* corporate profit rate for Germany, in comparison to the UK, albeit closely correlated decline and restoration *patterns* in profit rates during the period.[14] This suggests that, if the period prior to 1970 in Germany had a similar decline in profitability as the UK, which I suggest is a valid claim, this has occurred from a higher starting point. Figure 11.5 provides estimates for the pre-1970 period based on UK data and also provides a MELT adjusted measure. The evidence presented in chapter 9 suggests that following currency reform and debt write-downs, aided by Marshall Plan monies, German firms enjoyed healthy profits after WW2 and dynamic growth as a consequence.

It is argued in this study that these falling profit rate measures provide a plausible explanation (albeit indirect) of the financial liberalization, and corresponding loss of state financial sovereignty, that has taken place in recent decades. In the following diagram (Figure 11.7), for instance, the UK current cost profit rates, using net operating surplus, of the nonfinancial corporations are contrasted with the financial ones. It is interesting to note that during the BW era, the financial company profit rates were generally lower than the nonfinancial ones. In the neo-liberal era, conversely, financial firms have been far more lucrative for investors. This is *prima facie* evidence, it is argued in this book, of declining sovereignty.

Figure 11.5 German Corporate Profit Rate.

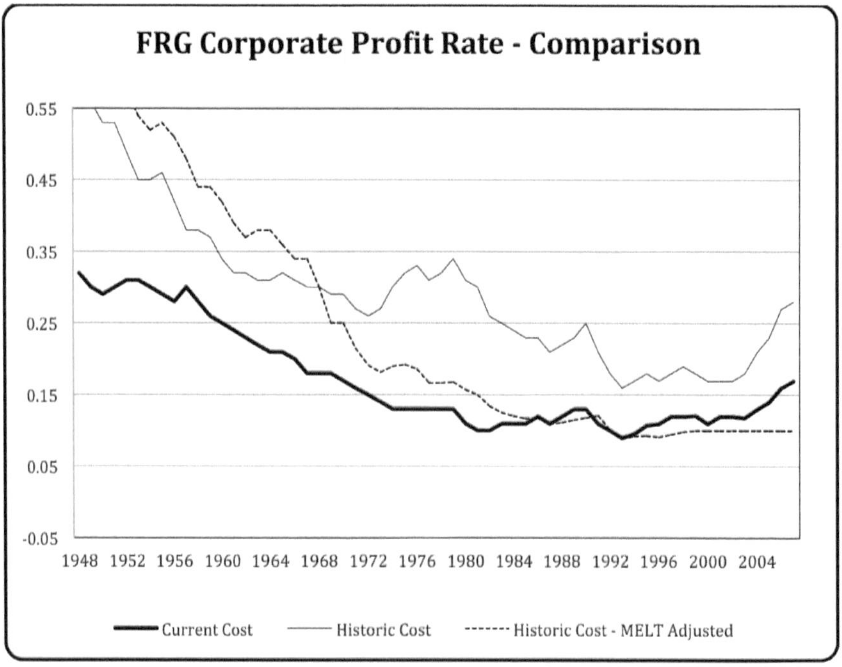

Figure 11.6 German Corporate Profit Rate Comparison.

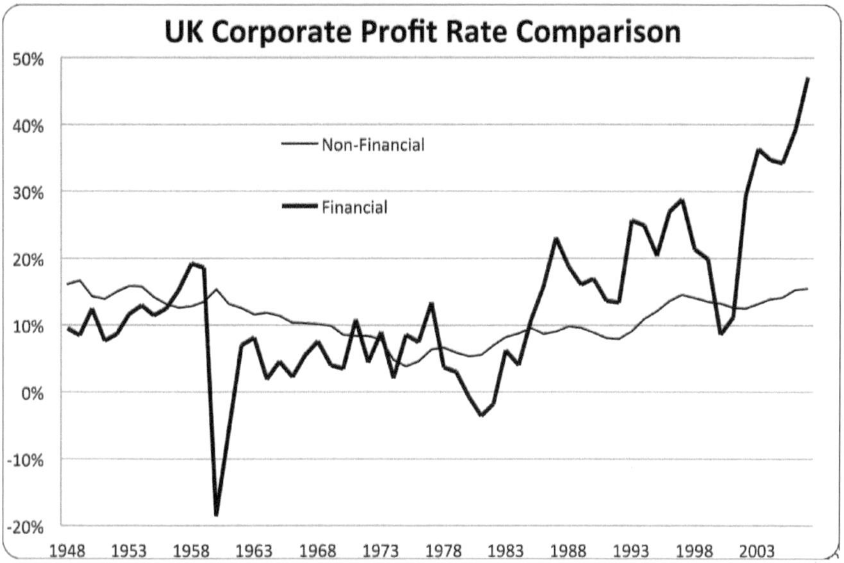

Figure 11.7 UK Profit Rate Comparison.

11.5 MORAL DEPRECIATION

Interestingly, moral depreciation discussed in chapter 5 has also become much more acute during the information age, with the advent of computer hardware and software engineering. Kliman has identified, for instance, a notable rise (from 7% to 11%) in US moral depreciation since the 1950s, which he attributes to computing, and the UK economy is very likely to display similar results (Kliman 2010: 75). This will raise profit rates after the initial fall as the fixed assets are marked down. The problem with the data used in this analysis from the Marxian perspective, however, is that the statistical authorities deduct obsolescence from profit figures (and fixed asset values) in *conjunction* with "wear and tear" and aging deductions.[15] Marx, conversely, did not consider moral depreciation and deterioration in the same way, in terms of his method of analysis, as a direct consequence of his law of value. As Marx claimed (p. 73), the value of a commodity derives from the living and dead labor *currently* needed to *reproduce* commodities of the same type. If a fixed asset experiences *moral* depreciation, therefore, a portion of the labor is no longer needed and the capitalist suffers loss. A portion of the monies expended, in other words, is not realized. Yet, if wear and tear is experienced, conversely, as long as commodities sell at labor values, all money (and value) is *realized* since they pass into the commodity. Moral depreciation does not reduce surplus value established in production because this derives from the labor, but it does reduce *realized* profit in *circulation* because some of the advanced capital is not realized, representing a loss for the capitalist. It can be argued that this is a key driver of any attempts to increase worker efficiency, during the neo-liberal era, as a consequence of faster information age moral depreciation. This certainly appears to be the case in the modern workplace. The now devalued fixed assets, conversely, reduce the value of advanced capital *in the next period* and profitability is raised. This process was illustrated in the Potts diagram in chapter 5 (Table 5.3) and has important implications for a Marxian profit rate study of this kind. The existence of shorter product life cycles must surely have an impact on entrepreneurial decision-making in the modern information era.

Kliman claims that *all* of the increase in moral depreciation during the neo-liberal era can be attributed to computing. He then contends, with the use of his estimated measures of *increased* moral depreciation, that capitalist losses, that is, unrealized surplus value, have been substantially higher since the 1980s as a consequence (Kliman 2010: 77).[16] His study has estimated *profit rates* using a *constant* rate of moral depreciation, by removing the recent *increase* of moral depreciation, and found unsurprisingly that the adjusted *fall* in the profit rate across the case-study period was even *more* marked as a consequence (Kliman 2010: 79). These results were confirmed using profits before and after tax, and his property income measure. This illustrates, therefore, that some firms have been compensated for the tendency of the profit rate to fall, by the shorter product life cycles of information age technologies. It might also be that some companies are able to predict that their firm will benefit from these new technologies in this way. In this latter stage of the capitalist mode of production, of course, given the LTFRP and rapid technological change, there are also more headaches for the statistical authorities in their calculation of fixed asset values.[17]

11.6 RENTIER INCOMES

Marx had discussed, as previously stated, the impact of the LTFRP on capitalist behavior. Firms will seek, for instance, to gain extra profit from productivity growth, at the expense of other firms, before profit equalization takes place even though actual equalization is unlikely, or seek out new investments and new markets, mergers or financial speculations. In addition, the incentive for elaborate forms of tax avoidance is enhanced. Michael Hudson, for example, has noted how *rentier* incomes, cunningly disguised as intermediate consumption in national accounts, have increased in recent years and the use of offshore financial centers has also risen (Hudson 2005).[18] As the reduced profit rates lead to a subsequent falling rate of accumulation that is, ratio of net investment to advanced capital, an increased activity also takes place in the financial markets.[19] Hudson explains that the current simultaneous models are simply inappropriate in describing these phenomena, in respect of their poor illustration of the financial markets. This also leads to a misleading view of how the real economy works (Hudson 2012: 1). Hudson contends that, since modern credit creation has inflated asset prices, which increase *rentier* incomes as well as debt-servicing levels, businesses then find that profitability is compromised and some firms at the margin then default. This then culminates in a debt deflation that then necessitates, Hudson argues, a debt write-down as an imperative for the regeneration of capitalism. Since this has consistently failed to materialize in recent times it suggests that capitalism is in crisis. In reality, most credit is provided in order to purchase assets that already exist, not to create new productive capacity. This partly explains why, in the modern era, recent quantitative easing has restored bank balance sheets, and helped to maintain high asset prices and *rentier* incomes, without stimulating the real economy or inflation. The impact of mainstream economics, therefore, is a failure to prevent recurring asset bubbles and provide adequate policies toward the real economy. Incomes that derive from the finance, insurance and real estate (FIRE) sector have clearly increased in the neo-liberal era. There is some evidence, as Stockhammer has identified and noted by Hudson, that rising capital gains in particular, are diverting finance away from real sector growth (Stockhammer 2004). The implication of this position, however, is that financialization is responsible for the stagnation rather than the LTFRP. The Stockhammer study has been challenged by Kliman, whose study of the US Bretton Woods to neo-liberal eras noted that the investment share of net profit has not fallen but risen in the neo-liberal period despite the financialization (Kliman and Williams 2015). This suggests that any stagnation is more likely to be driven by the LTFRP as claimed in the book and financialization is simply an indirect offshoot at best. The financialization position, in contrast, implies that capitalism can be *sustainable* if the real economy is able to thrive again through a restoration of profitability, providing that the finance sector is restricted. Yet, even if this were to be possible, the type of policies that would facilitate this has not been forthcoming in the capitalist economies.

I argue, in contrast, that if asset values were to be marked down leading *inter alia* to lower rents and associated costs, and finance expenses were also reduced, these measures would indeed mitigate falling profitability. However, they would perhaps only provide a short-term sticking plaster to the problems of capitalism. Marx probably would have argued that these types of policies could only provide temporary relief, delaying the real and financial economy crises that result from the LTFRP. Marx had commented, for example, in his critique of the French socialist Proudhon who had argued for the elimination of financial exploitation, that removing interest from lending did not eliminate surplus value and, therefore, the law of value will still ensure that the rate of profit has a propensity to fall across periods providing there were insufficient counter-tendencies (Marx 1972: 525). In any case, such abovementioned policy proposals for transforming capitalism, through the mitigation of financial sector incomes, would be unlikely to succeed since the reduced asset prices, and/or financial returns, would be strongly resisted by the investor classes anyway.

The changing financial system, in terms of the growth of the financial markets and reduced state sovereignty, thus creates more opportunities for profit for finance-sector agents, as surplus profits, hoarded wealth and credit expansion are directed toward it. In addition, as Potts notes, the transfer of surplus profits to the financial sector further fuels speculative activity and asset bubbles (Potts 2009).[20] Yet, since finance and tradable securities (as fictitious capital) do not create *extra* value according to Marx's definition, this is a zero-sum activity and profit opportunities are fleeting. This fosters instability, since speculative gains are not available to all, which then manifests in the form of burst asset bubbles and subsequent default on debt obligations or shortfalls of demand in the markets of the real economy. The financial markets, in terms of advances, derivatives, securitization, foreign exchange and international capital markets have all experienced substantial growth during the case-study period, particularly in the neo-liberal era, as an indirect consequence of falling nonfinancial corporate profit rates. The changing nominal volumes of foreign exchange trading and derivative contracts, for example,

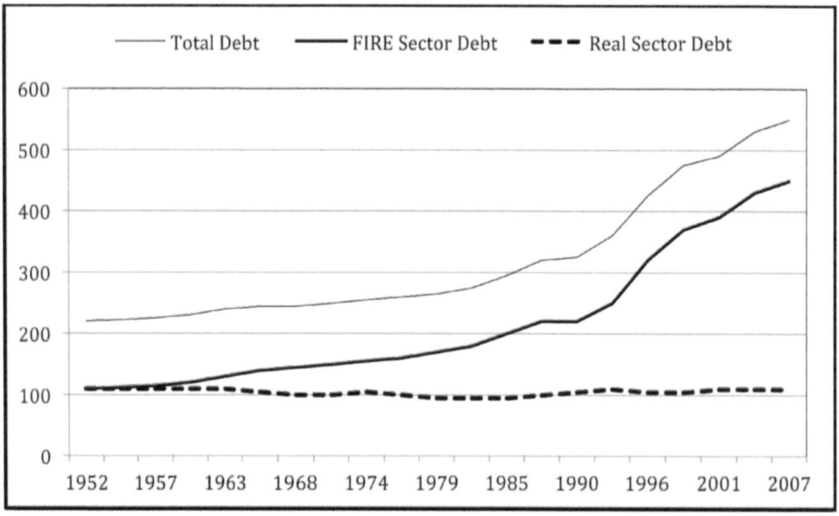

Figure 11.8 US Private Debt.

are illustrated in the diagrams Figures 11.9 and 11.10. Both markets have experienced phenomenal growth in the neo-liberal era.

A further problem with these financial sector developments, driven indirectly by the law of value, is that in a climate of general financial uncertainty, people also tend to hoard their monies. This means that overproduction takes place, as goods fail to sell in sufficient quantities. Marx had scoffed, as Harvey notes, at those who claimed "supply creates its own demand" (Say's law), since the capitalist frequently does not realize surplus value in such instances

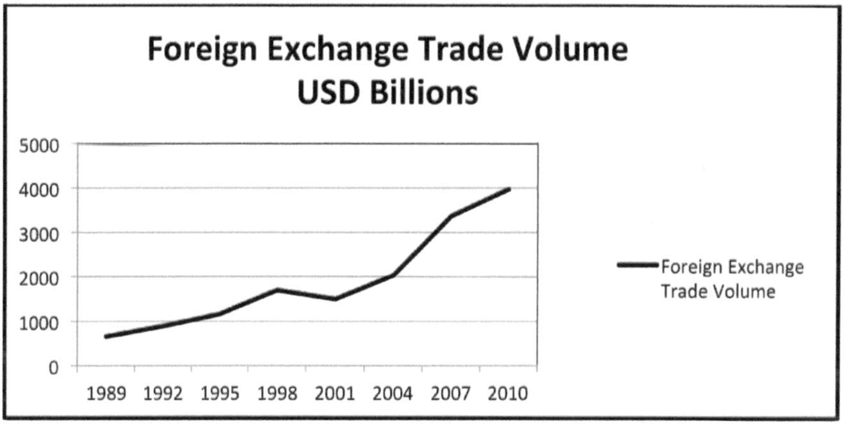

Figure 11.9 Global Foreign Exchange.

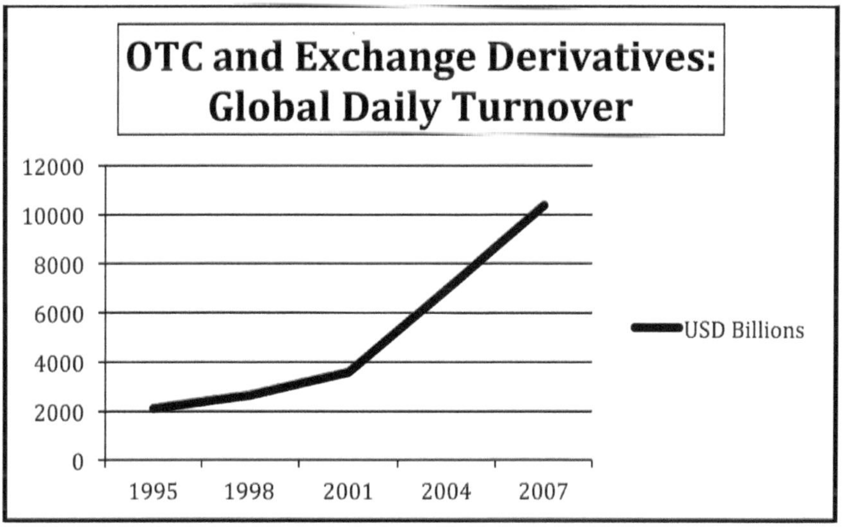

Figure 11.10 Global Derivative Contracts.

(Harvey 2010: 66). Prices are formed during production, and then circulation follows, but there is no guarantee that all commodities will sell and capitalist losses are experienced at this point of the period. Yet, paradoxically, many authors have sought to *explain* the existence of financial crises with reference to this lack of aggregate demand as a precursor to crisis. Yet, as stated earlier in 8.6, Kliman pointed out that the so-called *under-consumptionists* use circular tautological reasoning, since their explanation of crises seems to simply describe the *manifestations* of the various crises in question rather than the causes (Kliman 1999).[21] Marx, conversely, identified that the LTFRP was the underlying albeit indirect cause of the overproduction. The falling profit rate, via its impact on the credit system (and speculation), then leads to the financial instability and any shortfall of demand. The vagaries of market forces, driven by Keynes's *animal spirits*, are still important and Marx recognized this. However, they simply do not occur in a vacuum driven by random subjectivities, as argued in the book, but instead occur as a general consequence of the law of value in operation. This is the key distinctive between the PK and Marx perspectives on political economy. It is recognized that if economic agents experience stable expectations of low interest rates, this will to some extent compensate for falling returns on capital advanced. Yet, the mechanics of successive periods of production will tend toward falling profitability and, therefore, the *imperative* of counter-tendencies and/or crisis to sustain capitalism in the longer term still remains. For Keynes, to be consistent with his overall philosophy, this did not always need to be considered since in the long run we are all dead anyhow.

11.7 THE RISE OF THE NONBANKS

Yet, even if we reject the usual Marxian prediction for the capitalist trajectory, where firms seek to realize increasingly more surplus value to offset the falling rate of profit, the generally accepted corporate (financial and non-financial) imperative is still the pursuit of profit. In the banking sector, there are fresh challenges for firms today, since information age and innovation have led to new channels of financial circulation, and financial liberalization has contributed toward a more competitive global economy. The companies most likely to succeed in this modern environment, as Lietaer has noted, are the ones *most* able to combine electronic knowledge systems with production. If this is extended to the development of nonfinancial corporate monies, nonbanks and payment systems, which it has been, this will further strengthen their competitive position (Lietaer 2001). So, nonbanks are becoming increasingly significant in the modern financial system (Adams, 2010). Bradford *et al.* have examined their varied roles in payment activity, in both traditional and emerging systems, for example, and identified complex relations with the banks and payment system. In addition, since they are rarely directly involved with final settlements, they appear, at least, to be less associated with systemic risk. In the real world of today banks *and* nonbanks are both, however, susceptible to operational risk (Bradford, 2003). The non-bank activity is, I argue, further evidence of low profitability in the productive sector as traditional firms in the real economy seek out new avenues of profitability in an era of financialization.

Table 11.1 illustrates the profit rate differential measured as a proportion of net capital stock, between UK financial and nonfinancial corporations *reported* profitability, measured using gross trading profits, in the twelve years leading up to the financial crash of 2008. It is unlikely that these substantial profit differentials have escaped the attention of profit-aspiring industrial capitalists, providing clear incentives for the development of financial sector activities by nonbank firms for purposes of securing additional profit.

Marx, in his analysis of the *subjugation* of feudal lending practices, as capitalism developed, considered that since the function of interest-bearing capital was inextricably linked to the production process it was, therefore, dependent on it. Capitalist banking and credit developed, therefore, to service the accumulation process and, subsequently, replaced older forms of lending with a more efficient provision of financial resources Marx writes:

> The commercial and interest-bearing forms of capital are older than industrial capital, which, in the capitalist mode of production, is the *basic form* of the capital relations dominating bourgeois society—and all other forms are only derived from it or secondary: derived as is the case with interest-bearing capital;

Table 11.1 UK Financial and NonFinancial Corporate Profit Rate

Year	*Profits*		*Net Cap*[a]		*Profit Rate*	
Billions	*NonFinancial*	*Financial*	*NonFinancial*	*Financial*	*NonFinancial*	*Financial*
1995	100.896	27.465	778.9	58.3	0.13	0.47
1996	104.173	32.782	795.7	59.6	0.13	0.55
1997	113.524	34.878	811.3	59.7	0.14	0.58
1998	119.055	36.249	847.6	63.4	0.14	0.57
1999	120.474	42.186	889.7	68.4	0.14	0.62
2000	130.251	46.062	928.1	72.1	0.14	0.64
2001	132.888	42.997	965.8	73.7	0.14	0.58
2002	141.491	40.788	997.2	75.0	0.14	0.54
2003	150.810	44.320	1,031.60	76.7	0.15	0.58
2004	161.754	45.849	1,071.00	78.4	0.15	0.58
2005	172.009	53.984	1,106.50	80.1	0.16	0.67
2006	187.300	57.291	1,138.90	82.0	0.16	0.70
2007	197.155	56.350	1,187.90	84.9	0.17	0.66

Source: Net Capital Stock: ONS (2010), Profits: HMRC National Statistics (2015).
[a]Net capital stock is measured at current replacement cost (ONS tables CIXH/CIXI).

> secondary means that the capital fulfills a special function (which belongs to the circulation process) as for instance commercial capital. In the course of its evolution, industrial capital must therefore *subjugate* [my emphasis] these forms and transform them into derived or special functions of itself
>
> (Marx [1863] 1971: 468).

Yet, the modern financial sector has become more profitable (as the graphs show), or more exploitative depending on definition used, and with recent financial innovation and electronic trading, can appear more remote from (or so-called decoupled from) the *real* economy. There is an incentive, therefore, for modern nonfinancial capitalists, faced with squeezed profit margins, to move into the financial sector arena in the search for additional profit. This is analogous, in the modern era, to the development of early capitalist banking after feudalism that Marx was referring to in the passage cited above.

A study by the European Central Bank and Federal Reserve Bank of Kansas City further confirmed the growing importance and influence of non-banks. They note that:

> Retail payments systems throughout the world are undergoing fundamental change. Traditional paper-based forms of payment are giving way to electronic forms of payment. Technology advances are making possible new front-end payment instruments and new back-end processing methods. New products, business models, new markets, and new alliances are an everyday occurrence.
>
> (ECB/FRBKC 2007: 45)

The margins on Internet payment transactions, for instance, are lower than ones for traditional electronic retail banking and the corporations, through financial innovation, are therefore able to further encroach upon traditional bank business.[22] Another feature of the new financial landscape is that retailers have diversified into financial services, challenging banks in their core market. Since retailers have strong brands and customer responsiveness they often have stronger market knowledge. Yet, as Welch and Worthington have identified, retailers have so far adopted a selective approach to the provision of financial services and do not cover the wider range offered by banks (Welch 2007). Notwithstanding, the retailer threat to retail banking is likely to continue. Retailers have strong customer relations, provide services and tie in customers with reward schemes. In addition, a customer is more likely to meet a retail manager than a bank manager. Conversely, the trend in retail banking has been toward Internet banking services, driven by cost-saving motives, and customers rarely get to see banking personnel. In contrast, retail customers regularly visit their preferred retailer for weekly shopping or for a variety of other goods such as medicines, mobile phones, kitchen items, white goods, electronics goods, books and CDs. Much financial innovation by nonbanks, therefore, has been driven by the development of closer customer interaction.

The Centre for the Study of Financial Innovation, a London-based think-tank, at the end of the 1990s, initiated an investigation into the *nonbank* phenomenon within Europe and how this would impact the retail banking sector. The report concluded that the new entrant retail players did pose a serious threat for the long term, though the inroad made by retailers at the time into the financial sector was limited (Lascelles 1999). It could be argued that the corporate sector is poised to make a serious impact on the retail banking sector, and its systems, facilitated by technology-led innovation. These developments are changing, and indeed challenging, the existing financial power structure. The retail sector is not the only threat to the retail banking and financial sectors. Car manufacturers have found that the development of finance houses, for car finance, has been an anecdote to tighter margins in recent years. GM capital provides another example of multinational corporate finance houses (Houghton-Budd 2005).

Another threat to the traditional financial sector, and/or state financial sovereignty, is the development of alternative or complementary currencies. Edward De Bono, while writing for the Centre for the Study of Financial Innovation in 1993, had raised the future concept of the "IBM Dollar" or large corporation Dollar that might appear in generalized circulation. The idea was that corporate currency could be issued and linked to future company products and, a secondary market could ensure minimum risk for holding. In this manner the "targeted tied currency" could insure against inflation (De Bono 1993). Boyle has also suggested something similar to the concept of corporate money, that of new money systems for large metropolitan areas such as London. These would effectively form "regional-corporation" money covering a significant number of everyday expenditure items within that region, such as transport and local economic exchanges (Boyle 2000). There are already examples with the Oyster card system in London and the Octopus cards in Hong Kong, which can be used to purchase non-transport items. Similar systems are been applied in other cities around the world, one of the most recent being in Dubai (Octopus 2007). Alternative and complementary currencies, from local authority and grassroots sources, have also both received more interest of late as a result of the many uncertainties surrounding the financial systemic vulnerabilities (Lietaer 2001).

Notwithstanding these threats to their core activities, there have also been several innovations initiating from the banking sector itself (Mouatt 2011). Changes include telephone services or Internet banking for example. Yet, while the banking sector has been innovative in their core markets, an increased level of abstraction of money has occurred through securitization, and increased customer distance, as finance appears to be more divorced from actual production and the real economy. It seems clear that corporations are developing their own financial instruments, in parallel to the traditional bank financial services, which is evident from the proliferation of voucher systems and electronic transactions by retailers and corporations.

This market view of financial sector transformation could be considered consistent with Hayek's for free banking. The natural progression of a Hayekian philosophy is increasingly abstract levels of money, from the banking and financial sectors, in conjunction with any corporate monies and complementary currencies. Yet, the increasing volume and abstraction, without margins of safety, could lead to a point where there is substantial systemic risk—at least in the long term. In the Hayek view, the money competition in a relatively free market would eventually deliver a system that achieves the common trust necessary for stable money and fewer currencies (Houghton-Budd 2005). It could be argued, therefore, that currencies and credit backed by corporate commodities are likely to become predominant in the event of major financial instability. These new processes could lead, however, to a concentration of greater financial power among nonfinancial firms, with a subsequent state democratic deficit as capitalism develops. In addition, they may engender instability in the short term.

11.8 CONCLUSION

The key conclusion of the chapter is that the transformation of finance, leading to an erosion of state financial sovereignty, has not been driven by endogenous factors but has, instead, resulted from the tendency for the rate of profit to fall across periods of production. In the empirical study of the UK and German profit rates, it was discovered that the historic cost, current cost and MELT-adjusted historic profit rates have demonstrated a secular decline since the Great Depression when the means of production were marked down. In addition, any *restoration* of profit rates established, since the 1970s, has not been sustained suggesting that the crises of the post-WW2 era have been unsuccessful in this regard. As a consequence, firms have sought new avenues of profitability and a migration of surplus capital toward the financial sector has taken place, in conjunction with leverage (further credit expansion) in the financial sector itself. It is these processes that have led, it is argued, to the neo-liberal era of banking and the so-called financialization with the subsequent erosion of state financial sovereignty. It is noted, however, that there are various counter-tendencies, which have mitigated, or even eliminated, the falling profitability and some of these are noted. In the last three decades, for instance, the shorter product life cycles of information technology have led to increased *moral depreciation.* This has resulted in losses for some capitals, and increased centralization processes, but restored rates of profit for others. In this environment, as might be expected, the lead technology firms have had a competitive advantage. Finally, the rise of nonbanks, and competing currencies, is perhaps *prima facie* evidence of nonfinancial capitalist attempts to secure a larger share of the surplus value that was previously accruing to economic agents in the financial sector. This provides further indication that production is a key driver of outcomes in the capitalist economies and, of course, persistent low profitability. The finance sector is currently undergoing much innovation as a consequence. At the end of the case-study period considered in the book, as the reader is no doubt fully aware, the global financial crisis of 2008 was experienced as the US sub-prime defaults triggered a mark down of collaterized debt obligations that many of the commercial banks held on their balance sheets. The subsequent insolvency led to shockwaves of panic, state bailouts, credit squeezes, rising national debt and real economy stagnation. The policy response in the UK has been to instigate public sector spending cuts that seem to have prolonged stagnation, while simultaneously seeking to stimulate economic activity by engaging in quantitative easing and encouraging low interest rates. In addition, there has been much discussion among interested parties regarding the systemic regulation and even transformation of the finance sector in order to avert future crises of the same proportions. Yet, partly as a consequence of the sheer quantity of the recent financial phenomena, much of the finance narrative has focused on financialization *per se* without specifically discussing the likely causes of financialization itself. It is hoped that this book makes a small contribution toward remedying this oversight and the credit goes to Marx for leaving us with a holistic description of general capitalist mechanics that is rooted in the LTFRP.

In the next and final chapter, I summarize the key propositions and findings of the book and point toward possible scenarios for the future.

NOTES

1. The slumps of the early 1970s or 1980s, notes Kliman, failed to restore profitability (Kliman 2012: 48).

2. Changing expectations are responsible for *de facto* investment decision-making. I take the position that historic profit rates, and inflation-adjusted historic profit rates, are a reliable indicator of likely expectations, in conjunction with any "animal spirits" (Keynes' notion) and current interest rate element that exists.

3. It has been assumed that this is a reasonable estimate of the UK historic cost measures for fixed assets. The values of fixed assets, for example, are likely to be an *underestimation* of UK measures because some UK assets date further back than US figures and, therefore, an overestimation of profit rate if anything is likely.

4. The ONS net investments measured at constant 2006 prices are entered in to the Perpetual Inventory Method (PIM) model and then reflated (or deflated) in order to give an approximation of current prices. This is not quite the same approach as the US method since the PIM uses varying asset category indices (Omundsen 2010: 5).

5. Adjusting for inflation, using the MELT and RPI/CPI measures, led to very similar results in the Kliman study and, therefore, it was not considered necessary to replicate the calculations for the UK.

6. This is a much closer statistical measure to Marx's notion of surplus value.

7. It is for this reason that it was considered unnecessary to replicate the same data calculation.

8. Figure 11.2 also gives an indication that the rising organic composition of capital, and subsequent falling profit rates, occur in cycles that, as Roberts notes, are consistent with earlier periods of industrialization and financialization in the US. He identifies 16–18-year (approximate) cycles (Roberts 2009: 55).

9. Corporate decision-makers can use the information, for instance, as they consider the replacement cost of advanced capital for the future. Yet, historic cost profit rate are useful for decision-makers as they contemplate historic average profit rate trends and the repayment of any debt obligations pertaining to capital.

10. Since the historic cost advanced capital is measured at the start of the year, the calculations are based on the MELT deflator for the previous year.

11. Michel Husson, a supporter of the view that neo-liberalism has restored profit rates, has challenged Kliman's method of deflating historic depreciation costs in order to calculate net investment with the MELT suggesting that current depreciation costs should have been used. However, when Kliman recalculated US profit rates using current depreciation costs he discovered there was virtually no difference to results (Kliman 2012: 86).

12. The proliferation of patents facilitates the extraction of technology rents.

13. The statistics prior to 1970 were unobtainable.

14. The restoration of profit in the neo-liberal era, however, has not been as marked.

15. This makes estimating surplus value difficult because the relative magnitudes, of the two categories of depreciation, are unknown from official data.

16. Kliman uses BEA data, from between 1937 and 1951, to estimate the level of normal (wear and tear) depreciation of fixed assets and then extrapolates values to estimate the relative proportion of moral and other depreciation since 1951. Kliman then calculates that the percentage of surplus value not realized as profit (the *increased* moral depreciation) was: 28% for after-tax profits, 21% for before-tax profits and 12% for property income (Kliman 2010: 78).

17. In the UK, there is already, as Nehru and Dhareshwar have noted, a lack of methodological consensus on how to formulate statistics on capital stocks and the information age, therefore, is likely to make this more controversial (Nehru 1993). However, the ONS statistical authorities, in the UK, are conducting study in order to report the computer age technology impact more effectively (Omundsen 2010: 6).

18. Strange, among many others, had also noted the varied aspects of criminal money laundering, false accounting and tax evasion at work in the modern global economy (Strange 1998: 131; Blackburn 2002).

19. The LTFRP means that less new value is available for investment, capitalist consumption or transfer into the financial markets. However, as the organic concentration of capital increases, so individual capitals can (depending on circumstances) increase the mass of surplus value thus compensating individual entrepreneurs.

20. If the government intervenes with a cheap money policy, this will further encourage financial sector activity.

21. Robert Brenner, noted by Kliman, suggests that firms expand "faster than demand will permit." Yet, if the crisis (which involves insufficient demand) is solely explained (in terms of causality) with reference to the lack of demand this is tautological (Kliman 1999: 3).

22. This has been further enhanced by the development, licence and general use of public key cryptography.

Chapter 12

Concluding Analysis

12.1 INTRODUCTION

The ability to influence currency-creation and its purchasing power, financial power, is clearly a significant source of *social power* in any context. Historically, these matters have been jointly determined by state and market, in varying proportions. Yet, during the capitalist mode of production, private agents in the market and banking system have mostly wielded this financial power. In fact, I argue that capitalism itself had instigated a shift in financial power away from the state from the outset. It was identified in chapter 1 that it is not common, with the exception of the international political economy literature, to discuss the *political* ramifications associated with financial power or its erosion, especially in traditional monetary theory. This became, therefore, the key rationale for writing the book. In particular, a general aim has been to address some of the political economy issues of modern money, while remaining grounded in economic theory. Given that plutocratic elites largely determine the trajectory of global capitalism, and material relations arguably shape social life in general, I suggest that the subject is important.

In the last century the size, influence and scope of the state had grown, especially in the immediate period following WW2. In terms of the extension of the economic influence of the state, including financial, it has been assumed that the general tough conditions of the Great Depression and subsequent WW2 provided the catalyst for the BW era, with its underlying Keynesian *synthesis* ideology. This was manifested, *inter alia*, in the BW N-1 exchange rate system adopted in 1944, for instance, or in the nationalization of the BOE in the UK. Keynesian interventionist-minded people had become established in policy-making circles, and the private banking system was subjected to at least some measure of control. The book's title, *The Dissolution of the Financial State*, suggests that these people had to be removed if a *bourgeois* state, which represents the key interests of capital (including banks) was to be established. The banks sought an expansion of bank profits that would only have been possible if such an erosion of state financial sovereignty occurred. As the BW era passed through the 1970s to the neo-liberal era, this was exactly what happened. The question was then asked whether or not the state had *lost* capability to influence currency-creation and purchasing power in a way that could be empirically validated in the case-study period. The evidence presented in chapters 9 and 10 concluded that this, indeed, had been the case.

In response to this erosion of financial power, the book then investigated the prediction of Marx, regarding the *tendential* behavior of the capitalist economy, and asked whether *production* factors were the *key* drivers of any systemic transformation. The book then partly replicated a US profitability study undertaken by Professor Andrew Kliman, in the context of German and UK case studies, which were presented in chapter 11 (Kliman 2010). It was discovered that falling profit rates were evident, and also that the falling rate of accumulation were likely to be *indirect* causes of the *financialization* processes, changing *rentier* incomes, faster moral depreciation, increasing concentration/centralization and the propensity toward crisis in the neo-liberal era.[1] It could be that economic agents cut back on investment, and surplus capital migrates to the financial sector. In addition, it is posited that leverage in the financial sector also fuels activity. It is argued in the book, therefore, that the erosion of state financial power identified can be adequately explained with reference to these particular processes. One of the reasons for the migration of capital to the finance sector is the existence of boom. In a boom, real economy profitability in value terms (but not physical terms) is falling. The generally high expectations in boom, however, lead to higher asset prices and speculation that is, enhanced finance sector activity. In addition, the lower interest rates further fuel the credit expansion in the finance sector. Yet, while the financialization literature focuses on financial sector activity and claims the phenomena are the *source* of stagnation in wages and growth in the real economy (see Palley), the Marx perspective argues that causality is the other way around (Palley 2007). Marx instead posited that the LTFRP is the indirect cause of the financialization activity in the first place, while recognizing the disruptive nature of finance phenomena as proximate causes of economic outcomes. So, the law of value was paramount.

Finally, the discussion of monetary theory in chapter 4 concluded that there is a need to present modern money with reference to the EMT, if the objective is to better reflect reality. Credit money is created in response to demand at a given interest rate which the state has a reasonable (but not complete) ability to determine. Yet, this has been excluded from traditional

Marxian analysis that has preferred to utilize commodity money entities or use abstract money, in line with Marx, in theoretical reasoning. It was therefore posited, in response, that Marx's political economy *could* comfortably be theorized in conjunction with the EMT. The notion of using other money entities in Marxian analysis has been explored before, but has not been *developed* with a full discussion of the EMT and/or the TSSI. It is argued this is a useful theoretical framework since it is important for monetary discourse to reflect the reality.

12.2 PRIVATE FINANCIAL POWER

Financial power, as a form of social power, is not the *exclusive* source of power. However, as was argued in chapter 1, it can definitely be considered, in line with Strange, as a *primary* source of social power in a monetary economy (Strange 1988). In contrast to the mainstream view of neutrality, therefore, money has significant *instigative* and *fungible* features. Marx had appreciated this aspect of money stating, with reference to an absolute monarchy, that monetary resources form the "material lever" of social power (De Brunhoff 1976: 45). Marx continued (quoting Steuart), it also forms "the measure of power between nations" (De Brunhoff 1976: 46). Marx therefore implies that, in addition to financial power *per se*, social power derived from other sources also needs to be able to secure the actual property rights (ownership title is insufficient) to monetary resources in order to be exercised. Yet, perhaps regrettably, Marx did not pursue these specific ideas any further. His later musings on the financial role of the state, as De Brunhoff noted referred to the sometimes difficult task of setting the standard of price, that is, the convertibility ratios between paper notes and specie (De Brunhoff 1976: 46). It is argued in the book that Marx wanted to focus on capitalist accumulation as a driver of material relations rather than the existence of money *per se* in social power relations. In other words, money was of primary significance in social life, but was secondary albeit indispensable to the general production process. Yet, Marx's notion of the circuit of capital places money as the initial *catalyst* to production, despite the general primacy of productive agents in his political economy, and any appropriated profit is also measured in monetary terms.

These ideas are somewhat different to those of Hilferding, who had posited that integrated financiers constitute key decision-makers that determine the trajectory of capitalist production (Hilferding 1910). This was predicated on the rise of the joint-stock firm, and, social interaction between financiers and capitalists. Marx, it is worth noting, had also presented the idea of the credit system's role in the centralization and concentration process of capital (De Brunhoff 2006: 198). The problem with the Hilferding position is that it was not consistent with Marx's overall political economy. Marx had instead illustrated how emerging capitalist credit relations subjugated earlier feudal lending practices, in contrast to Hilferding, with productive agents remaining preeminent (Marx [1863] 1971: 468). Marx had clearly recognized that finance was *able* to disrupt capitalist production but this was not the same thing as a deterministic function (Marx [1894] 1981: 678). The book has conceded, however, that there is an *appearance* of increasing autonomy, or decoupling, of the financial realm, deriving from recent *financialization* in the neo-liberal era. Yet, it is argued that money, as a *claim* on real resources will always remain dependent on the real economy and, furthermore, there is recent evidence that production is re-exerting influence over finance.[2] This supports the view that the tendential behavior of the capitalist economy, as predicted by Marx, provides an adequate explanation of the financialization and erosion of state financial power evidenced in the case studies presented. Notwithstanding, it is clear to all that the financial markets have grown exponentially in recent times and this certainly (if only in appearance) suggests that the finance sector has been elevated in relation to the real economy in terms of the ability to determine outcomes. In addition, Palley claims there has been a recent continual transfer of income from the real economy to the finance sector and changes to macroeconomic variables as a consequence of financialization (Palley 2007: 3). Palley further points out that the FIRE sector share of GDP has risen from 15% to 20.4% from 1973 to 2005 and there is weaker investment now in relation to 1979 (Palley 2007: 10). Hudson also pointed out in reference to Figure 11.8 in chapter 11 that debt associated with the FIRE sector in the US has grown substantially in the neo-liberal era while debt associated with the real economy has remained stable (Hudson 2005). Despite all of the financialization discourse, it still tends to be presented as a collection of information about financial phenomena (as stated above), without the necessary analysis of the underlying causes. Instead of explaining the financial phenomena, and reflecting on their effect on a range of variables, I contend that the finance activity is used to explain the finance activity.

If it can be concluded that the *private* control of money has been increasing at the expense of the state, although not necessarily proportionate to any decline in state capability, then there are positive and negative ramifications.[3] If *increasing* accumulation and centralization of money resources in plutocratic elites has taken place in the modern era this will reflect in many aspects of economic society. This latter notion is consistent with some contemporary research. Hudson, for instance, as outlined in chapter 11, has discussed the increases of *rentier* incomes that have taken place during the neo-liberal order, while the real economy stagnates (Hudson 2005). In an era of inflated real estate prices, these incomes have derived from *inter alia* debt-servicing or increased rents. It was concluded that, while measures to reduce *rentier* income would serve as a counter-tendency to the LTFRP, the book claims Marx's law of value still exerts influence in the long-term and leads to the inevitable crisis, and interim influences on the financial sector.

12.3 MONETARY THEORY

Marx's political economy, and its derived monetary theory, is compatible with inconvertible modern credit-money. It has been claimed that others have discussed the possible use of fiat or credit-money in Marxian analysis but that it has not been theorized in conjunction with the EMT or TSSI. Most recently (2011), Moseley, for example, has recently identified a fiat-money version of the MELT, denoted as MV/L where M represents a measure of inconvertible fiat money (Rieu 2012: 2).[4] He derived this notion of the MELT from Marx's treatment of fiat money that exists alongside commodity money (Marx 1976: 225). Moseley then further posits that this can be extended to the treatment of modern credit-money, which he sees as partly exogenous and partly endogenously created (Moseley 2011: 100).[5] However, while Moseley's version (to its credit) was not predicated on the Marx notion of the *economizing* nature of credit monies that is, not money proper, and instead used *units* of bank credit-money, it was not combined with a full discussion of the EMT (Marx [1894] 1981: 653). It is posited that *ex nihilo* credit entities can also be used in the normal reproduction schema of Marx, by incorporating them in to the TSSI tradition that usually uses abstract money. Since, at least for the duration of time that the debt obligation(s) pertains to, credit monies can serve the full functionality of money as defined. Moseley's concept of the MELT, in contrast, is theorized using a SSSI of Marx that, as a consequence of its internal logic (as Kliman has explained), precludes the possibility of LTFRP and the profit rate is physically determined. (Kliman 2007: 53). Since, this study claims that the decline in state financial power, and the concurrent transformation of the financial sector, *can* be adequately explained by the LTFRP, the Moseley conception of the MELT has therefore not been accepted. The restored LTFRP of Marx, courtesy of Kliman *et al.*, is preferable to the purpose of the book.

It has also been argued that the difficulty of reducing credit-money into units of abstract social labor, rendering *changes* to commodity values expressed in monetary terms more complicated, may be the reason for their previous nonuse by Marxian economists. It may also have been problematic to model the credit-money system in general. Alternatively, it has been suggested in chapter 6, as Marx intimated, credit-money theory may not be used since it is only specie that has the *sustained* ability to transcend the boundaries of the nation-state (Marx [1867] 1976: 240). Notwithstanding its limitation, it is this monetary synthesis of EMT credit-money as *units* of money combined with Marx's political economy, as understood by the TSSI, that the book claims is theoretically valid. In the same way that the MELT allows us to express the produced and realized value of commodities either in labor-time or money, the MELT also allows us to estimate the production costs of circulation (credit-money) in labor-time or money. The costs of circulation will, therefore, be a deduction of surplus value for the productive economy and a source of income for the financial sector.

These monetary ideas were further expanded in the steam train analogy in chapter 8. In the PK conception, loans are created *ex nihilo*, simply in response to demand, at a given interest rate (Lavoie 2003: 507).[6] The supply conditions are, in turn, determined by various factors such as risk expectations or liability management that is, the ability of retail banks to increase their own borrowing without the forced sale of their marketable assets (Lavoie 2003: 521). The quantity of money to be added to the drive wheel circumference of the train, net of credit repayments and dishoarding levels, represents the amount of credit creation in each production period. This, in turn, is dependent on the prices of production, which represent completed profit equalization processes following Marx, and the changing profit rate and accumulation across periods. Yet, the train allows for unforeseen credit system problems to interfere with next period's production, and this period's circulation, in a disruptive manner, directly impacting the money supply for the period. The steam train analogy, for purposes of simplicity, also assumed a pure credit-money economy.

12.4 GERMAN AND UK SYSTEM TRANSFORMATION

It was argued in chapter 9 that Germany has undergone substantial change during the case-study period since WW2. After 1875, and prior to WW1, the financial power of the state was evident in its "direction" of the Reichsbank but, following WW2, the allies had placed restrictions on the political control of the bank by Weimar Republic politicians. In particular, the allies were concerned to ensure that the decision-making capability of the Reichsbank was *autonomous* from politicians. Yet, the central bank is seen as a semi-state institution, charged with the affairs of state. In this sense, even though the Weimar Republic politicians had less control than the earlier Reich, the German state begins the case-study period with a substantial amount of financial power in relation to the market. The BDL *Zentralbankrat*, formed in 1948, was revealed to have a reasonable grip on market interest rates, and hence credit-money and inflation, through their imposition of minimum reserve requirements and Lombard/discount rates of interest. In the early part of the BW era, for example, the BDL and Bundesbank inflation control had surpassed that of the later post-BW period.

Yet, as the 1960s progressed, noted by Franke, banks used different ways to bypass the monetary policy instruments, thus reducing state sovereignty (Franke 2013). Franke further notes that the DB tried to act more in line with market rates when deciding Lombard/discount rates in the neo-liberal era (Franke 2013). In addition, as noted in chapter 9, the introduction of new security repurchases, in Bundesbank open market operations, while motivated by the need to regain some interest rate control, the impact was tempered (as Baltensperger noted) by increased market sensitivity in DB decision-making (Baltensperger 1999). In terms of exchange-rate sovereignty, in the BW system, the interstate monetary regime can be considered to have represented greater FRG state capability, despite the fact that the allies rather than FRG state apparatus had instigated its compliance with the arrangements. In the neo-liberal era that followed, with floating exchange rates, it became increasingly difficult for the FRG/German state to effect currency values with the use of foreign exchange interventions. Notwithstanding, as Potts noted, the Deutschmark was a stable currency during the latter period of the case study, evidenced by its use as an anchor currency in the years leading to the introduction of the ERM in 1979 (Potts 1997).

The particular characteristics of the German financial system have also contributed toward a mitigation of more exploitative elements of the financial sector, which may account for the specific nature of the transformation of the banking sector during the case-study period. German banks, as Vitols notes, in comparison to the UK, provide more long-term finance and are less equity financed (Vitols 1998). They also tend to have a bigger role, as Soskice argued, in real economy decision-making due to their frequent equity stakes and proxy votes on executive boards (Soskice 1992). This is partly because, as Deeg noted, the big three commercial banks only have 10% of assets (1992), in comparison to 15% for the cooperative sector (*Genosseenschaftsbanken*) and 40% for the public savings banks (e.g., *Sparkassen*), and there has also been a shift to the latter in the post-WW2 era due to the demand from the *Mittelstand* small to medium firms for finance (Deeg 1992).[7] This is predicated on the idea that public and cooperative banks are likely to work more closely with nonfinancial executives, and that the practice of universal banking that is, the mixture of investment and retail banking further intensifies the integration of financial and real sector relations (Vitols 1998).

In the UK case study, a similar erosion of financial power was identified. The period had begun with the abandonment of the gold standard (reinstated in 1925) in 1931, leading to a sharp devaluation of Sterling.[8] This freed monetary policy from the constraints of gold convertibility.

The subsequent monetary policies pursued by the UK state authorities, until WW2, consisted primarily of a low Bank Rate at 2%, which achieved a measure of success in term of real growth.[9] At this time, and during the BW era as argued in chapter 10, the Bank Rate formed the definitive guide to the market interest rates and, therefore, the level of bank advances. This effectiveness of the official interest rate, defining state capability, continued until the growth of the interbank market in the 1960s, where it is argued greater market volumes and activity reduced agent dependency on discount rates.[10] It was also noted in chapter 10 that, during the BW period, the banks had at least a latent capability to substantially expand credit given the levels of liquidity in the system, as a direct consequence of the level of national debt securities held. During the 1970s, however, substantial credit expansion occurred and the state regulation of the financial sector became more market orientated. The deregulated neo-liberal era has since, therefore, represented a time of increased private financial power and an eroded state capability to determine credit levels, and by implication the allocation, and the value of currency.

The empirical part of the book that was concluded in chapter 11 with a study of UK/FRG profitability was partly replicated from a study by Professor Andrew Kliman conducted on the US economy from the time of the Great Depression to 2007. The LTFRP was considered by Marx to be his single most important contribution to political economy and, Marx claimed, it constituted the driver of systemic transformation in capitalism generally. Consistent low profitability, detrimental to the *modus operandi* of capitalism, is presented as leading, albeit indirectly, to stagnation and the desperate attempts by capitalists and government policy to counter the effects. In both Germany and the UK, faling profit rates were identified. This provided an explanation of the growth of financial markets in the neo-liberal era, as surplus capital migration fueled their activity, derived from firms cutting back on investment in conjunction with leverage in the financial sector. However, while productive and financial factors have a reflexive relationship, in the sense that they co-determine outcomes, the book maintains the position that productive factors, in particular Marx's law of value, is the key driver of outcomes and transformation. Yet, the German and UK case studies revealed a notable difference between the two economies. While general profitability has fallen in both countries, and in the case of the UK the MELT-adjusted profit rate failed to recover, Germany has experienced a higher level of profitability. It is claimed that this was partly due to the currency reform of 1948, and later debt write-downs, in conjunction with substantial technology rents and the maintenance of *lead* producer status, which enables firms to receive profit above the average rate in the sector. In addition, Germany has maintained international competitiveness through lower relative inflation and wage levels. It is concluded that this partly explains the existence of a relatively less exploitative universal banking sector, with large public and cooperative sector, that perhaps provides more stability than national financial systems in other parts of the global economy.

12.5 THE FUTURE

The book concludes that Marx's political economy, in combination with the EMT, provides us with the best lens through which we can view the capitalist mode of production, and its monetary system, and predict its future trajectory. The study findings also shed light on the need for government policy that takes account of the need to restore profitability, assuming that the intention is to sustain the mechanics of the current economic system. Marx, as noted in chapter 5, did not predict the inevitable collapse of capitalism although he maintained that class tensions derived from material relations of production *may* lead to the expropriation of the means of production following a period of political upheaval. The contradictory nature of the mechanical operation of market competition leads to endogenous, thus inevitable, crises that mark down the value of the means of production, in conjunction with other counter-tendencies to the LTFRP. These processes are not policy options but are indispensable for the system operation, and its sustainability in its current form, unless the system is sustained by more concerted political action of some kind. This latter scenario, some have argued, provides a possible explanation of the bank balance sheet bailouts of 2008. When systemic crisis requires it, the state steps in as *sustainer of last resort.* Capitalism is clearly more resilient than some of the radicals have given credit for. Given the global income and wealth inequalities, alienation from produce, negative social impacts from competition, waste and the relentless use of finite resources perhaps, for the sake of people and planet, the time has arrived to consider a new economic system. In the past, these types of ideas have been reserved for the radical fringe and the esoteric. It now appears that systemic change is becoming more of a mainstream consideration.

In the times of Henry VIII in the sixteenth century, the dissolution of the monasteries facilitated an already weakened Catholicist ideological stronghold in England, thus improving the chances of protestant thinking becoming preeminent. Yet, as many historians note, there were also economic motives. The monasteries had substantial assets, and monies were also being raised and diverted to Rome. The coffers of Henry VIII were subsequently greatly enhanced by the dissolution and the stand against the Papacy. In the same way, as the graph in chapter 11 illustrates, the dissolution of the financial state since WW2 has led to a substantial increase in private bank profits.

Yet, perhaps in a way that is analogous to the troubled reigns of Queen Mary and Elizabeth I after Henry VIII, the neo-liberal era has been marked by perennial financial crises. It is perhaps time to reconsider the need for a stronger financial state.

NOTES

1. In the study the rate of accumulation was assumed to track the rate of profit, as it does in Kliman's study.

2. The discussion of the increasing activity of nonbanks providing retail and investment banking services, discussed in chapter 11, is an example of production exerting more influence over the finance sector.

3. In our current globalized world, for instance, state financial power may diminish as a direct result of the interventions of multilateral institutions or other nation-states.

4. Moseley recognizes that the term fiat money is sometimes used to refer to credit money as well as forms created by the state. However, he posits, following Lapavitsas, that fiat money (as also defined in this book) is created by government, remains in circulation and is separate from credit-money (Moseley 2011: 98).

5. The Moseley paper appeared in *Review of Radical Economics* at the same time as my paper that outlines, albeit in the context of the EMT and TSSI, the same theoretical construct (Moseley 2011; Mouatt 2011).

6. The assumption in the study is that, in capitalist economies, the market interest rates are generally determined by the money market rates, which the central bank seeks to target with their open market operations and base rate policies. They have long since abandoned the intention of controlling the money supply and/or inflation by targeting monetary aggregates and solely rely on the use of interest rates (Fontana 2003: 45).

7. In the UK and US, in contrast, the joint-stock financial institutions have owned almost all of the bank assets since WW1 (Vitols 1998). However, it also needs to be mentioned that despite the specific nature of German bank relations with industry, the public banks in Germany are not permitted by law to take equity stakes in nonfinancial corporations (Vitols 1998). Cooperative banks are different.

8. The UK/US exchange rate recovered by 1934 and remained reasonably stable until WW2 (Middleton 2010).

9. In the 1920s the UK practice of following the US interest rate trends was implemented by the Treasury and the BOE. The cheap money policy of the 1930s, later marked a move toward the ideas of Keynes, albeit without a proactive fiscal policy (Middleton 2010).

10. The addition of nonfinancial corporation deposits in this market, in neo-liberal times, has further contributed toward the ability of the banks to circumnavigate the intended objectives of state open market operations. It is the contention of this study that this is *prima facie* evidence of more market-driven interest rate policy and, therefore, a reflection of declining state financial power as defined.

Appendix 1

Table A1.1 US Current Cost, US Historic Cost, UK Current Cost and Estimates for UK Net Capital Stock

Year	US[a] CC	US[b] Historic	UK CC	UK[c] Historic	Year	US CC	US Historic	UK CC	UK Historic
1948	204.3	105.2	12.30	6.3	1978	2046.1	1018.8	293.90	146.3
1949	208	115.9	13.20	7.4	1979	2360	1144	356.10	172.6
1950	233	124.2	14.80	7.9	1980	2717.4	1295.7	416.50	198.6
1951	252.7	133.3	17.00	9.0	1981	3077.8	1459	445.70	211.3
1952	267.2	145.4	18.40	10.0	1982	3267.8	1645.8	459.00	231.2
1953	280.4	157.8	19.20	10.8	1983	3362.4	1816.7	475.50	256.9
1954	288.5	171.3	20.60	12.2	1984	3563	1969.4	498.10	275.3
1955	317.4	183.1	22.80	13.2	1985	3763.4	2164.1	530.40	305.0
1956	352.2	196.4	24.70	13.8	1986	3933.6	2365.6	565.50	340.1
1957	377.8	214.1	26.60	15.1	1987	4140.3	2538.8	611.40	374.9
1958	385.2	233.3	27.70	16.8	1988	4406.2	2694.5	677.60	414.4
1959	402.5	246.5	29.10	17.8	1989	4670.3	2863	751.60	460.7
1960	410.6	261.2	31.10	19.8	1990	4937	3046.6	775.40	478.5
1961	420.8	278.2	34.90	23.1	1991	5050.3	3246.2	779.60	501.1
1962	434.4	293.5	37.10	25.1	1992	5217.8	3409.2	771.10	503.8
1963	448.2	310.6	39.60	27.4	1993	5474.1	3562.7	785.40	511.2
1964	473.3	328	42.90	29.7	1994	5778.8	3751.9	812.40	527.5
1965	506.1	349.5	46.60	32.2	1995	6114.1	3963.6	837.20	542.7
1966	551.3	377.7	50.10	34.3	1996	6437.8	4228.7	855.30	561.8
1967	597.8	412.3	53.40	36.8	1997	6808.3	4521.2	871.00	578.4
1968	658.3	445.2	58.30	39.4	1998	7192	4841.5	911.00	613.3
1969	725.6	481.5	64.80	43.0	1999	7613.8	5183.5	958.10	652.3
1970	798.8	522.6	73.90	48.3	2000	8137.6	5549.7	1000.20	682.1
1971	876.5	562.5	84.10	54.0	2001	8528.8	5952.1	1039.50	725.4
1972	951.9	602.2	97.60	61.7	2002	8743.4	6242.1	1072.20	765.5
1973	1075.4	648.3	120.90	72.9	2003	8999.8	6411.7	1108.30	789.6
1974	1320.4	708.4	157.30	84.4	2004	9687.7	6577.2	1149.40	780.4

Table A1.1 US Current Cost, US Historic Cost, UK Current Cost and Estimates for UK Net Capital Stock (*Contd...*)

Year	*US[a] CC*	*US[b] Historic*	*UK CC*	*UK[c] Historic*	*Year*	*US CC*	*US Historic*	*UK CC*	*UK Historic*
1975	1467.4	780	191.80	102.0	2005	10523.4	6774.9	1186.60	763.9
1976	1613.5	847.9	222.40	116.9	2006	11337.8	7046.6	1220.90	758.8
1977	1797.9	923.4	253.30	130.1	2007	11887.3	7430.1	1272.80	795.6

Author's calculations based on data from US (CC) and US (HC) Bureau of Economic Analysis, Kliman (2010b), UK (CC) Office for National Statistics (2010c).

[a]Current cost.

[b]US Historic cost measures are for the previous year since BEA reports at year end.

[c]UK historic cost is estimated by dividing the US HC by US CC times the UK CC.

Appendix 2

Table A2.1 US Depreciation at Current Cost, US Historic Cost Depreciation, UK Current Cost Depreciation and Estimates for UK Depreciation at Historic Cost

Year	US[a] DHC	US[b] DCC	UK DCC	UK[c] DHC	Year	US DHC	US DCC	UK DCC	UK DHC
1948	7.1	10.6	508	340	1978	93.2	135.4	15589	10730
1949	7.9	11.5	545	374	1979	108.1	157.7	18513	12690
1950	8.7	12.3	596	422	1980	121.8	181.3	22196	14912
1951	9.5	13.8	705	485	1981	138.1	209.9	25126	16531
1952	10.3	14.5	806	573	1982	156.5	232.9	27207	18282
1953	11.3	15.5	853	622	1983	171.7	241.1	29039	20680
1954	12.2	16.3	901	674	1984	189.6	254	30684	22904
1955	13.2	17.4	999	758	1985	211.8	273.2	32986	25573
1956	14.3	19.3	1121	831	1986	230.2	291	34997	27685
1957	15.6	21.4	1222	891	1987	249	308.3	38136	30801
1958	16.9	22.5	1297	974	1988	266.4	330.5	40664	32777
1959	17.9	23.4	1349	1032	1989	289.8	356.9	44748	36335
1960	18.7	24.1	1429	1109	1990	304.9	374.7	50118	40782
1961	19.8	24.7	1618	1297	1991	321.7	394.2	54988	44875
1962	21	25.7	1739	1421	1992	343.6	410.7	57480	48089
1963	22.4	26.8	1835	1534	1993	358.2	424.5	58599	49447
1964	24.1	28.3	1997	1701	1994	391.4	458.4	59638	50921
1965	26.2	30.5	2174	1868	1995	412.5	482.1	60447	51720
1966	29	33.6	2375	2050	1996	446.1	510.8	62718	54774
1967	31.7	36.9	2507	2154	1997	486.1	546.6	62393	55487
1968	34.6	40.8	2744	2327	1998	530.9	583.9	64803	58921
1969	38.1	45.4	3022	2536	1999	580.9	630.8	68147	62756
1970	41.5	50.3	3450	2846	2000	631.1	685.9	71017	65343
1971	44.7	55.3	4051	3274	2001	686.2	742.1	72910	67418
1972	50.2	61.4	4630	3785	2002	688.9	742.1	75406	70000
1973	54.6	67.5	5485	4437	2003	700.9	759.8	77682	71660

Table A2.1 US Depreciation at Current Cost, US Historic Cost Depreciation, UK Current Cost Depreciation and Estimates for UK Depreciation at Historic Cost (*Contd...*)

Year	*US[a] DHC*	*US[b] DCC*	*UK DCC*	*UK[c] DHC*	*Year*	*US DHC*	*US DCC*	*UK DCC*	*UK DHC*
1974	60.2	79.2	6929	5267	2004	722	797.1	80323	72755
1975	66.4	95.3	9078	6325	2005	752.3	858.9	82804	72527
1976	73.2	105.5	11173	7752	2006	766	892.8	85606	73448
1977	82.2	119	13323	9203	2007	807.3	945.3	87828	75006

Author's calculations based on data from US (DCC) and US (DHC) Bureau of Economic Analysis, Kliman (2010b), UK (DCC) Office for National Statistics (2010d).

[a] US depreciation at historic cost.

[b] US depreciation at current cost.

[c] UK depreciation at historic cost is estimated by dividing the US DHC by US DCC and then multiplying by the UK DCC.

Appendix 3

Table A3.1 The Calculation of the MELT and MELT Index

Year	*UK*[a] *EMPLO*	*UK GDP*	*UK MELT*	*MELT*[b] *Index*	Year	*UK EMPLO*	*UK GDP*	*UK MELT*	*MELT Index*
1948	21566	11974	555	N/A	1978	24940	169344	6790	1.15
1949	21728	12726	586	1.06	1979	25195	199220	7907	1.16
1950	22013	13308	605	1.03	1980	25086	233184	9295	1.18
1951	22220	14784	665	1.10	1981	24430	256279	10490	1.13
1952	22181	15983	721	1.08	1982	23951	281024	11733	1.12
1953	22298	17121	768	1.07	1983	23775	307207	12921	1.10
1954	22648	18126	800	1.04	1984	24285	329913	13585	1.05
1955	22943	19490	849	1.06	1985	24592	361758	14710	1.08
1956	23200	20956	903	1.06	1986	24746	389149	15726	1.07
1957	23291	22105	949	1.05	1987	25239	428665	16984	1.08
1958	23129	23050	997	1.05	1988	26070	478510	18355	1.08
1959	23242	24348	1048	1.05	1989	26749	525274	19637	1.07
1960	23711	25977	1096	1.05	1990	26871	570283	21223	1.08
1961	24044	27413	1140	1.04	1991	26162	598664	22883	1.08
1962	24232	28711	1185	1.04	1992	25540	622080	24357	1.06
1963	24250	30409	1254	1.06	1993	25303	654196	25854	1.06
1964	24527	33228	1355	1.08	1994	25504	692987	27172	1.05
1965	24770	35888	1449	1.07	1995	25818	733266	28401	1.05
1966	24913	38189	1533	1.06	1996	26060	781726	29997	1.06
1967	24509	40281	1644	1.07	1997	26526	830094	31294	1.04
1968	24326	43656	1795	1.09	1998	26795	879102	32808	1.05
1969	24386	47023	1928	1.07	1999	27168	928730	34185	1.04
1970	24446	51696	2115	1.10	2000	27484	976533	35531	1.04
1971	24507	57670	2353	1.11	2001	27710	1022[c]	36876	1.04
1972	24579	64621	2629	1.12	2002	27920	1076	38523	1.04
1973	24965	74545	2986	1.14	2003	28182	1140	40442	1.05

Table A3.1 The Calculation of the MELT and MELT Index (*Contd...*)

Year	*UK*[a] *EMPLO*	*UK GDP*	*UK MELT*	*MELT*[b] *Index*	*Year*	*UK EMPLO*	*UK GDP*	*UK MELT*	*MELT Index*
1974	25029	84513	3377	1.13	2004	28480	1203	42239	1.04
1975	24933	106717	4280	1.27	2005	28770	1254	43589	1.03
1976	24786	126274	5095	1.19	2006	29025	1328	45766	1.05
1977	24809	146973	5924	1.16	2007	29228	1405	48065	1.05

Author's calculations based on data from HM Stationery Office (1971), IMF (2010d), ONS (2015),
[a]UK employment.
[b]The MELT index measures the % change from the previous year.
[c]This and subsequent GDP measures are in £ billions.

Appendix 4

OTHER PUBLICATIONS BY THE AUTHOR

Mouatt, S., 2008. Evaluating Stephen Zarlenga's Treatment of Historical Monetary Thought, *International Journal of Social* Economics. 35 (11), 846–56.
Mouatt, S., 2010. The Case for Monetary Diversity. *The International Journal of Community Currency Research,* 14, 17–28.
Mouatt, S. and C. Adams, eds., 2011. *Corporate and Social Transformation of Money and Banking: Breaking the Serfdom.* Chippenham: Palgrave Macmillan.
Mouatt, S., 2011. Can Sequential and Non-Dualistic Interpretation of Marx's Monetary Thought be synthesized with the Endogenous Money Paradigm? *Critique: Journal of Socialist* Theory. 39 (2), 233–46.
Mouatt, S., 2015. Credit Cycles: Freewheeling, Driving or Driven? Forthcoming: *International Journal of Social Economics.*

References

Ackrill, M. and L. Hannah, 2001. *Barclays: The Business of Banking 1690–1996*. Cambridge: Cambridge University Press.

Adams, C. and S. Mouatt, 2010. Evolution of Mobile Business and Service: Government Support of M-Payment Services. *International Journal of E-Services and Mobile Applications*, 2 (2), 58–0.

Adams, C. and S. Mouatt, 2011. Alternatives to the Global Financial Sector: Local Complementary Currencies, LETS and Time-Backed Currencies. In: Z. Luo, ed. *Advanced Analytics for Green and Sustainable Economic Development: Supply Chain Models and Financial Technologies*. Hershey, PA: IGI Global, pp. 64–78.

Adams, C. and S. Mouatt, 2010. The Rise of Complementary Currencies and Corporafinance: E-Commerce driven Competition in the Financial Sector. *The Journal of Internet Banking and Commerce*, 15 (1), 1–12.

Adams, N., 1993. *World's Apart – The North/South Divide and the International System*. Guildford: Zed.

Adams, P., 1991. *Odious Debts: Loose Lending, Corruption and the Third World's Environmental Legacy*. London: Earthscan.

Allen, J., 2003. *Lost Geographies of Power*. Bodmin: Blackwell.

Amin, S., 1997. *Capitalism in an Age of Globalisation*. Guildford: Zed.

Arrow, K. J. and G. Debreu, 1954. Existence of an Equilibrium for a Competitive Economy. *Econometrica*. 22 (3), 265–90.

Arestis, P. and M. Sawyer, 2002. The Bank of England Macroeconomic Model: Its Nature and Implications. *Journal of Post Keynesian Economics*. 24 (4), 529–46.

Argy, V., 1994. *International Macroeconomics: Theory and Policy*. United Kingdom: Routledge.

Arthur, C., 2001. Value, Labour and Negativity. *Capital and Class*, (73), 15–39.

Atkinson, J., 1984. Manpower Strategies for Flexible Organisations. *Personnel Management*, August, pp. 28–31.

Atwell, J., M. Milgate and P. Newman, 1990. *Marxian Economics*. Hong Kong: Macmillan.

Ball, A., 1977. *Modern Politics and Government*. 2nd ed. Hong Kong: Macmillan.

Balogh, T., 1956. Debate on Monetary Control: Dangers of the New Orthodoxy. *The Banker,* 106 (365), 347–53.

Baltensperger, E., 1999. Monetary Policy Under Conditions of Increasing Integration (1979–96). In: Bundesbank, ed. *50 Years of the Deutsche Mark: Central Bank and the Currency in Germany since 1948*. Guildford: Oxford University Press, pp. 439–523.

Bank of England, 2007. *Annual Report* [Viewed 2 December 2014]. Available from: http://www.bankofengland.co.uk/publications/Documents/annualreport/2007/2007report.pdf.

Bank of England, 2009. *Market Notice: Sterling Monetary Framework* [Viewed 7 December 2014]. Accessed from: http://www.bankofengland.co.uk/markets/Documents/marketnotice090806smf.pdf.

Bank of England, 2010. *Minimum Lending Rates* [Viewed 15 April 2010]. Available from: http://www.bankofengland.co.uk/mfsd/iadb.

Bank of England, 2011. *Documentation for the Bank of England's Operations under the Sterling Monetary Framework* [Viewed 7 December 2014]. Available from: http://www.bankofengland.co.uk/markets/Documents/money/documentation/110701operating.pdf.

Bank of England, 2012. *Explanatory Notes – Wholesale* [Viewed 7 December 2014]. Available from: http://www.bankofengland.co.uk/statistics/Pages/iadb/notesiadb/wholesale.

Barrow, C., 1993. *Critical Theories of the State*. Madison: University of Wisconsin.

Batra, R., 2002. Neutrality and Non-Neutrality of Money in a Classical-Type Model. *Political Economic Review,* 7 (3), 489–503.

Batten, D., M. Blackwell, I. Kim, S. Noceru and Y. Ozeki, 1990. *The Conduct of Monetary Policy in the Major Industrial Countries: Instruments and Operating Procedures*. United States: International Monetary Fund.

Begg, D., S. Fisher and R. Dornbusch, 2000. *Economics*. Turin: McGraw-Hill.

Bello, W., K. Malhotra, N. Bullard and M. Mezzera, 2000. Notes on the Ascendancy and Regulation of Speculative Capital. In: W. Bello, N. Bullard and K. Malhotra, eds. *Global Finance: New Thinking on Regulating Speculative Capital Markets*. Malaysia: Zed, pp. 1–26.

Bhaskar, R., 1989. *Reclaiming Reality: A Critical Introduction to Contemporary Philosophy*. London: Verso.

Bibow, J., 2009. On the Origin and Rise of Central Bank Independence in West Germany. *The European Journal of the History of Economic Thought,* 16 (1), 155–90.

Bird, G., 1989. *Loan-Loss Provisions and Third World Debt: Essay in International Finance*. 176, United States: Princeton University.

Bank for International Settlements, 2002. *Triennial Central Bank Survey: March*. [Viewed 7 December 2014]. Available from: http://www.bis.org/publ/rpfx02t.pdf.

Bank for International Settlements, 2007. *Triennial Central Bank Survey: December*. [Viewed 7 December 2014]. Available from: http://www.bis.org/publ/rpfxf07t.pdf.

Blackburn, R., 2002. The Enron Debacle and the Pension Crisis. *New Left Review,* 14, (March–April), 26–51.

Blaug, M., 1995. Why is the Quantity Theory of Money the Oldest Surviving Theory in Economics? In: G. Wood, ed. *The Quantity Theory of Money – From Locke to Keynes and Friedman*. Chippenham: Edward Elgar, pp. 27–49.

Bortkiewicz, L., 1949. On the Correction of Marx's Fundamental Theoretical Construction in the Third Volume of Capital. In: P. Sweezy, ed. *Bohn-Bawerk. Karl Marx and the Close of his System*. New York: Augustus M Kelley, pp. 199–222.

Bottomore, T., 1991. *A Dictionary of Marxist Thought*. 2nd ed. Bodmin: Blackwell.

Boyle, D., 2000. *Why London Needs Its Own Currency*. United Kingdom: New Economics Foundation.

Boyle, D., ed. 2002. *The Money Changers*. Ebbw Vale: Earthscan.

Bradford, T., M. Davies and S. Weiner, 2003. *Nonbanks in the Payments System*. United States: Federal Reserve Bank of Kansas City.

Brett, E. A., 1983. *International Money and Capitalist Crisis*. Guildford: Heinemann.

Brewer, A., 1984. *A Guide to Marx's Capital*. Cambridge: Cambridge University Press.

Brown, E., 2007. *The Web of Debt*. Baton Rouge: Third Millennium Press.

Bryman, A., 2008. *Social Research* Methods. 3rd ed. Italy: Oxford University Press.

Buchheim, C., 1999. The Establishment of the Bank deutcher Lander and the West German Currency Reform. In: Deutsche Bundesbank, ed. *Fifty Years of the Deutsche Mark – Central Bank and the Currency in Germany since 1948*. Guildford: Oxford University Press, pp. 55–102.

Buckle, M. and J. Thompson, 2004. *The UK Financial System: Theory and Practice*. 4th ed. Glasgow: Manchester University Press.

Bundesbank, ed. 1999. *Fifty Years of the Deutsche Mark: Central Bank and the Currency in Germany since 1948*. Guildford: Oxford University Press.

Bundesbank, 2013. *Geldmenge und Kreditvolumen*. [Viewed 19 January 2013]. Deutsche Bundesbank Eurosystem. Available at: http://www.bundesbank.de/download/statistik/wirtschaftsentwicklung/geldmenge_kreditvolumen.xls

Burkett, P., 2004. Marx's Reproduction Schemes and the Environment. *Ecological Economics*, 49 (4), 457–67.

Burnham, P., 2007. The Politicisation of Monetary Policy-Making in Post-war Britain. *British Politics*, 2 (3), 395–419.

Cairncross, A., 1995. *The British Economy since 1945*. Bodmin: Blackwell.

Capie, F. and A. Webber, 1985. *A Monetary History of the United Kingdom, 1870–1982: Data, Sources, Methods*. Chatham: George Allen and Unwin.

Capie, F. H., 2010. *The Bank of England 1950's to 1979*. United States: Cambridge University Press.

Capie, F. H., 1998. The Long-Run Relationship between Money and Prices. In: G. Wood, ed. *Money, Prices and the Real Economy*. Bodmin: Edward Elgar, pp. 19–33.

Carchedi, G., 1996. Non-Equilibrium Market Prices. In: A. Freeman and G. Carchedi, eds. *Marx and Non-Equilibrium Economics*. Cheltenham: Edward Elgar, pp. 164–82.

Cerny, P. G., 1993. *Finance and World Politics – Markets, Regimes and States in the Post-Hegemonic Era*. Cambridge: Edward Elgar.

Cerny, P. G., 1998. Politicising International Finance. *Millennium: Journal of International* Studies, 27 (2), 353–61.

Challen, P., S. Mouatt and R. Shakespeare, 2011. The State-Issue of Money without Usury. In: S. Mouatt and C. Adams, eds. *Corporate and Social Transformation of Money and Banking: Breaking the Serfdom*. Chippenham: Palgrave Macmillan, pp. 205–18.

Chick, V., 1986. *The Evolution of the Banking System and the Theory of Saving, Investment and Interest*. Discussion Paper No. 86–01, University College London.

Chick, V., 2000. Money and Effective Demand. In: J. Smithin, ed. *What is Money?* London: Routledge, pp. 124–38.

Clarke, A., 1992. *The Micro politics of Free Market Money: A Proposal*. United Kingdom: Libertarian Alliance [Viewed 7 December 2014] Available from: http://www.libertarian.co.uk/lapubs/econn/econn039.pdf.

Cohen, B., 1998. *The Geography of Money*. London: Cornell University Press.

Cohen, B., 2006. *The Future of* Money. United States: Princeton University Press.

Cohen, B., 2008. *Global Monetary Governance*. United States: Routledge.

Collins, M., 2012. *Money and Banking in the UK: A History*. Abingdon: Routledge.

Cooper, R. N., 1982. The Gold Standard: Historical Facts and Future Prospects. *Brookings Papers on Economic* Activity. 1, pp. 1–56.

Cox, R., 1987. *Production, Power and World Order*. United States: Columbia University Press.

De Bono, E., 1993. The IBM Dollar. In: D. Boyle, ed. *The Money Changers*. Ebbw Vale: Earthscan, pp. 168.

De Brunhoff, S., 1976. *Marx on Money*. New York: Urizen.

De Brunhoff, S. and D. Foley, 2006. Karl Marx's Theory of Money and Credit. In: P. Arestis and M. Sawyer, eds. *Handbook of Alternative Monetary Economics*. Cheltenham: Edward Elgar, pp. 188–204.

Deeg, R., 1992. *Banks and the State in Germany*. PhD Thesis, MIT, Cambridge, Mass.

De Meulenaere, S., 2008. 2007 Annual Report of the Worldwide Database of Complementary Currency Systems. *International Journal of Complementary Currency Research*, 12, 2–19.

Desai, M., 2002. *Marx's Revenge: The Resurgence of Capitalism and the Death of Statist Socialism*. Guildford: Verso.

De Soto, J. H., 2009. *Money, Bank Credit and Economic Cycles* [Viewed 9 December 2014]. Ludwig von Mises Institute. Available from: http;//www.mises.org.

Destatis, 2010a. *Net Fixed Assets: Statistisches Bundesamt, Fachserie 18, Reihe S.29/ D108*. Wiesbaden, Germany: Federal Statistical Office.

Destatis, 2010b. *Employment by Sectors of Economy: D210*. Wiesbaden, Germany: Federal Statistical Office.

Destatis, 2011a. *National Accounts GDP: Long Term Series since 1950*. Wiesbaden, Germany: Federal Statistical Office.

Destatis, 2011b. *Net Operating Surplus: 3.1.1 Wertschopfung Inlandsprodukt und Einkommen, Fachserie 18, Reihe S.29*. Wiesbaden, Germany: Federal Statistical Office.

Dimsdale, N. H., 1991. British Monetary Policy Since 1945. In: N. Crafts and N. Woodward, eds. *British Economy Since 1945*. Bath: Oxford University Press, pp. 89–140.

Docherty, P., 2008. Basel II and the Political Economy of Banking Regulation – Monetary Policy Interaction. *International Journal of Political Economy,* 37 (2), 82–106.

Dowd, K. and Greenway, D., 1993. Currency Competition, Network Externalities and Switching Costs: Towards an Alternative View of Optimum Currency Areas. *Economic Journal*, 103 (September), 1180–89.

Duchrow, U. and F. J. Hinklelammert, 2004. *Property for People, not for Profit: Alternatives to the Global Tyranny of Capital.* London: Zed.

Dumenil, G., 1984. The so-called "Transformation Problem" revisited: A brief comment. *Journal of Economic Theory* 33, 340–348.

Dunning, J. E., 2004. *Making Globalisation Good: The Moral Challenges of Capitalism.* King's Lynn: Oxford University Press.

ECB and FRBKC 2007, *Nonbanks in the Payments System: European and US Perspectives. Proceedings of Nonbanks in the Payments System: Innovation, Competition and Risk*, Santa Fe, New Mexico.

Eichengreen, B., 2011. *Exorbitant Privilege: The Rise and Fall of the Dollar and the Future of the International Monetary System.* United States: Oxford University Press.

El Diwany, T., 2003. *The Problem with Interest.* 2nd ed. Birmingham: Kreatoc.

El Gamal, M. A., 2006. *Islamic Finance: Law, Economics and Practice.* United States: Cambridge University Press.

Emry, S., 1984. *Billions for the Bankers, Debts for the People,* Sandpoint, Idaho. America's Promise Ministries.

Fama, E., 1970. Efficient Capital Markets – A Review of Theory and Empirical Work. *Journal of Finance,* 25 (2), pp. 383–417.

Ferguson, N., 2002. *The Cash Nexus: Money and Politics in Modern History, 1700–2000.* St Ives: Penguin.

Fforde, J., 1992. *The Bank of England and Public Policy 1941–1958.* Cambridge: Cambridge University Press.

Filipovic, M., 1997. *Governments, Banks and Global Capital: Securities Markets in Global Politics.* Aldershot: Ashgate.

Fisher, I., 1993. The Debt Deflation Theory of Great Depressions. *Econometrica,* 1 (4), 337–57.

Fohlin, C., 2007. *Finance Capitalism and Germany's Rise to Industrial Power.* United States: Cambridge University Press.

Foley, D. K., 1982. The Value of Money, the Value of Labor Power and the Transformation Problem. *Review of Radical Political Economics,* 14 (2), 37–47.

Fontana, G. and A. Palacio-Vera, 2003. Modern Theory and Practice of Central Banking: An Endogenous Money Perspective. In: L. Rochon and S. Rossi, eds. *Modern Theories of Money: The Nature and Role of Money in Capitalist Economies.* Bodmin: Edward Elgar, pp. 40–66.

Foucault, M., 1982. The Subject and Power. In: H. L. Drefus and P. Rabinow, eds. *Michel Foucault: Beyond Structuralism and Hermeneutics.* Brighton: Harvester, pp. 208–26.

Franke, G., 1999. The Bundesbank and Financial Markets. In: Bundesbank, ed. *Fifty Years of the Deutsche Mark – Central Bank and the Currency in Germany since 1948.* Guildford: Oxford University Press, pp. 219–66.

Franke, G., 2013. *Personal Communication* (26 February 2013). Professor of International Financial Management, Konstanz University, Germany.

Freeman, A., 1996. The Psychopathology of Walrasian Marxism. In: A. Freeman and G. Carchedi, eds. *Marx and Non-Equilibrium Economics*. eds. Cheltenham: Edward Elgar, pp. 1–29.

Freeman, A., 2004. *Geld (Money)*. Personal REPEC (MPRA) Archive Paper. Munich.

Freeman, A., 2008. *Speech at the Annual Conference of Heterodox Economics*. Cambridge, July.

Freire, M. V., 2009. Social Economy and Central Banks: Legal and Regulatory Issues on Social Currencies (Social Money) as a Public Policy Instrument Consistent with Monetary Policy. *International Journal of Complementary Currency Research,* 13, 76–94.

Friedman, M., 1953. The Case for Flexible Exchange Rates. In *Essays in Positive Economics*. Chicago: Chicago University Press.

Friedman, M., 1956. *Studies in the Quantity Theory of Money*. Chicago: University of Chicago Press.

Friedman, M., 1957. *A Theory of the Consumption Function*. Princeton: Princeton University Press.

Friedman, M. and Friedman, R., 1985. *The Tyranny of the Status Quo*. Bungay: Penguin.

Friedman, M. & Schwartz, A., 1993. *A Monetary History of the United States, 1867–1960*. Princeton: Princeton University Press.

Fuller, N., 1990. *Fundamental Economics*. Newcastle on Tyne: Tudor.

Galbraith, J. K., 1975. *Money: From Whence it Came and Where it Went*. London: Andre Deutsch.

Gaspar, V., G. Quiros and H. Mendizabal, 2004. *Interest Rate Determination in the Inter-Bank Market: Working Paper 351*. Frankfurt: European Central Bank.

George, S., 1992. *The Debt Boomerang*. Worcester: Pluto.

Germain, R. D., 1998. *The International Organisation of Credit: States and Global Finance in the World-Economy*. Cambridge: Cambridge University Press.

Gerschenkron, A., 1962. *Economic Backwardness in Historical Perspective*. Cambridge, MA: Harvard University Press.

Gesell, S., 1913. Why Money has to Rust. In: D. Boyle, ed. *The Money Changers: Currency Reform from Aristotle to e-Cash*. Ebbw Vale: Earthscan, pp. 40–42.

Gnos, C., 2004. Circuit Theory as an Explanation of the Real World. In: L. Rochon and S. Rossi, eds. *Modern Theories of Money: The Nature and Role of Money in Capitalist Economies*. Bodmin: Edward Elgar, pp. 322–38.

Gramsci, A., 1991. *Prison* Notebooks. Trowbridge: Lawrence and Wishart.

Graziani, A., 2003. *The Monetary Theory of Production*. Cambridge: Cambridge University Press.

Griffith-Jones, S., 1988. *Managing World Debt*. Worcester: Harvester Wheatsheaf.

Griffith-Jones, S., 1998. *Global Capital Flows*. Chippenham: Macmillan.

Grossmann, H., 1929. *The Law of the Accumulation and Collapse of the Capitalist System: Also a Theory of Crisis*, Leipzig: Hirschfeld.

Grossmann, H., 1977 (1941). Marx, Classical Economy and the Problem of Dynamics. *Capital and Class,* 2 (Summer), 32–55.

Grossmann, H., 1992. *The Law of Accumulation and Breakdown of the Capitalist System: Being also a Theory of Crisis*. London: Pluto.

Guinnane, T., 2004. *The 1953 London Debt Agreement.* Economic Growth Centre, Yale University, Discussion Paper No 880.

Gurley, J. and E. Shaw, 1960. *Money in a Theory of Finance*. Washington DC: The Brookings Institute.

Hagen, J., 1999. A New Approach to Monetary Policy (1971–8). In: Bundesbank, ed. *50 Years of the Deutschemark: Central Bank and the Currency in Germany since 1948*. Guildford: Oxford University Press, pp. 403–38.

Hahn, F., 1987. The Foundations of Monetary Theory. In: M. Cecco and J. Fitoussi, eds. *Monetary Theory and Economic Institutions*. London: Palgrave Macmillan, pp. 21–43.

Hampton, M. and J. Abbott, eds., 1999. *Off-shore Finance Centres and Tax Havens: The Rise of Global Capital*. Chippenham: Macmillan.

Hanson, J. L., 1970. *Monetary Theory and Practice*. 4th ed. Bungay: The Chaucer Press.

Harris, L., 1981. *Monetary Theory*. Singapore: McGraw-Hill.

Harvey, D., 2010. *A Companion to Marx's Capital*. United States: Verso.

Hawtrey, R. G., 1919a. *Currency and Credit*. London: Longmans, Green and Co.

Hawtrey, R. G., 1919b. The Gold Standard. *The Economic Journal,* 29 (116), 428–42.

Hayek, F., 1990. *Denationalisation of Money: The Argument Refined: An Analysis of the Theory and Practice of Concurrent Currencies*. 3rd ed. Lancing: The Institute of Economic Ideas, Hobart Paper (Special) 70.

Helleiner, E., 1992. States and the Future of Global Finance. *Review of International Studies,* 18, 31–49.

Helleiner, E., 1994. *States and the Re-emergence of Global Finance: From Bretton Woods to the 1990's*. United States: Cornell University Press.

Helleiner, E., 2008. The Evolution of the International Monetary and Financial System. In: J. Ravenhill, ed. *Global Political Economy*. 2nd ed. Italy: Oxford University Press, pp. 213–40.

Hengsbach, F., 2002. The Global Financial Markets: No 5th Power. In: J. Ammann, M. Pohl, W. Seifert and L. Weidenfeld, eds. *A Banker of Our Time: Business is Movement*. London: Weidenfeld and Nicolson, pp. 163–71.

Herdt, H., 2002. Corporations in the Global Financial Market Economy. In: J. Ammann, M. Pohl, W. Seifert and L. Weidenfeld, eds. *A Banker of Our Time: Business is Movement*. London: Weidenfeld and Nicolson, pp. 14–23.

Hetzel, R., 2002a. German Monetary History in the First Half of the Twentieth Century. *Economic Quarterly: Federal Reserve Bank of Richmond,* 88 (1), 1–35.

Hetzel, R., 2002b. German Monetary History in the Second Half of the Twentieth Century: From the Deutsche Mark to the Euro. *Economic Quarterly: Federal Reserve Bank of Richmond,* 88 (2), 29–64.

Hicks, J. R., 1967. *Critical Essays in Monetary Theory*. Oxford: Oxford University Press.

Hilferding, R., 1981 (1910). *Finance Capital: A Study in the Latest Phase of Capitalist Development*. London: Routledge and Kegan Paul.

HM Stationery Office, 1971. *British Labour Statistics: Historical Abstract: 1886–1968*. Department of Employment and Productivity. Poole: J.Looker Ltd.

HMRC National Statistics, 2015. *Table11.2*. [Viewed 28 February 2015]. Available from: https://www.gov.uk/government/statistics/corporation-tax-income-allowances-deductions-and-tax-liabilities-by-company-sector

Hobbes, T., 1968 (1651). *Leviathan*. Aylesbury: Penguin.

Hodgman, D., 1973. *Credit Controls in Western Europe: An Evaluative Review*. Boston Federal Reserve Bank. Credit Allocation Techniques and Monetary Policy Conference Proceedings [Viewed 9 December 2014]. Available from: http:\\www.bos.frb.org/economic/conf/conf11/conf11h.pdf.

Holtfrerich, C., 1999. Monetary Policy Under Fixed Exchange Rates. In: Bundesbank, ed. *50 Years of the Deutsche Mark: Central Bank and the Currency in Germany since 1948*. Guildford: Oxford University Press, pp. 307–401.

Hotson, A., 2010. *British Monetary Targets, 1976–1987: A View from the Fourth Floor of the Bank of England*. Special Paper 190, Financial Markets Group, London School of Economics and Political Science, ISSN 1359-9151-190.

Houghton-Budd, C., 2005. *Auditorial Central Banking – Monetary Themes for the 21st Century*. PhD Thesis. London: City University.

Howells, P. and K. Bain, 2002. *The Economics of Money, Banking and Finance: A European Text*. 2nd ed. Gosport: Prentice-Hall.

Howells, P. and K. Bain, 2004. *Financial Markets and Institutions*. 4th ed. Gosport: Prentice Hall.

Howells, P. and K. Bain, 2008. *Economics of Money, Banking and Finance*. 4th ed. Gosport: Pearson.

Huber, J. and J. Robertson, 2000. *Creating New Money: A Monetary Reform for the Information Age*. London: New Economics Foundation.

Hudson, M., 2005. *How Rent Gets Buried in the National Income Accounts* [Viewed 9 December 2014]. Available from: http://archives.econ.utah.edu/archives/a-list/2005w52/docw0ZMWYgp3A.doc.

Hudson, M., 2003. The Creditary/Monetarist Debate in Historical Perspective. In: E. N. S. BELL, ed. *The State, the Market and the Euro*. London: Edward Elgar.

Hudson, M. and D. Bezemer, 2012. Incorporating the *Rentier* Sectors into a Financial Model. *World Economic Review,* 1, 1–12 [Viewed 7 March 2015]. Available from: http://wer.worldeconomicsassociation.org/files/WER-Vol1-No1-complete.pdf

Hufner, F., 2010. The German Banking System: Lessons from the Financial Crisis. *OECD Economic Department Working Papers* (788).

Hulme, D. and P. Mosley, 1996. *Finance against Poverty*. Padstow: Routledge.

Ingham, G., 2001. Fundamentals of a Theory of Money: Untangling Fine, Lapavitsas and Zelizer. *Economy and Society*, 30 (3), 304–23.

IMF, 2010a. *International Financial Statistics: Inflation Rates Table 64.D.ZF and Table 64.7F* [Viewed 10 January 2010]. Available at: http://esds80.mcc.ac.uk/WDS_IFS.

IMF, 2010b. *International Financial Statistics: UK/German Base/Call Money Interest Rates* [Viewed 15 April 2010]. Available at: http://esds80.mcc.ac.uk/WDS_IFS/TableViewer.aspx.

IMF, 2010c. *International Financial Statistics: Deutsche Mark Dollar Exchange Rate* [Viewed 15 April 2010]. Available at: http://esds80.mcc.ac.uk/WDS_IFS/TableViewer.aspx.

IMF, 2010d. *International Financial Statistics: UK/German USD Reserves and GDP* [Viewed 15 April 2010]. Available at: http://esds80.mcc.ac.uk/WDS_IFS/TableViewer.aspx.

IMF, 2015a. *International Financial Statistics* [Viewed 7 March 2015]. 19MC-ZF (M0) and 59MD-ZF (M4). Available at: http://www.ukdataservice.ac.uk.

IMF, 2015b. *International Financial Statistics: USD Exchange Rate* [Viewed 7 March 2015]. Available at: https://stats.ukdataservice.ac.uk/

Ishizaka, A., 1999. The Monetary Policy of the Bank Deutsche Lander (Bank of the German State) during Germany's Post-War Re construction (1948–52). *Socio-Economic History,* 65 (3), 315–35.

Itoh, M. and C. Lapsvitsas, 1999. *The Political Economy of Money and Finance.* Chippenham: Macmillan.

Ivanova, M., 2011. Can it Happen Again: The Limits of Money Artistry. *Critique: Journal of Socialist Theory,* 39 (2), 211–32.

James, H., 1999. The Reichsbank 1876–1945. In: Bundesbank, ed. *50 Years of the Deutsche Mark: Central Bank and the Currency in Germany since 1948.* Guildford: Oxford University Press, pp. 3–49.

Janssen, N. and P. Andrew, 2005. *Publication of Narrow Money Data: the Implications of Money Market Reform.* Bank of England [Viewed 9 December 2014]. Available from: http://www.bankofengland.co.uk/publications/Documents/quarterlybulletin/qb050304.pdf.

Jayadev, A. and G. Epstein, 2007. The Correlates of Rentier Returns in OECD Countries. *Political Economy Research Institute*, Working Paper Series, No 123, University of Massachusetts [Viewed 9 December 2014]. Available from: http://www.peri.umass.edu/fileadmin/pdf/working_papers/working_papers_101-150/WP123.pdf.

Johnson, C. E., 1991. *Monetarism and the Keynesians.* Bristol: Pinter.

Jurgilas, M. and F. Zikes, 2012. *Implicit Intraday Interest Rate in the UK Unsecured Overnight Money Market.* Working Paper 447, London, Bank of England [Viewed 9 December 2014] Available from: http://www.bankofengland.co.uk/research/Documents/workingpapers/2012/wp447.pdf.

Kaen, F. and H. Sherman and H. Tehranian, 1997. The Effects of Bundesbank Discount and Lombard Rate Changes on German Bank Stock. *Journal of Multinational Financial Management*, 7, 1–25 [Viewed 9 December 2014]. Available from: https://www2.bc.edu/~tehranih/Hassan%20published%20paper/The%20Effect%20of%20Bundesbank%20Discount.pdf.

Kelso, L. and M. Adler, 1958. *The Capitalist Manifesto.* New York: Random House.

Kenen, P., 1960. *British Monetary Policy and the Balance of Payments 1951–1957.* United States: Harvard University Press.

Kennedy, M., 1995. *Inflation and Interest Free: Creating an Exchange Medium that Works for Everyone and Protects the Earth*. Canada: New Society Publisher.

Keynes, J. M., 1919. *The Economic Consequences of the Peace*. London: Macmillan.

Keynes, J. M., 1924. *A Tract on Monetary Reform*. London: Macmillan.

Keynes, J. M., 1930. *A Treatise on Money*. London: Macmillan.

Keynes, J. M., 1936. *The General Theory of Employment, Interest and Money*. London: Macmillan.

Keynes, J. M., 1937. Alternative Theories of the Rate of Interest. *Economic Journal,* 47(186), 241–52.

Killick, T., 1995. *The Flexible Economy*. London: Routledge.

Kindleberger, C., 1973. *The World in Depression 1929–1939*. United States: University of California Press.

Kindleberger, C., 1987. *International Capital Movements*. Cambridge: Cambridge University Press.

Kindleberger, C., 2000. *Manias, Panics and Crashes: A History of Financial Crises*. Eastbourne: Macmillan.

Kliman, A., 1999. Debt, Economic Crisis and the Tendential Fall in the Profit Rate: A Temporal Perspective [Viewed 9 December 2014]. *Seminario Internacional Complutense (S.I.C) Nuevas Direcciones en el Pensamiento Economico Critico, Campus de Somosaguas, Universidad Complutense de Madrid, Madrid, Spain, May 10–13, 1999*, May. Available from: http://www.akliman.squarespace.com/storage/P%20DECTFPR%20lg%205.3.99.doc.

Kliman, A., 2007. *Reclaiming Marx's Capital: A Refutation of the Myth of Inconsistency*. United States: Lexington.

Kliman, A., 2008. *Worse than They Want you to Think – A Marxist Analysis of the Economic Crisis* [Viewed 9 December 2014] Talk: 21 October. New York: The New Space. Available from: http://akliman.squarespace.com/crisis-intervention.

Kliman, A., 2009. The Destruction of Capital and the Current Economic Crisis. *Socialism and Democracy,* 23 (2), 47–54.

Kliman, A., 2010a. *The Persistent Fall in Profitability Underlying the Current Crisis: New Temporalist Evidence*. New York: Marxist Humanist Initiative.

Kliman, A., 2010b. *Bureau of Economic Analysis Data: The Persistent Fall in Profitability Underlying the Current Crisis: New Temporalist Evidence*. [Viewed 1 July 2011]. New York: Marxist Humanist Initiative. Available from: http://akliman.squarespace.com/persistent-fall.

Kliman, A., 2012. *The Failure of Capitalist Production: Underlying Causes of the Great Recession*. Chippenham: Pluto Press.

Kliman, A. and S. Williams, 2015. Why 'Financialization' hasn't Depressed US Productive Investment. *Cambridge Journal of Economics*, forthcoming 2015.

Knapp, G. F., 1924. *The State Theory of Money*. London: Macmillan.

Kregel, J., 2008. *Using Minsky's Cushions of Safety to Understand the Sub-Prime Mortgage Crisis*. Lecture. London: School of Oriental and African Studies, 23 April.

Krehm, W., 2007. How NAIRU Became NEIRU When BIS Fell Asleep at the Switch. *COMER: The Journal of the Committee on Monetary and Economic Reform,* 19 (4), 19–20.

Lapavitsas, C., 1991. The Theory of Credit Money: A Structural Analysis. *Science and Society*. 55 (3), 291–322.

Lapavitsas, C., 1994. The Banking School and the Monetary Thought of Karl Marx. *Cambridge Journal of Economics,* 18 (5), 447–61.

Lapavitsas, C., 2009. Financialised Capitalism: Crisis and Financial Expropriation. *Historical Materialism,* 17 (2), 114–48.

Lascelles, D., 2000. *Europe's New Banks: The "Non-Bank" Phenomenon.* London: Centre for the Study of Financial Innovation.

Lavoie, M., 2003. A Primer on Endogenous Credit-Money. In: L. Rochon and S. Rossi, eds. *Modern Theories of Money: The Nature and Role of Money in Capitalist Economies*. Bodmin: Edward Elgar, pp. 506–43.

Lavoie, M., 2010. Changes in Central Bank Procedures during the Sub-Prime Crisis and Their Repercussions on Monetary Theory. *International Journal of Political Economy,* 39 (3), 3–23.

Lavoie, M., 2012. *Personal Communication.* 23 October 2012. Canada: University of Ottawa.

Lawson, T., 1994. A Realist Theory for Economics. In: R. E. Backhouse, ed. *New Directions in Economic Methodology*. Chatham: Routledge, pp. 257–85.

Lenin, V., 1996. *Imperialism: The Highest Stage of Capitalism.* Bristol: Pluto.

Lietaer, B., 2011. Monetary Monopoly as Structural Cause for Systemic Financial Instability? In: S. Mouatt and C. Adams, eds. *Corporate and Social Transformation of Money and Banking: Breaking the Serfdom.* Chippenham: Palgrave Macmillan, pp. 25–55.

Lietaer, B., 2001. *The Future of Money – Creating New Wealth, Work and a Wise World.* Guildford: Random House.

Lipietz, A., 1983. *The Enchanted World – Inflation, Credit and the World Crisis.* Thetford: Verso.

Liu, H. C. K., 2005. *Nazism and the German Economic Miracle*, 24 May [Viewed 9 December 2014] Hong Kong: Asia Times, Available from: http://www.atimes.com/atimes/Global_Economy/GE24Dj01.html.

Lukauskas, A., 1999. Managing Mobile Capital: Recent Scholarship on the Political Economy of International Finance. *Review of International Political Economy,* 6 (2), 262–87.

Luxemburg, R., 1971 [1913]. *The Accumulation of Capital.* London: Routledge.

Malkiel, B. G., 2003. The Efficient Market Hypothesis and its Critics. *The Journal of Economic Perspectives*. 17 (1), 59–82.

Mandel, E., 1969. *An Introduction to Marxist Economic Theory.* New York: Merit.

Mandel, E., 1987. Karl Marx. In: J. Eatwell, M. Milgate and P. Newman, eds. *Marxian Economics*. Hong Kong: Macmillan, pp. 1–38.

Mandeville, B., 1997. *Fable of the Bees and Other Writings*. Indianapolis: Hackett.

Mann, M., 1986. *Sources of Social Power: Volume One: A History of Power from the Beginning to AD1760*. United States: Cambridge University Press.

Marglin, S. and J. Schor, eds. 2000. *The Golden Age of Capitalism.* Bath: Oxford University Press.

Marsh, D., 1993. *The Bundesbank: The Bank that Rules Europe*. Reading: Mandarin.

Marshall, A., 1890. *Principles of Economics.* New York: Macmillan.

Marshall, A., 1923. *Money, Credit and Commerce*. London: Macmillan.

Marx, K., [1844] 2014. *Economic and Philosophical Manuscripts* [Viewed 18 December 2014]. Marxists Internet Archive. Available from: https://www.marxists.org/archive/marx/works/download/epub/index.htm

Marx, K., [1848] 1996. *The Communist Manifesto*. St Ives: Phoenix.

Marx, K., [1858] 1973. *Grundrisse – Foundations of a Critique of Political Economy*. Penguin, Aylesbury.

Marx, K., [1859] 1970. *A Contribution to the Critique of Political Economy*, Lawrence & Wishart, Union of Soviet Socialist Republics.

Marx, K., [1863] 1971. *Theories of Surplus Value: Part Three*. Moscow: Progress.

Marx, K., [1867] 1976. *Capital: Volume One*. St Ives: Penguin.

Marx, K., [1885] 1978. *Capital: Volume Two*. Aylesbury: Penguin.

Marx, K., [1894] 1981. *Capital: Volume Three*. Bungay: Penguin.

Maunder, P., D. Myers, N. Wall and R. Miller, 1995. *Economics Explained*. 3rd ed. Musselburgh: Harper Collins.

McLeay, M., A. Radia and R. Thomas, 2014. *Money Creation in the Modern Economy* [Viewed 16 December 2014] Bank of England. Accessed from: ww.bankofengland.co.uk/publications/Documents/quarterlybulletin/2014/qb14q1prereleasemoneycreation.pdf

Meltzer, A. H., 1998. What is Money? In: G. Wood, ed. *Money, Prices and the Real Economy*. Bodmin: Edward Elgar.

Menger, C., 1871. *Principles of Economics*. Ludvig von Mises Institute [Viewed 9 December 2014]. Available from: http://mises.org/sites/default/files/Principles%20of%20Economics_5.pdf.

Middleton, R., 2010. *British Monetary and Fiscal Policy in the 1930's*. British Academy Conference: Lessons from the Great Depression for the Making of Economic Policy [Viewed 9 December 2014] Available from: http://www2.warwick.ac.uk/fac/soc/economics/research/centres/cage/events/conferences/lessons/papers/british_monetary_and_fiscal_policy_in_the_1930s_ver_1_13.04.10.pdf.

Miliband, R., 1969. *The State in Capitalist Society: An Analysis of the Western System of Power*. Aylesbury: Quartet.

Miliband, R., 1977. *Marxism and Politics*. Oxford: Oxford University Press.

Mill, J. S., [1859] 1974. *On Liberty*. Bungay: Penguin.

Minsky, H. P., 1978. *The Financial Instability Hypothesis: A Restatement*. Thames Papers in Political Economy. [Viewed 9 December 2014] Available at: http://digitalcommons.bard.edu/hm_archive/180.

Mises, L. V., 1953. *The Theory of Money and Credit*. New Haven: Yale University Press.

Mishkin, F. and A. Posen, 1997. German Monetary Targeting: A Precursor to Inflation Targeting. *Federal Reserve Bank of New York: Economic Policy Review*, August, pp. 21–34.

Mishkin, F., 2007. How Did We Get Here? In: F. Mishkin, ed. *Monetary Policy Strategy*. United States: MIT Press Books.

Mohun, S., 1984. Abstract Labour and its Value Form. *Science and Society*, 48 (4), 388–406.

Moore, B., 2006. *Shaking the Invisible Hand: Complexity, Choices and Critiques*. Basingstoke: Palgrave Macmillan.

Moore, B., 1991. Has the Demand for Money been Mislaid? A Reply to "Has Moore become too Horizontal?" *Journal of Post Keynesian Economics,* 14 (1), 125–33.

Moore, B., 1988. *Horizontalists & Verticalists: The Macroeconomics of Credit Money*. New York: Cambridge University Press.

Moseley, F., 2009. The US Economic Crisis: Causes and Solutions. *International Socialist Review*. [Viewed 9 December 2014] 64 (March–April). Available from: http://isreview.org/issue/64/us-economic-crisis.

Moseley, F., 2011. The Determination of the "Monetary Expression of Labor Time" ("MELT") in the Case of Non-Commodity Money. *Review of Radical Political Economics,* 43 (1), 95–105.

Mouatt, S., 2004. *Global Financial Power, Capitalist Crisis and Uneven Development*. Association of Heterodox Economics Conference, United Kingdom, Leeds University.

Mouatt, S., 2008. Evaluating Stephen Zarlenga's Treatment of Historical Monetary Thought. *International Journal of Social Economics,* 35 (11), 846–56.

Mouatt, S., 2010. The Case for Monetary Diversity. *The International Journal of Community Currency Research,* 14, A17–28.

Mouatt, S. and C. Adams, eds., 2011a. *Corporate Transformation of Money and Banking: Breaking the Serfdom*. Chippenham: Palgrave Macmillan.

Mouatt, S., 2011b. The Corporate Subjugation of Money and Banking. In: S. Mouatt and C. Adams, eds. *Corporate and Social Transformation of Money and Banking: Breaking the Serfdom*. Chippenham: Palgrave Macmillan, pp. 103–18.

Mouatt, S., 2011c. The Dissolution of the Financial State. In: S. Mouatt and C. Adams, eds. *Corporate Transformation of Money and Banking: Breaking the Serfdom*. Chippenham: Palgrave Macmillan, pp. 87–102.

Mouatt, S., 2011d. Can Sequential and Non-Dualistic Interpretation of Marx's Monetary Thought be Synthezised with the Endogenous Money Paradigm? *Critique: Journal of Socialist Theory,* 39 (2), 233–46.

Mushin, J., 2012. *The Sterling Area*. Encyclopaedia of Economic and Business History, United States: Miami University. Available from: http://www.ssrn.com/abstract=2102939.

Naito, A., 2008. Money, Credit and the State: Post Keynesian Theory of Credit Money and Chartalism. *Association of Heterodox Economics Conference*. Anglia Ruskin University: Cambridge.

Narourei, S., 2011. An Empirical Investigation into the UK Profit Rate, 1949–2003. Association of Heterodox Economics, Nottingham University, United Kingdom, July.

Nehru, V. and A. Dhareshwar, 1993. A New Database on Physical Capital Stock: Sources, Methodology and Results. *Revista de Analisis Economico,* 8 (1), 37–59.

Niebyl, K. H., 1946. *Studies in the Classical Theories of Money*. New York: Columbia University Press.

Obstfeld, M. and A. Taylor, 2004. *Global Capital Markets: Integration, Crisis and Growth*. Cambridge: Cambridge University Press.

Octopus, 2007. *Octopus to Provide Major Transport Smartcard System in Dubai.* [Viewed 9 December 2014]. Available from: http://www.octopus.com.hk/release/detail/2007/en/20071122.html.

Office for National Statistics, 2010a. *Inflation. CZBHH.RPI.* [Viewed 10 January 2010]. Available from: http://www.statistics.gov.uk/statbase.

Office for National Statistics, 2010b. *Statistical Bulletin: Capital Stocks, Capital Consumption and Non-Financial Balance Sheets.* [Viewed 7 March 2015]. Available from: http://www.ons.gov.uk.

Office for National Statistics, 2010c. *Net Capital Stock: Tables CIXJ, CIXH and CIXI* [Viewed 15 December 2011] Available from: http://www.ons.gov.uk.

Office for National Statistics, 2010d. *Net Operating Surplus: Tables NQBE, NQNV, NSRM, NSRK and NHCE.* [Viewed 15 December 2011] Available from: http://www.ons.gov.uk.

Office for National Statistics, 2015. *Employment: Table MGRZ.* [Viewed 10 March 2015] Available from: http://www.ons.gov.uk/ons/datasets-and-tables/data-selector.html?cdid=MGRZ&dataset=lms&table-id=1

Olin-Wright, E., 2002. *Seminar on Theories of the State.* [Viewed 9 December]. Madison: University of Wisconsin. Available from: http://www.ssc.wisc.edu/~wright/924-02.pdf.

Olson, W. and A. Groom, 1991. *International Relations Then and Now: Origins and Trends in Interpretation.* London: Routledge.

Omundsen, B., C. Mcclaren, B. Saunders and T. Ware, eds., 2010. *Capital Stocks, Capital Consumption and Non-Financial Balance Sheets.* United Kingdom: Office for National Statistics.

Ormazabal, K. M ., 2004. Adam Smith on Labour and Value: Challenging the Standard Interpretation [Viewed 9 December 2014] *Department of Foundations of Economic Analysis.* Spain: University of the Basque Country. Available from: http://www.ehu.es/documents/2276258/2294671/il2006_26.pdf.

Overy, R. J., 1982. *The Nazi Economic Recovery 1932–1938.* Hong Kong: Macmillan.

Owen-Smith, E., 1994. *The German* Economy. United States: Routledge.

Palley, T., 2004. From Keynesianism to Neo-Liberalism: Shifting Paradigms in Economics. In: A. Saad-Filho and D. Johnstone, eds. *Neo-Liberalism: A Critical Reader.* Chippenham: Pluto Press.

Palley, T., 2003a. *The Economic Case for the Tobin Tax.* [Viewed 9 December 2014]. Economics for Democratic and Open Societies: Open Society Institute. Available from: http://www.thomaspalley.com/docs/articles/international_markets/Tobin%20Tax_New%20Rules.pdf.

Palley, T., 2003b. Monetary Control in the Presence of Endogenous Money and Financial Innovation: the Case for Asset-Based Reserve Requirements. In: L. Rochon and S. Rossi, eds. *Modern Theories of Money: The Nature and Role of Money in Capitalist Economies.* Cheltenham: Edward Elgar, pp. 67–83.

Palley, T., 2007. *Financialization: What it is and Why it Matters.* (Viewed 9 December 2014] United States: The Levy Economics Institute, No 525. Available from: http://www.levyinstitute.org/pubs/wp_525.pdf.

Patinkin, D., 1965. *Money, Interest and Prices.* 2nd ed. New York: Harper and Row.

Patomaki, H., 2003. *Democratising Globalisation: The Leverage of the Tobin Tax*. Malaysia: Zed.

Pesek, B. and T. Saving, 1967. *Money, Wealth and Economic Theory*. New York: Macmillan.

Petrella, R., 2001. *The Water Manifesto: Arguments for a World Water Control*. Reading: Zed.

Pettifor, A., 2006. *The Coming First World Debt Crisis*. Chippenham: Palgrave Macmillan.

Pilbeam, K., 2005. *Finance and Financial* Markets. 2nd ed. China: Palgrave Macmillan.

Polanyi, K., 1944. *The Great Transformation*. New York: Octagon Books.

Pontzen, M. and F. Schobert, 2008. Episodes in German Monetary History – Lessons for Transition Countries [Viewed 9 December 2014] *The Experience of Exchange Rate Regimes in South-eastern Europe in a Historical and Comparative Perspective: Second Conference of the South-Eastern European Monetary History Network*. Oesterreichische Nationalbank, April 13, 2007, pp. 145–160. Available from: www.oenb.at/dms/oenb/Publikationen/.../pontzen_tcm16-80927.pdf.

Positive Money, 2014. [Viewed 11 December] Available from: http://www.postive-money.org/

Potts, N., 1997. National Economic Sovereignty and the Single European Currency. *European Business Review*, 97 (1), 11–23.

Potts, N., 2005a. *The Political Economy of Money, Profitability and Value*. PhD Thesis. University of London.

Potts, N., 2005b. The Relevance of Marx to Students of Economics, no Matter the Level. *International Journal of Social Economics*, 32 (9), 827–51.

Potts, N., 2007. Some Preliminary Thoughts on Knowledge-based Production: 49 Seconds on Mustafar. *Critique: Journal of Socialist Theory*, 35 (3), 357–73.

Potts, N., 2009a. Trying to Rescue Value for Everyone. *Critique: Journal of Socialist Theory*, 37 (2), 177–99.

Potts, N., 2009b. Back to the C19th Business as Usual: A Surprise? *Association for Heterodox Economics Conference*, Kingston, London, July.

Potts, N., 2010. Surplus Capital: The Ultimate Cause of the Crisis. *Critique: Journal of Socialist Theory*, 38 (1), 35–49.

Potts, N., 2011a. Valuation in the Presence of Stocks of Commodities: Exploring the Temporal Single System Interpretation of Marx. *Critique of Political Economy*, 1, 89–119.

Potts, N., 2011b. Marx's Big Idea. In: S. Mouatt and C. Adams, eds. *Corporate Transformation of Money and Banking: Breaking the Serfdom*. Chippenham: Palgrave Macmillan, pp. 56–70.

Potts, N., 2011c. When is a Financial Crisis not a Financial Crisis? In: S. Mouatt and C. Adams, eds. *Corporate Transformation of Money and Banking: Breaking the Serfdom*. Chippenham: Palgrave Macmillan, pp. 71–86.

Potts, N., 2013. Keynesian Economics: In Search of Unnatural Stability. *Critique: Journal of Socialist Theory*. 41 (2), 183–97.

Potts, N., 2014. *'Surplus Profits' and Progressive Land Ownership: A Marxist Perspective*. [Viewed 11 December] Association of Heterodox Economics conference,

July, Greenwich University. Available from: http://hetecon.net/documents/ConferencePapers/2014/Potts_451-651-1-RV.pdf.

Poulantzas, N., 1974. *Classes in Contemporary Capitalism*. Thetford: Verso.

Preparata, G. G., 2002. Hitler's Money: The Bills of Exchange of Schacht and Rearmament in the Third Reich. *American Review of Political Economy,* 1 (1), 15–27.

Pringle, R., 2001. *Key Events in Central Banking 1609–2001*. London: Central Banking Publications.

Ramos-Martinez, A., 2004. Labour, Money, Labour-Saving Innovation and the Falling Rate of Profit. In: A. Freeman, J. Wells and A. Kliman, eds. *The New Value Controversy and the Foundations of Economics*. Cheltenham: Edward Elgar, pp. 67–84.

Rabushka, A., 2004. Representation without Representation. *Policy Review*, December 2003 & January 2004 [Viewed 9 December 2014]. Hoover Institution, Stanford University, United States. Available from: http://www.hoover.org/research/representation-without-representation.

Reszat, B., 2003. Financial Reform in Germany. In: M. J. B. Hall, ed. *The International Handbook of Financial Reform*. King's Lynn: Edward Elgar, pp. 88–112.

Reuten, G., 1993. The Difficult Labor of a Theory of Social Value: Metaphors and Systematic Dialectics at the beginning of Marx's "Capital". In: F. Moseley, ed. *Marx's Method in Capital: a re-examination*. Atlantic Highlands, NJ, Humanities Press, pp. 89–113.

Ricardo, D., [1821] 1962. *Principles of Political Economy and Taxation*. London: Cambridge University Press.

Ricardo, D., 1824. *Plan for the Establishment of a National Bank*. London: John Murray.

Rieu, D., K. Lee and H. Ahn, 2012. The Determination of the Monetary Expression of Labor Time under the Inconvertible Credit Money System. Association of Heterodox Economics Conference, Paris, France, July.

Rius, 1999. *Introducing Marx*. Australia: Icon Books.

Roberts, M., 2009. *The Great Recession: Profit Cycles, Economic Crisis. A Marxist View*. London: Lulu Enterprises.

Rochon, L. and S. Rossi, 2007. Monetary Policy without Reserve Requirements: Central Bank Money as a Means of Final Payment on the Inter-Bank Market. CEMF Conference: *Post-Keynesian Principles of Economic Policy*, University of Burgundy, Dijon, December.

Rochon, L., 1999. The Creation and Circulation of Endogenous Money: A Circuitist Dynamique Approach. *Journal of Economic Issues,* 33 (1), 1–21.

Roley, V. and R. Troll, 1984. The Impact of Discount Rate Changes on Market Interest Rates. *Economic Review*, Federal Reserve Bank of Kansas City, Issue Jan, pp. 27–39.

Ross, D. M., 1992. British Monetary Policy and the Banking System in the 1950's. *Business and Economic History,* 21, 199–208.

Rousseas, S., 1998. *Post Keynesian Monetary Economics*. Chippenham: Macmillan.

Rousseau, J., [1762] 1968. *The Social Contract*. London: Penguin.

Saros, D., 2007. The Price-Form as a Fractional Reflection of the Aggregate Value of Commodities. *Review of Radical Political Economics,* 39 (3), 407–15.

Saunders, M., P. Lewis and A. Thornhill, 2007. *Research Methods for Business Students: Fourth Edition*. Spain: Prentice-Hall.
Sawyer, M., 2001. Kalecki on Money and Finance. *European Journal of the History of Economic Thought,* 8 (4), 487–508.
Schacht, H., 1967. *The Magic of Money*. London: Oldbourne.
Schraven, J., 2000. The Economics of Local Exchange and Trading Systems: A Theoretical Perspective. *International Journal of Community Currency Research,* 4, 1–8.
Schroeder, R. F. H., 2006. Community Exchange and Trading Systems in Germany. *International Journal of Community Currency Research,* 10, 24–42.
Schumpeter, J. A., 1954. *History of Economic Analysis*. Guildford: Routledge.
Shakespeare, R. and P. Challen, 2002. *Seven Steps to Justice*. Chippenham: New European Publications.
Shuklian, S., 2002. Karl Marx on the Foundations of Monetary Theory. *Lewis School of Business: Marshall University, West Virginia,* no. 00–02.
Silverman, D., 1998. *Hitler's Economics*. United States: Harvard University Press.
Singer, H., 1988. International Financial Reform and the Third World: The Continuing Relevance of Keynes' Proposals. In: H. Singer, N. Hatti and K. Tandon, eds. *Resource Transfer and the Debt Trap*. Part One. New Delhi: Ashish, pp. 3–19.
Skidelsky, R., 2005. *John Maynard Keynes 1883 –1946 Economist, Philosopher, Statesman*. United States: Penguin.
Skidelsky, R., 1995. J. M. Keynes and the Quantity Theory of Money. In: G. Wood, ed. *The Quantity Theory of Money – From Locke to Keynes and Friedman*. Chippenham: Edward Elgar, pp. 80–96.
Smith, A., 2003 (1776). *The Wealth of Nations*. New York: Bantam Dell.
Soskice, D., 1993. The Institutional Infrastructure for International Competitiveness: A Comparative Analysis of the UK and Germany. In: A. Atkinson and R. Brunetta, ed. *The Economics of the New Europe*. London: Macmillan, pp. 45–66.
Sraffa, P., 1960. *Production of Commodities by Means of Commodities: Prelude to a Critique of Economic Theory*. Cambridge: Cambridge University Press.
Steedman, I., 1977. *Marx after Sraffa*. London: New Left Books.
Stern, K., 1999. The Note-Issuing Bank within the State Structure. In: Bundesbank, ed. *Fifty Years of the Deutsche Mark – Central Bank and the Currency in Germany since 1948*. Guildford: Oxford University Press, pp. 103–64.
Stockhammer, E., 2004. Financialisation and the Slowdown of Accumulation. *Cambridge Journal of Economics*. 28 (5), 719–41.
Strange, S., 1988. *States and Markets*. London: Pinter.
Strange, S., 1990. Finance, Information and Power. *Review of International Studies*.16 (3), 259–74.
Strange, S., 1996. *The Retreat of the State – The Diffusion of Power in the World Economy*. Cambridge: Cambridge University Press.
Strange, S., 1997. *Casino Capitalism*. Manchester: Manchester University Press.
Strange, S., 1998. *Mad Money*. Guildford: Manchester University Press.
Straw, J., 2008. Islamic Financial and Trade Conference. United Kingdom: Park Plaza Hotel Victoria.

Suter, C., 1992. *Foreign Loans, Financial Crisis and Debt Settlement, 1820–1990.* Oxford: Westview.

Tabb, W., 1999. *Reconstructing Political Economy: The Great Divide in Economic Thought.* London: Routledge.

Taylor, J., 2009. *How Government Actions and Interventions Caused, Prolonged and Worsened the Financial Crisis.* United States: Hoover Institution Press.

Taylor, J., 1993. Discretion Versus Policy Rules in Practice. *Carnegie-Rochester Conference Series on Public Policy,* vol. 39, pp. 195–214.

Thirlwall, A. P., 1985. *Keynesian Economic Development: 7th Keynes Seminar,* Hong Kong: Macmillan.

Tickell, A., 1997. Don't Panic Mr Mainwaring: Restructuring the British Financial Sector into the Twenty-First Century. *Capital and Class,* 62, 13–19.

Tily, G., 2005. The British Labour Party and Finance Capital: New Labour – Old Finance. *Association of Heterodox Economics Conference,* London: City University, July.

Tily, G., 2007a. *Keynes General Theory, the Rate of Interest and Keynesian Economics,* Macmillan, Chippenham.

Tily, G., 2007b. Keynes, the Post-Keynesians and the Curious Case of Endogenous Money. *Association of Heterodox Economics Conference,* Bristol: University of the West of England.

Tobin, J., 1978. A Proposal for International Monetary Reform. *Eastern Economic Journal,* 4, 153–59.

Toporowski, J., 2010. Marx's Grundrisse and the Monetary Business Cycle [Viewed 11 December 2014]. *International Initiative for Promoting Political Economy: Financialisation Working Paper,* 7. Available from: http://www.iippe.org/wiki/images/b/bd/Toporowski-Grundrisse.pdf.

Towell, P., A. Scott and C. Oates, 2007. *Web 2.0: How the next generation Internet is changing financial services.* London: The Centre for the Study of Financial Innovation.

Triffin, R., 1960. *Gold and the Dollar Crisis,* Yale University Press, New Haven.

Turnbull, S., 2009. *Options for Rebuilding the Economy and the Financial System* [Viewed 9 December 2014]. International Institute for Self Governance, Sydney, Australia. Available from: http://papers.ssrn.com/sol3/papers.cfm?abstract_id=1460086.

Vincent, A., 1987. *Theories of the State.* Worcester: Basil Blackwell.

Vitols, S., 1998. Are German Banks Different? *Small Business Economics,* 10, (2), 79–91.

Wadsworth, J., 1973. *The Banks and the Monetary System in the United Kingdom.* Abingdon: Routledge.

Wallerstein, I., 1983. *Historical Capitalism.* Guildford: Verso.

Walras, L., 1926. *Elements of Pure Economics.* Paris: Pichon.

Walter, A., 1993. *World Power and World Money.* Exeter: Harvester Wheatsheaf.

Weber, M., [1919] 2004. Politics as Vocation. In: D. Owen and T. B. Strong, eds. *The Vocation Lectures.* Indianapolis: Hackett Publishing Company.

Weber, M., [1922] 1978. *Economy and Society: Volume One.* United States: University of California Publications.

Welch, P. and S. Worthington, 2007. Banking at the Checkout 2007–08: Evaluating the Provision of Financial Services by Retailers. *Journal of Financial Services Marketing,* 2 (3), 230–45.

Werner, R., 2005. *New Paradigm in Macroeconomics: Solving the Riddle of Japanese Macro-Economic Performance.* Chippenham: Palgrave Macmillan.

Wicksell, J. G. K., 1936. *Interest and Prices.* London: Macmillan.

Williamson, J., 1985. Bancor and the Developing Countries: How Much Difference Would It Have Made? In: A. P. Thirlwall, ed. *Keynes and Economic Development: The Seventh Keynes Seminar, University of Kent, 1985.* New York: St Martins Press, pp. 92–106.

Williamson, D. G., 1982. *The Third Reich.* Singapore: Longman.

Wray, R., 2007. *Endogenous Money: Structuralist and Horizontalist.* Working Paper 512, United States: The Levy Institute.

Wray, R., 2004. *When are Interest Rates Exogenous?* Working Paper 30, United States: The Levy Institute.

Yin, R., 1993. *Applications of Case Study Research.* California: Sage Publishing.

Zarlenga, S., 1994. *A Refutation of Menger's Theory of The Origin of Money* [Viewed 9 December 2014]. United States: American Monetary Institute Charitable Trust. Available from: http://www.monetary.org/a-refutation-of-mengers-theory-of-the-origin-of-money-abridged/2010/12.

Zarlenga, S., 1999. Germany's 1923 Hyperinflation: A Private Affair. [Viewed 9 December 2014] *The Barnes Review,* July-August, pp. 61–67. Available from: http://www.wintersonnenwende.com/scriptorium/english/archives/articles/hyperinflation-e.html.

Zarlenga, S., 2002. *The Lost Science of Money – The Mythology of Money: The Story of Power.* United States: The American Monetary Institute.

Index

About the Author

Simon Mouatt has taught economics at Southampton Solent University for twenty-two years and enjoys engaging with the students and general university life. He is an active researcher and is also a member of the Association of Heterodox Economics and the Transition movement. Simon lives in West Sussex, UK, with his wife and children and, in his spare time, enjoys walking, music, comedy, and surfing. His research interests include monetary economics, international financial markets, Marxist economics, post-Keynesian economics and economic development.

www.ingramcontent.com/pod-product-compliance
Ingram Content Group UK Ltd.
Pitfield, Milton Keynes, MK11 3LW, UK
UKHW040154091026
15587UKWH00018B/240

9 780739 190371